Smells Like Dead Elephants

Also by Matt Taibbi

The Great Derangement: A Terrifying True Story of War, Politics, and Religion at the Twilight of the American Empire

Spanking the Donkey: Dispatches from the Dumb Season

The Exile: Sex, Drugs, and Libel in the New Russia

Smells Like Dead Elephants

Dispatches from a Rotting Empire

—

Matt Taibbi

Black Cat

a paperback original imprint of Grove/Atlantic, Inc.

New York

Published simultaneously in Canada
Printed in the United States of America

FIRST EDITION

ISBN-10: 0-8021-7041-2
ISBN-13: 978-0-8021-7041-5

Black Cat
a paperback original imprint of Grove/Atlantic, Inc.
841 Broadway
New York, NY 10003

Distributed by Publishers Group West

www.groveatlantic.com

07 08 09 10 11 12   10 9 8 7 6 5 4 3 2 1

Contents

Contents

Introduction

I missed the beginning of the Bush years. When the Gore-Bush electoral mess blew up in the news I was living in Moscow, Russia, editing an English-language paper called the *eXile* and also writing for a mudslinging Russian tabloid called *Stringer*. While America was busy counting hanging chads and careening toward a constitutional crisis, what I mostly remember is sitting in the *Stringer* offices pounding vodka with Russian colleagues Leonid Krutakov and Alexei Fomin, and listening to them howl with delight at the news that the mighty U.S.A. was now officially as fucked up and directionless as the Russian state. "Let's see you bastards try to lecture us about our elections now!" I remember Leonid saying, shaking his head with contempt. "We may be a third-world country, but at least we know it!"

Nearly a year later, when 9/11 happened, America was still far away enough for me—I had been gone from it for most of ten years—that I still couldn't quite relate to what was going on back home. In Russia, and in particular in Moscow, terrorist bombings were sort of a regular event. I had twice been within a football field of massive explosions on Tverskaya Avenue, the capital's main drag. In one, a bomb blew up the twentieth floor of the Intourist hotel in what apparently was an unsuccessful attempt to assassinate Iosif Kobzon, a wig-wearing mobbed-up crooner often described as the "Russian Sinatra." I was eating an ice cream cone and walking toward Red Square

when that one hit; I was close enough to see glass shards landing on the street. Not long after that I was on line at the original Russian McDonald's when the Pushkin Square Metro
station exploded; I remember that scene well because so many
of the McDonald's customers used the confusion after the blast
as an opportunity to cut in line. Terrorist attacks were a part
of everyday life in Russia, a regular annoyance to go with industrial disasters, coups d'etat and currency collapses—something to joke about, like the weather.

As such my response to 9/11 was typical for a Muscovite of
that period. My paper, the *eXile,* covered the bombings by running a cover photo showing a businessman bending over his
naked secretary high up in a World Trade Center office. Bent
over and looking out the window, she sees a plane approach-
ing fast. The headline read: OH GOD, IT'S SO BIG!!!

At the time, I thought that was funny. My clients did not,
however—we lost pretty much every corporate advertiser we
had because of that goddamn cover. Business decisions like
these left me increasingly impoverished and as I steamed toward my mid-thirties I began to recognize the necessity of getting my head screwed on a little straighter, and perhaps even
coming back to America to try to earn an actual living.

So in early 2002 I returned to the United States for the first
time in nearly a decade, repatriating in the red-hot vigilant
period of the Bush years. At first, the culture shock was so intense, I might as well have been on Mars. The post-9/11 war
hysteria and paranoia, drummed up on the airwaves by absurd
fascist-mouthpiece caricatures of the O'Reilly and Hannity ilk,
struck me at first as ridiculous comedy, some bad director's half-
baked, overdone rendition of an Orwellian dystopia, as dumb
and unbelievable as *V for Vendetta.*

But as I traveled the country taking up my first freelance assignments on the campaign trail for a project that would eventually turn into an election diary called *Spanking the Donkey*, it slowly sunk in that this was *not* a joke, that a great many people in this country were taking this campy, goofball conservatism seriously, that the so-called "Bush revolution" was for real.

By the time the 2004 election ended I had fairly settled in to life back in the States. Like many returning expatriates, my readjustment period came at a cost of a nervous breakdown and the near-total disintegration of my personal life. Once those things were out of the way, however, I emerged transformed into more or less a typical American bourgeois geek, with a huge-screen television, a Gap credit card, a mild hydrocodone habit, no friends, and . . . a job.

Having gone for nearly a dozen years without a boss—my last experience with regular employment had been a study in incompetence as a bumbling assistant at a private-eye firm in Boston in the early nineties—my first response to being hired to write regular political features for *Rolling Stone* was sheer terror. Among other things, I was still totally mystified by the whole Bush phenomenon and had serious doubts that I could find anything intelligent to say about it.

On the surface, Bush looked to me just like a stammering dipshit with a third-grade education barely equal to the task of playing the president on television. I felt sure that there had to be some more sophisticated hidden force behind his presidency, some kind of powerful evil brain behind the dumb face, but the people my new colleagues in the American press were touting as "geniuses" and "Svengalis" and "visionaries" behind the regime turned out to be half-bright slobs like Karl Rove

Introduction

(whose "genius" was that he was mean enough to accuse his opponents of having a drug addict wife or an illegitimate daughter) and the president's famed circle of "neocon" advisers, a group of people so stupid, they could only have been bred in expensive graduate schools.

The Wolfowitzes and Cheneys and Feiths who were the alleged brains behind Bush's Iraq campaign were "intellectuals" in the same way that Koko the signing gorilla is a "linguist"— in a technical sense, sure, they used their brains to come up with these silly ideas about spreading democracy in the Muslim Middle East by dropping bombs and marching in to welcoming parades, but the idea that anyone, much less the majority of the country, could be impressed by their erudition struck me as totally amazing.

But people were impressed, and those neocons sure were proud of themselves and their academic chops, giving themselves gigantic polysyllabic titles at the various right-wing think-tanks, accepting many an academic award, giving many a commencement speech in honorific caps and gowns, and publishing scads of verbose books and monographs while wearing important-looking tweed and wire-rimmed glasses for their jacket photos. And while they were doing this, their little Iraq adventure was already blowing up in their faces, an obviously dumb idea about to be turned spectacularly on its ear—but in those early years after 9/11 no one wanted to admit that yet, we wanted to believe these guys had a plan, that they weren't the pompous, preening boneheads they ought to everyone to have seemed to be at the time. Like everyone else, I too made the mistake of thinking there had to be more there, something more behind the unnervingly unimpressive visible reality.

It was like that with almost everything I ended up covering for *Rolling Stone*. At each of the big events of the Bush era I kept thinking that there had to be something else to the story, some other layer I was missing. Sent to attend the trial of the Enron executives, for instance, I kept looking for that other layer to the conspiracy, the details that would add up to characters of Shakespearean depth—for surely someone who can steal a billion dollars is a very interesting person on *some* level.

But it wasn't there. Ken Lay and Jeff Skilling just weren't interesting people. Lay was your typically unremarkable mealy-executive type, the kind of person you would expect to be eaten first in any lifeboat situation, while Skilling was just an ordinary corporate egomaniac, the kind of dime-a-dozen asshole you see just about everywhere in America, holding forth with his sleeves rolled up about the "art of selling" for crowds of drooling junior associates in an Applebee's or a Sheraton ballroom somewhere.

Their only "genius" was that they spent a dozen years or so kicking mishit balls back onto the fairway when no one was looking, until they got caught and it all came crashing down and they weren't geniuses anymore but more like supreme all-time retards, two new captains of a modern *Titanic* prepped to spend all eternity ridiculed for driving themselves and thousands of others into an iceberg—except you'd never know it from the press coverage. For even very late in the Bush era we treated people who were merely exceptionally greedy or exceptionally self-important or exceptionally wrong-headed with reverence and awe, sometimes doing so even after they got caught or indicted or exposed, or after their acts left us broke or underwater or on fire or otherwise in a state of total, irreversible fuckedness.

I remember being at the Enron trial and reading a *USA Today* article that described Lay and Skilling as standing "stoically" as the verdicts were announced. I was there; there was nothing "stoic" about the way either of them were standing. Both of these numbskulls were wide-eyed and frightened, mute and with their mouths slightly open, looking like they'd just been whacked across the face with a pine board. Lynndie England had the same face at her trial. The way they were standing could more appropriately have been described as *stupidly*. And such a posture was as good a metaphor as any I could see for the way the Bush years ended up winding down.

Looking back now, after three years criss-crossing the country for the magazine, I can see that there never really was more to the story. Under the editorial direction of the vaunted National Affairs Desk at *Rolling Stone* I felt all along an intense pressure to pin down and describe that dark, slimy, ever-present *thing* about the Bush years that might connect, say, the circus around the Michael Jackson trial to a hurricane disaster area to a once-proud Texas farm town grimly reborn as a privatized, neo-American gulag. There was a curious logic to the assignments I was given that seemed to me to be relentlessly searching out a thesis/theory about the nature of life in the new Republican paradise. In the beginning my failure to really grasp that theory was a source of considerable stress, as I often wondered whether my belated attempt to join the responsible workforce would end in disaster, and escape to another third-world hole where I would be less confused and frightened by my surroundings.

But in the end I understood that there was a good reason that I never tapped into what the hidden truth of the Bush years was, and the reason for that is that there never was anything to tap into. The tragedy of the Bush era is that there was never any depth under its absurd surface—and when the ridiculous exterior washed away, in scandal and indictment and disaster and failure and ignominy, we were left with nothing but emptiness, disorganization, and chaos. If I indulged in any conscious use of metaphor anywhere in these reports it was in the section about hurricane Katrina, where the whole country saw how tenuous our grip on civilization really is, and where those of us who happened to get a close-up look at New Orleans after the flood saw what America in these years looked like behind what turned out to be a very thin curtain.

The Bush administration burst onto the scene like a carnival, full of grand plans and crazy schemes, wars and Patriot Acts, suspensions of laws and habeas corpus and international standards—but in the late years, the years covered in this book, all those plans blew up, and we were left to stare at the wreckage, and stare at each other, and wonder what the fuck happened.

More than once during this time, and especially one dark night as I trudged through the black water of New Orleans in search of a place to sleep in a friend's waterlogged chapel, I recalled a poem by Archibald MacLeish called "The End of the World." The poem is about a circus where freaks and midgets and lions are all performing, and everything is going grandly and circuslike, until suddenly the top of the tent blows off—and there overhead, hanging over the thousands of white faces and dazed eyes, Macleish writes:

There in the starless dark, the poise, the hover,
There with vast wings across the cancelled skies,
There in the sudden blackness the black pall
Of nothing, nothing, nothing—nothing at all.

That was the big joke of the Bush years. Our leaders during this time were dumb as rocks, they couldn't see beyond a few feet in front of their faces, their plans were infantile and embarrassingly mean-spirited, and as it turned out they screwed us all over very badly for at least a generation to come. But when they finally knocked themselves out of the picture, hanging themselves with a rope of their own rapacious incompetence, we were forced to remember that we were the ones who put them in charge in the first place. If *those* guys were that dumb, what does that say about us, the ones left holding the bag? We now get to spend the next four years considering that question, and God help anyone who looks forward to finding out the answer.

Smells Like Dead Elephants

Jacko on Trial

Inside the strangest show on Earth

April 7, 2005

It is the first day of witness testimony in the Michael Jackson trial, and I am stuck in the overflow room of the Santa Barbara County Courthouse—a windowless trailer at the edge of the court compound, where fifty journalists are crouched around a closed-circuit broadcast of the trial, poised to catch the word *masturbate* should it fly out of the TV monitor.

The figures on the screen are tiny and barely recognizable. Jackson attorney Thomas Mesereau is the only one who is easy to spot, his mane of blow-dried white hair flowing back and forth across the screen like a cursor.

"Please to tell, veech von ees Jackson?" whispers a European reporter.

"He's the little dot on the left," snaps an American TV reporter, not averting his eyes from the monitor.

The screen goes dark. District Attorney Tom Sneddon, a humorless creep whose public persona recalls the potbellied vice principal perched on the gym bleachers watching you slow-dance, has chosen to open proceedings with a screening of *Living with Michael Jackson,* the sensational documentary put out by Hobbit-like self-promoting British tabloid creature Martin Bashir—a smug blob we can just make out sitting with folded hands in the witness dock.

It's fitting that Bashir is the first witness in this case. The whole trial is peopled with the amoeboid life-forms one finds swimming in the sewer of the celebrity industry: publicists, personal assistants, B-list entertainment lawyers. The species Bashir represents is the pompous hack who peers through the bedroom windows of famous people and imagines he is curing cancer.

Bashir is so pretentious, he affects not to understand what Sneddon means when he uses the term "video documentaries" to describe his work. "I call them *cultural-affairs programs,*" Bashir says.

The theory of the prosecution, for those few who can follow it, is that the airing of this documentary in Britain in February 2003 set in motion a sinister conspiracy that ultimately led to Michael Jackson sticking his hands down a boy's underpants. The prosecution presents the film as the dramatic opening chapter of a labyrinthine tale of moral decay; it follows that the darkening of the courtroom is intended to have symbolic import, a sign that we are entering a world of shadows.

But the effect is ruined when the film starts. As the camera pans across the gates of Jackson's Neverland ranch, the audio track booms out the familiar bass groove of "Billie Jean"—and in the overflow room, the sea of aging reporters instantly begins bobbing cheerfully to the beat.

"I love this song," the TV reporter whispers to me.

The Jackson trial is a goddamn zoo, a freak show from sunup to sundown. By six-thirty every morning, when the sheriff's deputies hold their lottery for public seating, a small vaudeville act of pro-Jackson protesters has already assembled in front of the Santa Barbara County Courthouse, and every day they fight the press and each other for the cameras, from the opening bell straight through to the end of testimony.

Like snowflakes, no two protesters are alike, or even similar. About the only connection one can imagine them having is that each was the 95,000th caller on the eighties radio station in his hometown. A kindly young black woman who quit her job teaching kindergarten in Los Angeles to support her favorite artist, a fat white psychopath from Tennessee who thinks Jackson is Jesus, and a rotund Latino in a FREE MICHAEL T-shirt who lives in his mother's basement a few miles from the courthouse—they've all joined hands, circling wagons against the press and against the equally weird self-appointed child-abuse victim advocates who occasionally show up to fuck up their action. Police apparently had to intervene one afternoon when the basement-dwelling Latino reportedly scuffled with a middle-aged blonde housewife carrying a sign that read HANDS OFF MY PRIVATE PARTS.

This small group, generally numbering not more than thirty, represents the sum total of public interest in the trial here. Though forty-five courtroom seats are reserved for the general public every day, on most days, California v. Jackson is outdrawn by the games of lawn bowling held for Santa Maria's retired elderly on the Astroturf lot at the rear of the court compound.

The utter lack of buzz adds to the sordid, depressing feel of the whole trial. As public attractions go, it ranks somewhere below a bearded-lady tent and one of those mules in Tijuana painted to look like a zebra—pay a dollar to have a Polaroid taken. Only the media still take the trial seriously.

The courtroom routine is established early on. Jackson, usually dressed in an armband and a dazed smile, makes his way in at about 8:15 AM most days. He comes with his parents and one of his brothers, embracing them as they take their seats, then glides over to the defense table to begin his pretrial rituals. He shakes hands with his lawyers, then drifts to the right-front corner of the courtroom, behind a small partition, and does a brief calisthenics routine, squatting up and down about five times as he faces the wall. By the time he is finished, the defense has laid out a bowl of peppermints for him; he walks up to the mints, slowly unwraps one and then another, sucks on them, then finally sits down in his seat and stares ahead impassively. Most days he sits like that, motionless, all day. He might be engaged in the case, he might be waiting for the spaceship to land. It's impossible to tell.

Beginning with Bashir, the early days of testimony feature a parade of absurd lackeys and celebrity parasites. A typical Sneddon witness is the froglike Ann Gabriel, who had been employed as a Jackson publicist for about a week around the time the alleged crime took place. Sneddon brought her in to testify that one of Jackson's lawyers had told her they could make the mother of Jackson's accuser "look like a crack whore."

During her brief testimony, Gabriel manages to plug her only other "celebrity" client, a Las Vegas magician and "noted self-hypnosis expert" named Marshall Sylver. Sylver, I would later find out, reached the peak of his fame when he gave a woman an orgasm on the *Montel Williams Show* by touching her knee. But in court, Gabriel speaks about him as though he is a candidate for pope. "That's Marshall Sylver," she repeats into the microphone. "S-y-l-v-e-r. . . ." You half-expect her to direct the jury to his Web site.

Jackson looks disengaged during this succession of clowns, but when the real witnesses start appearing, he begins acting out. On the fourth day of the trial, while Mesereau is cross-examining the accuser's big sister—who, among other things, testified that she saw the pop star repeatedly kiss her brother on the forehead—Jackson suddenly gets up and walks out of the courtroom.

The move momentarily staggers Mesereau, a hired killer of the first order, and he looks uncharacteristically sheepish as he chases after his client. He returns a minute later to inform eternally exhausted Judge Rodney Melville that "Mr. Jackson has to go to the bathroom, Your Honor."

A week later, Jackson simply fails to show up in court on a day when his actual accuser is scheduled to testify, forcing a clearly rattled Mesereau to tell Judge Melville that his client has "severe back pains"; Jackson eventually arrives to court in pajamas. But for all of Jackson's fabled eccentricity, he is, astonishingly, not the dominant personality at the trial. That honor belongs to District Attorney Sneddon, whose convoluted indictment is a Frankenstein's monster of incongruous parts every bit as luridly fascinating as the defendant's surgically altered face.

The prosecution's case, seldom satisfactorily explained in the mainstream media, goes as follows. On February 6, 2003, the Bashir documentary, in which Jackson is seen admitting that he sleeps in his bedroom with young boys, is shown on British TV. Among the children who appear in the video is his accuser in this case, a thirteen-year-old cancer survivor who had been introduced to Jackson during his chemotherapy treatments several years before.

According to the prosecution, Jackson had not molested the boy at the time the Bashir documentary aired, but he was sufficiently concerned that the boy might make such allegations that he and a band of Neverland courtiers entered into an elaborate conspiracy to "falsely imprison" the boy and his family for nearly five weeks (in luxury hotels, at Neverland ranch, and other places), during which time they coerced the family into denying, on camera, that anything untoward had ever happened between Jackson and the boy.

Jackson's five alleged coconspirators—none of whom were indicted—seem to be the sort of people who show up full of ideas at the bedside of fading greatness: junior Nazis who get Hitler to sign off on a new T-shirt design during the last days in the bunker. "Business associate" Dieter Wiesner, for instance, owns sex clubs in Germany and sank gobs of the pop star's money into a doomed Michael Jackson soft drink, to be marketed in Europe, called the MJ Mystery Drink. (Wiesner's former partner, coconspirator Ronald Konitzer, has since been accused by Mesereau of stealing Jackson's money.) Marc Schaffel came to Jackson after September 11 with plans to market an antiterror-theme "We Are the World"–type charity single through the McDonald's corporation; Schaffel later turned out to have been a former gay-porn producer. Rounding out the conspiracy are Vincent Amen and Frank Tyson, a pair of young Neverland gofers, who, until this case, appeared destined to star in a movie called *Harold and Kumar Pick Up Michael Jackson's Dry Cleaning*.

At any rate, it was only after the filming of this so-called rebuttal video—which, incidentally, Jackson then sold to the Fox Network for $3 million—and after authorities had begun an investigation into Jackson's relationship with the boy, that Jackson allegedly molested the child, in early March.

The prosecution's case therefore boils down to this: In a panic over negative publicity, Jackson conspires to kidnap a boy and force him to deny acts of molestation that in fact never happened, and then he gets over his panic just long enough to actually molest the child at the very moment when the whole world is watching.

It is a fantastic argument, a bilious exercise in circular prosecutorial logic: conspiracy to commit conspiracy, false imprisonment for the sake of it, followed by a sudden act of utter self-destructive madness. And none of it makes sense, until you actually watch Sneddon operate in court.

Day six of the trial. Sneddon, a splotchy-faced doughy man whose body could only look good on an autopsy table, is conducting his direct examination of the alleged victim's younger brother. It is a crucial moment in the trial, with Sneddon drawing out the only eyewitness to the alleged molestation. The pudgy-cheeked boy claims to have twice entered Jackson's bedroom late at night and seen the aging star fondling his brother and masturbating.

In a trial full of roundly unsympathetic characters, it is hard not to feel for this kid. A raspy-voiced fourteen-year-old with the sad eyes of a habitually ignored younger brother, this witness looks like every fat kid who's ever had his milk money stolen or his underwear pulled over his head. Whatever he's doing here, it's sad.

If his story is true, he is recounting an immensely painful personal experience in front of the entire world. If it is false, then his appearance here is a tragedy, an overmatched adolescent mind coached to mutter a litany of sordid implausibilities in the service of an ugly confluence of low-rent adult ambitions: grown-ups pulling his underwear over his head.

Sneddon practically drools when the boy finally says what he saw Jackson doing: "He was, uh, masturbating."

"Can you demonstrate that?" Sneddon says. "Can you show us what you saw?"

"What do you mean?" the boy whispers.

"Can you show us how he was masturbating?" Sneddon repeats.

The boy balks, but Sneddon presses. Finally the boy moves his hand up and down.

"Can you do it again?" Sneddon asks.

The boy hesitates, then gives another fleeting demonstration. It's still not enough for Sneddon.

"OK," he snaps. "For the record, you're moving your hand up and down, kind of opening and closing your palm."

Such episodes become increasingly common in the next few days of testimony, as the prosecution sinks further and further into a mushy mix of unapologetic crotch-sniffing and rhetorical hysterics. It is hard not to escape the impression that Sneddon hates Jackson. He clearly has not forgotten the debacle of 1993, when Jackson and the family of thirteen-year-old Jordan Chandler reached a $15.3 million settlement before Sneddon could bring Jackson to trial on molestation charges.

His key witnesses, meanwhile—the accuser and his family, whom we'll call the Riveras—are an astounding bunch. Any sane prosecutor would drown himself before building a case around witnesses like these, but they were all Sneddon had. A single mom and her three kids, an older daughter and two boys. They're poor but not ghetto poor—just poor like eighty percent of America is poor, making their way through life with a shabby cocktail of nowhere jobs, disability, Zoloft, Jesus, diets, and, one guesses, a vast collection of self-help books.

This family has been burdened first by an abusive father, then by a horrible cancer that struck the older boy; by the age of ten, he had a sixteen-pound tumor in his stomach. Through a series of charitable foundations and recovery programs, the boy's terrible predicament put the family in touch with a number of celebrities: George Lopez, Chris Tucker, Jay Leno, and Michael Jackson. The Jackson fiasco did not really begin until the boy, hereafter referred to as Freddy, had miraculously recovered and the family returned to its mean pre-crisis existence, armed only with a suddenly impressive Rolodex.

One hates to be uncharitable, but this is the special ugliness of the Jackson case: Even the poor are undignified. Once they enter this world, the Riveras become just another subspecies of the Bashirs, Gabriels, and Wiesners: a Dickensian family adopted as a curiosity by the royals.

The mother—we'll call her Agnes Rivera—seems to be the key figure in the accuser's camp. At this writing, she has only appeared in the trial via the rebuttal video, which Mesereau introduced as evidence during cross-examination. A plump, dewy-eyed woman with heavy makeup who looks like a Latina version of Bernadette Peters (only with a few more miles), she expresses herself almost exclusively in saccharine, retch-inducing platitudes of the sort one might hear on *Oprah* or at a motivational retreat for recovering glue addicts—using words like *God* and *love* and *hope* the way most normal people use connecting words like *and* and *the*.

The video is a low-tech production filmed in some dismal studio in West Hills; it's a single tripod shot of the four family members bunched in front of a gray dropcloth. The prosecution claims that Agnes and the children were dragged to this ugly place by Wiesner and told exactly what to say. But in the outtakes shown in court, the jury sees Agnes clearly making her own enthusiastic directorial contributions.

During the period of "false imprisonment" in which this film was shot, Agnes was put up in the Calabasas Country Inn, where at Jackson's expense she managed to fit in a full body wax and a shopping spree at, among other places, the Topanga Canyon Mall; she spent $454 on Jockey underwear at one stop, $415 at Banana Republic and another $450 at the Jeans Outlet. The family also got in a showing of *Old School* at a Calabasas movie theater and a $175 dinner at the Black Angus restaurant in Woodland Hills. Agnes also managed to avoid calling the police for the five hours she spent waiting in an orthodontist's office in Solvang while Freddy's braces were removed on Jackson's tab.

If Agnes seemed to handle her false imprisonment with aplomb, it might be because she had plenty of experience with it. Twice in the past she filed lawsuits claiming false imprisonment: once against her ex-husband (whom she also accused of murdering the family's pet ferret) and once against a pair of security guards at a JC Penney, who stopped her after finding Freddy in the store parking lot with unpaid merchandise. In the latter case, Agnes claimed that the guards not only falsely imprisoned her but brazenly fondled her breasts in front of the children; she won $150,000 in damages.

In any event, it is Sneddon's contention that after her latest false imprisonment at the hands of Jackson in Calabasas, Agnes and the children voluntarily returned to Neverland for a two-week stay that would turn into yet another false imprisonment in which Agnes believed she and her children were being held against their will. Even though she supposedly spent this time trying to escape, for some reason she did not even ask where her children were sleeping at night.

Thus she was unaware that Freddy was spending his nights in Michael's bedroom, engaging in mutual masturbation with the pop star not once but on two different occasions, both times in front of Freddy's pudgy little brother—who happened to creep to the bedroom and open the locked door just long enough to witness the hideous act through the darkness without being detected by either Michael or his brother.

Pudge, in his testimony, is very specific about how long he watched both sex acts. The first time, he says, it was four seconds. The second time? "Three seconds—it was shorter," he says.

You can dismiss Sneddon as a monomaniacal, headline-hungry bureaucrat and his witnesses as scheming, lying-ass gold diggers, but there's no avoiding the fact that Michael Jackson is, undeniably, one seriously weird motherfucker. As implausible and suspicious as the prosecution timeline sounds, many details of the boys' testimony about life at Jackson's Neverland lair are just too strange and wildly improbable to be anything but true.

At one point during the trial, the jury is shown a picture of a frighteningly lifelike mannequin of a small black girl with braided hair. Recovered during one of the two searches of Neverland ordered by Sneddon, this mannequin apparently was fashioned in the image of a little cousin of Jackson's. The accuser's brother testifies that on their first night at Neverland, Jackson jumped on the mannequin and simulated sex with it. "He was, uh, having intercourse with it," says Pudge.

Sneddon then leaves the picture of the mannequin onscreen for a few long moments. It looks exactly like a real girl. Nobody in the courtroom can take their eyes off the thing. My own heart skips a beat; I half-expect the picture to start steaming from the ears and speaking in tongues.

In scenes from the Bashir documentary shown to the jury, Jackson is depicted as the father of three utterly Caucasian "real" children who never see their mother. He insists he's had only one small nose job; he says with a straight face that he is Peter Pan and that he will never die. And he thinks everybody understands when he says that sleeping in beds with kids is OK because there should be "more love in the world." And it gets even more disturbing. He talks about the nicknames he gave the kids: "Blow Hole" for Pudge and "Doo Doo" or "Apple Head" for Freddy. Pudge testifies that Jackson called another boy who came to the ranch "Baby Rubber."

If you buy this part of the story, and it's pretty close to impossible not to, it doesn't require a great leap of logic to connect the remaining dots. It is a short step from Doo Doo

11

and Apple Head to a late-night hand down your underpants. This is the kind of thing that is running through the collective mind of the courtroom at the trial's first decisive moment: when Freddy takes the stand.

No longer a frail cancer victim, Jackson's accuser is now a strapping fifteen-year-old with a thick neck and a military-style buzz cut. But in his direct examination, he mumbles and hangs his head quite a lot and seems to grow smaller and more child-like on the stand as he is led through the tale of his terrible ordeal at Neverland.

It is a horrifying story, a tale of long nights of Jesus juice— Jackson's name for the red wine he fed the boy—porn, and late-night groping in the dark room full of mannequins. In the pivotal moment, Jackson and the boy guzzle booze in the Neverland arcade, then retreat to Jackson's bedroom, where the pop star asks the boy about masturbation. Jackson tells him that if he doesn't know how, "he would do it for me." He then mastur-bates the boy and himself as the two lie side by side.

"About a day later," Freddy says, the scenario repeats itself; only this time, Jackson tries to place the boy's hand on Jackson's genitals. Freddy says he resisted this but that he still ejaculated in both incidents. He felt bad about this, but, he says, Jackson "comforted me."

Through all this, Sneddon can't resist a little of his trade-mark crotch-sniffing. The prosecutor seems disappointed both legally and libidinously when Freddy fails, after being prompted, to remember seeing Jackson walk into the bedroom with an erection while he and his brother were watching television. A visibly frustrated Sneddon ends up pulling out a transcript of the boy's own grand-jury testimony and showing him the ref-erence to Jackson's erection, effectively shoving Jackson's erec-tion in the boy's face.

12

When the kid refuses to comply—saying only: "Me and my brother were kind of like '*Eww,*' because we had never seen a grown man naked before"—Sneddon frowns, clearly pissed, and moves on.

Still, by the time Sneddon is finished with this witness, Jackson looks fucked. Reporters scramble outside to do "Prosecution Roars Back" stand-ups, and even the most skeptical members of the press corps concede that Sneddon might not have to lift a finger for the rest of the trial.

During this testimony, Jackson scarcely moves. Mesereau, for his part, simply bides his time and waits in a seething posture for his cross examination. His demolition of Sneddon's star witness would prove to be one of the more merciless legal fraggings you'll ever see in an American courtroom. He gets Freddy to admit that something he had testified Michael Jackson told him—that "if a man doesn't masturbate, he can get to the point where he might rape a girl"—had actually been told to him by his grandmother.

He gets the boy to admit that he told the dean of his middle school, a Mr. Alpert, that "nothing had ever happened sexually with Mr. Jackson."

Mesereau asks about the alleged period of false imprisonment at Calabasas and Neverland. Sneddon sinks in his chair when Freddy answers, "I never wanted to leave. I was having too much fun."

Then there is the timeline of the actual abuse: Mesereau gets the boy to admit that he initially told investigators that the abuse had happened before the alleged false imprisonment and the rebuttal video, then later changed his story. "To this day," Freddy says, "I don't remember exactly when everything happened."

Mesereau then does a cunning thing. He leads the boy through a history of all his disciplinary problems in middle school. Freddy, it appears, was a pain in the ass to almost every teacher in his junior high: talking back and being disruptive and generally disrespecting authority. Mesereau slyly assumes the role of an accusing teacher and manages to coax out on the stand the above-it-all classroom smartass who only a few days before played the part of the mute, helpless child ruthlessly taken advantage of by an adult sexual predator.

Every disagreement he had ever had with a teacher, Freddy contends, was the teacher's fault. Mr. Geralt ran his class like a drill sergeant, which was why the boy had stood up in class and said that Mr. Geralt "had his balls in his mouth." He brags about arguing in Mrs. Slaughter's class ("A lot of the times, I would stand up to the teachers, and the kids would, like, congratulate me").

"Did you have problems in Mr. Finklestein's class?" Mesereau asks.

"Everyone had problems in Mr. Finklestein's class," Freddy snaps.

"Did you have problems in Mr. Finklestein's class?" Mesereau coldly repeats.

"If everyone had a problem," the boy sneers, "then I'd be one of them, right?"

Later, Mesereau plays the entire rebuttal video for Freddy, stopping every few moments. Since it is the prosecution's case that the family was told to lie in the video, Mesereau decides to get the boy to explain to the jury exactly where everyone was lying and where everyone was telling the truth—the obvious point being that it was very difficult to tell.

It's a savage courtroom scene, and the boy withers visibly as it wears on. When the jury sees Freddy claiming on the video that "he used to pray that he would meet Michael Jackson," Mesereau stops the DVD and asks, "Were you lying here?"

"I didn't actually pray to meet Michael Jackson," the boy mutters.

It goes on like this for another forty minutes. Freddy's performance is so atrocious that even Judge Melville wakes up. Until this point, Melville seldom looked anything but pained, apparently mourning the lost dignity of the legal profession. But during Freddy's cross examination, Melville's impatience with the prosecution is suddenly palpable. Usually, he takes ten quiet seconds before ruling on any objection, but after a few hours of this witness, his trigger finger gets very itchy, instantly blasting even the more reasonable of Sneddon's occasional objections. At one point, Mesereau asks the boy about his history teacher: "She complained that you were defiant on a regular basis and disrespectful, is that correct?"

Even I expect an objection to this; Mesereau is asking and answering.

"Your Honor, objection," Sneddon says. "Asked and answ—"

"Overruled," Melville snaps, glaring at the boy. "You may answer."

By the end of the day, Sneddon is slumped so far in his seat that his shoulders are almost below the armrests. His humiliation is total when Mesereau asks the boy if it is true that he once wanted to be an actor. "Yes," he says. "But now that I've seen other careers, I want to be in law enforcement."

By the time Freddy steps down, the trial is only twelve days old. It was impossible to say who was winning or losing; one forgets, after all, that these things are decided by a jury, which in this case looks mostly like a row of immobile elderly white women who might think they're judging the Lindbergh kidnapper.

Or one hopes they think that, for their sake. The elderly should be spared spectacles like the Jackson trial. This case is the ultimate sizzling shit pile of American society: It is what our culture of gross celebrity worship looks like when it comes out the other end. A pop star gone sideways under the lights, maggots nibbling at his fortune, hourly underpants updates on cable, industry insiders trading phone numbers over drinks, and boy orgasms. And people like me writing about it all. We're the worst America has to offer—and we're all here.

Four Amendments and a Funeral
A month inside the house of horrors that is Congress

August 25, 2005

It was a fairy-tale political season for George W. Bush, and it seemed like no one in the world noticed. Amid bombs in London, bloodshed in Iraq, a missing blonde in Aruba, and a scandal curling up on the doorstep of Karl Rove, Bush's Republican Party quietly celebrated a massacre on Capitol Hill. Two of the most long-awaited legislative wet dreams of the Washington Insiders Club—an energy bill and a much-delayed highway bill—breezed into law. One mildly nervous evening was all it took to pass through the House the Central American Free Trade Agreement (CAFTA), for years now a primary strategic focus of the battle-in-Seattle activist scene. And accompanied by scarcely a whimper from the Democratic opposition, a second version of the notorious USA Patriot Act passed triumphantly through both houses of Congress, with most of the law being made permanent this time.

Bush's summer bills were extraordinary pieces of legislation, broad in scope, transparently brazen, and audaciously indulgent. They gave an energy industry drowning in the most obscene profits in its history billions of dollars in subsidies and tax breaks, including $2.9 billion for the coal industry. The highway bill set new standards for monstrous and indefensibly wasteful spending, with Congress allocating $100,000 for a single traffic light in Canoga Park, California, and $223 million for the construction of a bridge linking the mainland to an Alaskan island with a population of just fifty.

17

It was a veritable bonfire of public money, and it raged with all the brilliance of an Alabama book burning. And what fueled it all were the little details you never heard about. The energy bill alone was 1,724 pages long. By the time the newspapers reduced this Tolstoyan monster to the size of a single headline announcing its passage, only a very few Americans understood that it was an ambitious giveaway to energy interests. Yet the drama of the legislative process is never in the broad strokes but in the bloody skirmishes and power plays that happen behind the scenes.

To understand the breadth of Bush's summer sweep, you had to watch the hand fighting at close range. You had to watch opposition gambits die slow deaths in afternoon committee hearings, listen as members fell on their swords in exchange for favors, and be there to see hordes of lobbyists rush in to reverse key votes at the last minute. All of these things I did— with the help of a tour guide.

"Nobody knows how this place is run," says Representative Bernie Sanders. "If they did, they'd go nuts."

Sanders is a tall, angular man with a messy head of gull-white hair and a circa-1977 set of big-framed eyeglasses. Minus the austere congressional office, you might mistake him for a physics professor or a journalist of the Jimmy Breslin school.

Vermont's sole representative in the House, Sanders is expected to become the first Independent ever elected to the U.S. Senate next year. He is something of a cause célèbre on both the left and the right these days, with each side overreacting to varying degrees to the idea of a self-described "democratic socialist" coming so near to a seat in the upper house.

Some months before, a Sanders aide had tried to sell me on a story about his boss, but over lunch we ended up talking about Congress itself. Like a lot of people who have worked on the

Hill a little too long, the aide had a strange look in his eyes—the desperate look of a man who's been marooned on a remote island, subsisting on bugs and abalone for years on end. You worry that he might grab your lapel in frustration at any moment. "It's unbelievable," he said. "Worse than you can possibly imagine. The things that go on . . ."

Some time later I came back to the aide and told him that a standard campaign-season political profile was something I probably couldn't do, but if Sanders would be willing to give me an insider's guided tour of the horrors of Congress I'd be interested.

"Like an evil, adult version of *Schoolhouse Rock*," I said.

The aide laughed and explained that the best time for me to go would be just before the summer recess, a period when Congress rushes to pass a number of appropriations bills. "It's like orgy season," he said. "You won't want to miss that."

I thought Sanders would be an ideal subject for a variety of reasons but mainly for his Independent status. For all the fuss over his "socialist" tag, Sanders is really a classic populist outsider. The mere fact that Sanders signed off on the idea of serving as my guide says a lot about his attitude toward government in general: he wants people to see exactly what he's up against.

I had no way of knowing that Sanders would be a perfect subject for another, more compelling reason. In the first few weeks of my stay in Washington, Sanders introduced and passed, against very long odds, three important amendments. A fourth very nearly made it and would have passed had it gone to a vote. During this time, Sanders took on powerful adversaries, including Lockheed Martin, Westinghouse, the Export-Import Bank, and the Bush administration. And by using the basic tools of democracy—floor votes on clearly posed questions, with the aid of painstakingly built coalitions of allies from both sides of the aisle—he, a lone Independent, beat them all.

It was an impressive run, with some in his office calling it the best winning streak of his career. Except for one thing.

By my last week in Washington all of his victories had been rolled back, each carefully nurtured amendment perishing in the grossly corrupt and absurd vortex of political dysfunction that is today's U.S. Congress. What began as a tale of political valor ended as a grotesque object lesson in the ugly realities of American politics—the pitfalls of digging for hope in a shit mountain.

Sanders, to his credit, was still glad that I had come. "It's good that you saw this," he said. "People need to know."

Amendment 1

At 2 p.m. on Wednesday, July 20, Sanders leaves his office in the Rayburn Building and heads down a tunnel passageway to the Capitol, en route to a Rules Committee hearing. "People have this impression that you can raise any amendment you want," he says. "They say, 'Why aren't you doing something about this?' That's not the way the system works."

Amendments occupy a great deal of most legislators' time, particularly those lawmakers in the minority. Members of Congress do author major bills, but more commonly they make minor adjustments to the bigger bills. Rather than write their own antiterrorism bill, for instance, lawmakers will try to amend the Patriot Act, either by creating a new clause in the law or by expanding or limiting some existing provision. The bill that ultimately becomes law is an aggregate of the original legislation and all the amendments offered and passed by all the different congresspersons along the way.

Sanders is the amendment king of the current House of Representatives. Since the Republicans took over Congress in 1995, no other lawmaker—not Tom DeLay, not Nancy Pelosi—has passed more roll-call amendments (amendments that actually went to a vote on the floor) than Bernie Sanders. He accomplishes this by on the one hand being relentlessly active and on the other by using his status as an Independent to form left-right coalitions.

On this particular day, Sanders carries with him an amendment to Section 215 of the second version of the Patriot Act, which is due to go to the House floor for a reauthorization vote the next day. Unlike many such measures, which are often arcane and shrouded in minutiae, the Sanders amendment is simple, a proposed rollback of one of the Patriot Act's most egregious powers. Section 215 allows law enforcement to conduct broad searches of ordinary citizens—even those not suspected of ties to terrorism—without any judicial oversight at all. To a civil libertarian like Sanders, it is probably a gross insult that at as late a date as the year 2005 he still has to spend his time defending a concept like probable cause before an ostensibly enlightened legislature. But the legislation itself will prove not half as insulting as the roadblocks he must overcome to force a vote on the issue.

The House Rules Committee is perhaps the free world's outstanding bureaucratic abomination—a tiny, airless closet deep in the labyrinth of the Capitol where some of the very meanest people on earth spend their days cleaning democracy like a fish. The official function of the committee is to decide which bills and amendments will be voted on by Congress and also to schedule the parameters of debate. If Rules votes against your amendment, your amendment dies. If you control the Rules Committee, you control Congress.

The committee has nine majority members and four minority members. But in fact only one of these thirteen people matters. Unlike on most committees, whose chairmen are usually chosen on the basis of seniority, the Rules chairman is the appointee of the Speaker of the House.

The current chairman, David Dreier, is a pencil-necked Christian Scientist from southern California, with exquisite hygiene and a passion for brightly colored ties. While a dependable enough yes-man to have remained Rules chairman for six years now, he is basically a human appendage, a prosthetic attachment on the person of the House majority leader, Tom DeLay. "David carries out the wishes of the Republican leadership right down the line," said former Texas congressman Martin Frost, until last year the committee's ranking Democrat.

There is no proven method of influencing the Rules Committee. In fact, in taking on the committee, Democrats and Independents like Sanders normally have only one weapon at their disposal.

"Shame," says James McGovern, a Massachusetts Democrat and one of the minority members on the committee. "Once in a great while we can shame them into allowing a vote on something or other."

The Rules Committee meets in a squalid space the size of a high school classroom, with poor lighting and nothing on the walls but lifeless landscapes and portraits of stern-looking congressmen of yore. The grim setting is an important part of the committee's character. In the vast, majestic complex that is the U.S. Capitol—an awesome structure where every chance turn leads to architectural wonderment—the room where perhaps the most crucial decisions of all are made is a dark, seldom-visited hole in the shadow of the press gallery.

The committee is the last stop on the legislative express, a kind of border outpost where bills are held up before they are allowed to pass into law. It meets sporadically, convening when a bill is ready to be sent to the floor for a vote.

Around 3 p.m., Sanders emerges from this hole into the hallway. For the last hour or so he has been sitting with his hands folded on his lap in a corner of the cramped committee room, listening as a parade of witnesses and committee members babbled on in stream-of-consciousness fashion about the vagaries of the Patriot Act. He heard, for instance, Texas Republican Pete Sessions explain his "philosophy" of how to deal with terrorists, which includes, he said, "killing them or removing them from the country."

Tom Cole of Oklahoma, another Republican committee member, breathlessly congratulated witnesses who had helped prepare the act. "This is a very important piece of legislation," he drawled. "Y'all have done a really good job."

Nodding bashfully in agreement with Cole's words was Wisconsin Republican James Sensenbrenner Jr. As chairman of the Judiciary Committee, Sensenbrenner is the majority lawmaker in whose scaly womb the Patriot Act gestated until its recent delivery to Rules. Though he was here as a witness, his obvious purpose was to bare his fangs in the direction of anyone or anything who would threaten his offspring.

Sensenbrenner is your basic Fat Evil Prick, perfectly cast as a dictatorial committee chairman. He has the requisite moist-with-sweat pink neck, the dour expression, the penchant for pointless bile and vengefulness. Only a month before, on June 10, Sensenbrenner suddenly decided he'd heard enough during a Judiciary Committee hearing on the Patriot Act and went completely Tasmanian devil on a group of Democratic witnesses who had come to share stories of abuses at places such as

Guantánamo Bay. Apparently not wanting to hear any of that stuff, Sensenbrenner got up mid-meeting and killed the lights, turned off the microphones, and shut down the C-Span feed before marching his fellow Republicans out of the room— leaving the Democrats and their witnesses in the dark.

This lights-out technique was actually pioneered by another Republican, former Commerce Committee chairman Thomas Bliley, who in 1995 hit the lights on a roomful of senior citizens who had come to protest Newt Gingrich's Medicare plan. Bliley, however, went one step further than Sensenbrenner, ordering Capitol police to arrest the old folks when they refused to move. Sensenbrenner might have tried the same thing in his outburst, except that his party had just voted to underfund the Capitol police.

Thus it is strange now, in the Rules Committee hearing, to see the legendarily impatient Sensenbrenner lounging happily in his witness chair like a giant toad sunning on nature's perfect rock. He speaks at length about the efficacy of the Patriot Act in combating the certain evils of the free-library system ("I don't think we want to turn libraries into sanctuaries") and responds to questions about the removal of an expiration date on the new bill ("We don't have sunsets on Amtrak or Social Security, either").

Such pronouncements provoke strident responses from the four Democratic members of the committee—Doris Matsui of California, Alcee Hastings of Florida, Louise Slaughter of upstate New York, and McGovern of Massachusetts—who until now have scarcely stirred throughout the hearing. The Democrats generally occupy a four-seat row on the far left end of the panel table, and during hearings they tend to sit there in mute, impotent rage, looking like the unhappiest four heads of lettuce ever to come out of the ground. The one thing they are allowed to do is argue. Sensenbrenner gives them just such an opportunity, and soon he and McGovern fall into a row about gag orders.

In the middle of the exchange, Sanders gets up and, looking like a film lover leaving in the middle of a bad movie, motions for me to join him in the hallway. He gestures at the committee room. "It's cramped, it's uncomfortable, there isn't enough room for the public or press," he says. "That's intentional. If they wanted people to see this, they'd pick a better hall."

Sanders then asks me if I noticed anything unusual about the squabbling between Sensenbrenner and McGovern. "Think about it," he says, checking his watch. "How hard is it to say, 'Mr. Sanders, be here at 4:30 p.m.'? Answer: not hard at all. You see, a lot of the things we do around here are structured. On the floor, in other committees, it's like that. But in the Rules Committee they just go on forever. You see what I'm getting at?"

I shrug.

"It has the effect of discouraging people from offering amendments," he says. "Members know that they're going to have to sit for a long time. Eventually they have to choose between coming here and conducting other business. And a lot of them choose other business. That's what that show in there was about."

Amendment 2

As he waits for his chance to address the Rules Committee, Sanders is armed with not one but two amendments. The measures are essentially the same, both using identical language to prohibit warrantless searches of libraries and bookstores. The only difference is that the amendment Sanders is trying to get past the committee would permanently outlaw such searches under the Patriot Act. The second amendment takes a more temporary approach, denying the Justice Department funding in next year's budget to conduct those types of searches.

This kind of creative measure—so-called limitation amendments—are often the best chance for a minority member like Sanders to influence legislation. For one thing, it's easier to offer such amendments to appropriations bills than it is to amend bills like the Patriot Act. Therefore, Sanders often brings issues to a vote by attempting to limit the funds for certain government programs—targeting a federal loan here, a bloated contract there. "It's just another way of getting at an issue," says Sanders.

In this case, the tactic worked. A month earlier, on June 15, the House passed Sanders's amendment to limit funding for library and bookstore searches by a vote of 238–187, with 38 Republicans joining 199 Democrats.

The move wasn't a cure-all; it was a short-term fix. But it enabled Sanders to approach the Rules Committee holding more than his hat in his hand. With the June vote, he had concrete evidence to show the committee that if his amendment to permanently alter the Patriot Act were allowed to reach the floor it would pass. Now, if Tom DeLay & Co. were going to disallow Sanders's amendment, they were going to have to openly defy a majority vote of the U.S. Congress to do so.

Which, it turns out, isn't much of a stumbling block.

While Sanders was facing the Rules Committee, House leaders were openly threatening their fellow members about the upcoming vote on CAFTA. "We will twist their arms until they break" was the Stalin-esque announcement of Arizona Republican Jim Kolbe. The hard-ass, horse-head-in-the-bed threat is a defining characteristic of this current set of House leaders, whose willingness to go to extreme lengths to get their way has become legend. In 2003, Nick Smith, a Michigan legislator nearing retirement, was told by Republican leadership that if he didn't vote for the GOP's Medicare bill, the party would put forward a primary challenger against his son Brad, who was planning to run for his seat.

Members who cross DeLay & Co. invariably find themselves stripped of influence and/or important committee positions. When Representative Chris Smith complained about Bush's policy toward veterans, he was relieved of his seat as the Veterans' Committee chairman. When Joel Hefley locked horns with Dennis Hastert during the Tom DeLay ethics flap, Hefley lost his spot as the House Ethics Committee chairman.

In other words, these leaders don't mind screwing even their friends any chance they get. Take the kneecapping of Arizona Republican Jeff Flake, whose surrender on the Patriot Act issue paved the way for the trashing of the Sanders amendment.

Flake, who sits on Sensenbrenner's Judiciary Committee, had been one of the leading Republican critics of the Patriot Act. He was particularly explicit in his support for sunset provisions in the law, which would prevent it from being made permanent. In April, for instance, a Flake spokesman told the *Los Angeles Times*, "Law enforcement officials would be more circumspect if they were faced with the prospect of having to come to Congress every couple of years and justify the provisions."

When Sanders offered his amendment to deny funding for warrantless searches, Flake was right there by his side. But now, only a few weeks later, Flake suddenly offers his own amendment, aimed at the same provision of the Patriot Act as Sanders's but with one big difference: it surrenders on the issue of probable cause. The Flake amendment would require only that the FBI director approve any library and bookstore searches.

It is hard to imagine a more toothless, pantywaist piece of legislation than Flake's measure. In essence, it is a decree from the legislative branch righteously demanding that the executive branch authorize its own behavior—exactly the kind of comical "compromise" measure one would expect the leadership to propose as a replacement for the Sanders plan.

Flake clearly had made a deal with the House leadership. It is not known what he got in return, but it appears that his overlords made him pay for it. Before the final vote on any bill, the opposition party has a chance to offer what is called a "motion to recommit," which gives Congress a last chance to reexamine a bill before voting on it. When the Democrats introduced this motion before the final vote, the House Republican leadership had to ask someone to stand up against it. They, naturally, turned to Flake, the chastened dissenter, to run the errand.

Flake is a sunny-looking sort of guy with a slim build and blow-dried blond hair. He looks like a surfer or maybe the manager of a Guitar Center in Ventura or El Segundo: outwardly cheerful yet ill-suited, facially anyway, for the real nut-cutting politics of this sort. When it comes time for him to give his speech, Flake meanders to the podium like a man who has just had his head clanged between a pair of cymbals. The lump in his throat is the size of a casaba melon. He begins, "Mr. Speaker, I am probably the last person expected to speak on behalf of the committee or the leadership in genera . . ."

When Flake mentions his own amendments, his voice drops as he tries to sound proud of them—but the most he can say is, "They are good." Then he becomes downright philosophical: "Sometimes, as my hero in politics said once . . . Barry Goldwater said, 'Politics is nothing more than public business . . . You don't always get everything you want.'"

It is a painful performance. Later, commenting on the Flake speech, Sanders shakes his head. "They made him walk the plank there," he says.

Flake denies he cut a deal to sell out on the Patriot Act. But his cave-in effectively spelled the end of the Sanders amendment. The Republicans point to the Flake amendment to show that they addressed concerns about library and bookstore searches. Essentially, the House leaders have taken the Sanders measure, cut all the guts out of it, bullied one of their own into offering it in the form of a separate amendment, and sent it sailing through the House, leaving Sanders—and probable cause—to suck eggs.

Amendment 1 Redux

Late in the afternoon, after waiting several hours for his turn, Sanders finally gets a chance to address the Rules Committee. His remarks are short but violent. He angrily demands that the committee let Congress vote on his amendment, noting that the appropriations version of it had already passed the House by fifty-one votes. "I would regard it as an outrageous abuse of power to deny this amendment the opportunity to be part of this bill," he shouts. "We had this debate already—and our side won."

In response, Republicans on the committee cast a collective "whatever, dude" gaze. "Sometimes, you can engage them a little," Sanders says later. But most of the time it works out like this.

Shortly after Sanders finishes his remarks, the Rules Committee members scurry to begin what will be a very long night of work. To most everyone outside those nine majority members, what transpires in the committee the night before a floor vote is a mystery on the order of the identity of Jack the Ripper or the nature of human afterlife. Even the Democrats who sit on the committee have only a vague awareness of what goes on. "They can completely rewrite bills," says McGovern. "Then they take it to the floor an hour later. Nobody knows what's in those bills."

A singular example of this came four years ago, when the Judiciary Committee delivered the first Patriot Act to the Rules Committee for its consideration. Dreier trashed that version of the act, which had been put together by the bipartisan committee, and replaced it with a completely different bill that had been written by John Ashcroft's Justice Department.

The bill went to the floor a few hours later, where it passed into law. The Rules Committee is supposed to wait out a three-day period before sending the bill to the House, ostensibly in order to give the members a chance to read the bill. The three-day period is supposed to be waived only in case of emergency. However, the Rules Committee of DeLay and Dreier waives the three-day period as a matter of routine. This forces members of Congress essentially to cast blind yes-or-no votes to bills whose contents are likely to be an absolute mystery to them.

There is therefore an element of Christmas morning in each decision of the committee. On the day of a floor vote, you look under the tree (i.e., the Rules Committee Web site) and check to see if your amendment survived. And so, on the morning of July 21, Sanders's staff goes online and clicks on the link H.R. 3199—USA PATRIOT AND TERRORISM PREVENTION REAUTHORIZATION ACT OF 2005. Twenty of sixty-three amendments have survived, most of them inconsequential. The Sanders amendment isn't one of them.

On a sweltering Tuesday morning in the Rayburn Building, a bookend location in the multibuilding home of the House of

Representatives, a very long line has formed in the first-floor corridor, outside the Financial Services Committee. In the ongoing orgy of greed that is the U.S. Congress, the Financial Services Committee is the hottest spot. Joel Barkin, a former press aide to Sanders, calls Financial Services the "job committee," because staffers who work for members on that committee move into high-paying jobs on Wall Street or in the credit-card industry with ridiculous ease.

"It seems like once a week, I'd get an e-mail from some staffer involved with that committee," he says, shaking his head. "They'd be announcing their new jobs with MBNA or MasterCard or whatever. I mean, to send that over an e-mail all over Congress—at least try to hide it, you know?"

On this particular morning, about half of the people in the line to get into the committee appear to be congressional staffers, mostly young men in ties and dress shirts. The rest are disheveled, beaten-down-looking men, most of them black, leaning against the walls.

These conspicuous characters are called "line standers." A lot of them are homeless. This is their job: they wait in line all morning so some lobbyist for Akin, Gump, or any one of a thousand other firms doesn't have to. "Three days a week," says William McCall (who has a home), holding up three fingers. "Come in Tuesday, Wednesday, and Thursday. Get between twelve and forty dollars."

When a photographer approaches to take a picture of the line, all the line standers but McCall refuse to be photographed and cover their faces with newspapers. I smile at this. Only the homeless have enough sense to be ashamed of being seen in Congress.

In reality, everybody in Congress is a stand-in for some kind of lobbyist. In many cases it's difficult to tell whether it's the companies that are lobbying the legislators or if it's the other way around.

Amendment 3

Across the Rayburn Building on the second floor, a two-page memo rolls over the fax machine in Sanders's office. Warren Gunnels, the congressman's legislative director, has been working the phones all day long, monitoring the Capitol Hill gossip around a vote that is to take place in the Senate later that afternoon. Now a contact of his has sent him a fax copy of an item making its way around the senatorial offices that day. Gunnels looks at the paper and laughs.

The memo appears to be printed on the official stationery of the Export-Import Bank, a federally subsidized institution whose official purpose is to lend money to overseas business ventures as a means of creating a market for U.S. exports. That's the official mission. A less full-of-shit description of Ex-Im might describe it as a federal slush fund that gives away massive low-interest loans to companies that a) don't need the money and b) have recently made gigantic contributions to the right people.

The afternoon Senate vote is the next act in a genuinely thrilling drama that Sanders himself started in the House a few weeks before. On June 28, Sanders scored a stunning victory when the House voted 313–114 to approve his amendment to block a $5 billion loan by the Ex-Im Bank to Westinghouse to build four nuclear power plants in China.

The Ex-Im loan was a policy so dumb and violently opposed to American interests that lawmakers who voted for it had serious trouble coming up with a plausible excuse for approving it. In essence, the United States was giving $5 billion to a state-subsidized British utility (Westinghouse is a subsidiary of British Nuclear Fuels) to build up the infrastructure of our biggest trade competitor, along the way sharing advanced nuclear technology with a Chinese conglomerate that had, in the past, shared nuclear know-how with Iran and Pakistan.

John Hart, a spokesman for Oklahoma Republican Senator Tom Coburn (who would later sponsor the Senate version of the Sanders amendment), laughs when asked what his opponents were using as an excuse for the bill. "One reason I got," Hart says, "was that if we build nuclear power plants in China, then China would be less dependent on foreign oil, and they would consume less foreign oil, and so as a result our oil prices would go down." He laughs again. "You'd think there would be more direct ways of lowering gas prices," he says.

Oddly enough, Coburn, a hard-line pro-war, pro-life conservative who once advocated the death penalty for abortion doctors, is a natural ally for the "socialist" Sanders on an issue like this one. Sanders frequently looks for cosponsors among what he and his staff call "honest conservatives," people such as California's Dana Rohrabacher and Texas libertarian Ron Paul, with whom Sanders frequently works on trade issues. "A lot of times, guys like my boss will have a lot in common with someone like Sanders," says Jeff Deist, an aide to Representative Paul. "We're frustrated by the same obstacles in the system."

In the case of Westinghouse, the bill's real interest for the Senate had little to do with gas prices and a lot to do with protecting a party member in trouble. Many of the 5,000 jobs the loan was supposed to create were in Pennsylvania, where Rick Santorum, the GOP incumbent, was struggling to hold off a challenger. "Five billion for five thousand jobs," Sanders says, shaking his head in disbelief. "That's a million dollars per job. And they say I'm crazy."

This morning, with the Senate vote only a few hours away, the lobbying has kicked into very high gear. That lobbyists for

Westinghouse are phone-blitzing senatorial offices is no surprise. Somewhat more surprising are reports that the Ex-Im Bank itself is hustling the senatorial staff.

"Technically speaking, government agencies aren't allowed to lobby," says Gunnels. "But they sure do a lot of informing just before big votes."

The document that has just spilled over the Sanders fax line is printed with a cover sheet from the Ex-Im Bank. It looks like an internal memo, sent by Ex-Im's "senior legislative analyst," Beverley Thompson.

The document contains a series of cheery talking points about the Ex-Im loan to China, which taken together seem to indicate that the loan is a darn good idea. Nowhere does the document simply come out and say, "We recommend that the Sanders amendment against this loan be defeated." But the meaning is fairly clear.

One odd feature of the document is a notation at the top of the page that reads, "FYI—this info has not been cleared." In government offices, documents must be cleared for public consumption before they can be distributed outside the agency. What this memo seems to suggest, then, is that the recipient was being given choice inside info from the Ex-Im Bank, a strange thing for the bank to be doing out in the open.

The Sanders office has seen this kind of thing before. In the summer of 2003, it received a very similar kind of document purportedly from the Treasury. Printed on Treasury stationery, the document contained, like the Ex-Im memo, a list of talking points that seemed to argue against a Sanders amendment. The issue in that case involved a set of new Treasury regulations that would have made it easier for companies to convert their employees' traditional pension plans into a new type of plan called a cash-balance pension plan.

Among the companies that would have been affected by the regulations was IBM, which stood to save billions by converting to this new system. And guess who turned out to have written the "Treasury Department memo" that was circulated to members of Congress on the eve of the vote?

That's right: IBM.

"It was hilarious," recalls Gunnels. "The Treasury Department logo was even kind of tilted, like it had been pasted on. It looked like a third-grader had done it."

Persistent questioning by Sanders's staff led to an admission by the Treasury Department that the document had indeed been doctored by IBM. The company, in turn, issued an utterly nonsensical mea culpa ("We believed that we were redistributing a public document that we had understood was widely distributed by the Treasury") that has to rank as one of the lamer corporate nonapologies in recent years.

It seemed obvious that the company had acted in conjunction with one or more Treasury employees to create the phony document. But no Treasury employee has ever been exposed, nor has IBM ever been sanctioned. "They turned the case over to the Inspector General's Office," says Gunnels. Jeff Weaver, Sanders's chief of staff, adds, "And they've done absolutely nothing."

So long as the investigation is still open, Gunnels explains, there is no way to request documents pertaining to the case through the Freedom of Information Act. "That investigation will probably stay open a long time," he says.

Every time Congress is ordered to clean up its lobbyist culture, its responses come off like leprechaun tricks. For instance, when the Lobby Disclosure Act of 1995 ordered the House and the Senate to create an electronic lobbyist registry system, so that the public could use the latest technology to keep track of

Washington's 34,000-plus lobbyists and whom they work for, the two houses only half complied.

The secretary of the Senate created an electronic database, all right, but what a database. The system was little more than a giant computerized pile of downloadable scanned images of all the individual registration forms and semiannual reports. The Senate system, however, was a significant improvement over the House system. The House responded to the 1995 law by entirely ignoring it.

All of Washington seems to be in on the lobbyist leprechaun game. News even leaked that corporations had managed to convince the local sports teams the Wizards and the Capitals to create special courtside or rinkside tickets. The tickets would not be available to the general public but would have an official list price of $49.50 and could be purchased by corporate customers. Why the low list price? Because congressional rules prohibit gifts to congressmen with a cost above fifty dollars.

Amendment 4

The Ex-Im amendment was not the only victory Sanders had scored on the government-waste front that month. In fact, just two days after he passed the Ex-Im amendment, Sanders secured another apparent major victory against a formidable corporate opponent. By a vote of 238–177, the House passed a Sanders amendment to cancel a $1.9 billion contract that the Federal Aviation Administration had awarded to Lockheed Martin to privatize a series of regional Flight Service Stations.

Several factors went into the drafting of this amendment. For one thing, the FAA-Lockheed deal would have resulted in the loss of about 1,000 jobs around the country from the closure of thirty-eight Flight Service Stations, which are basically small regional centers that give out weather information and provide some basic air-traffic assistance. Thirty-five of those projected job losses would have come from a station in Burlington, Vermont, so in opposing the deal Sanders was behaving like a traditional congressman, protecting his home turf.

But there were other concerns. The FAA deal was an early test run for a Bush policy idea called "competitive sourcing," which is just a clunky euphemism for the privatization of traditionally government-run services. Sanders is generally opposed to competitive sourcing, mainly on cost and quality grounds.

Beyond that, Sanders sees in issues like the Westinghouse deal and the Lockheed Martin deal a consistent pattern of surrender to business interests by Congress. Too often, he says, Congress fails to tie government assistance to the company's record in preserving American jobs.

"I have no problem with the argument that we should help businesses out," Sanders says. "But if you go to these hearings, no one ever asks the question 'How many jobs have you exported over the years? If we give you money, will you promise not to export any more jobs?'"

He laughs. "It's funny. Some of these companies, they'll be straight with you. General Electric, for instance. They come right out and say, 'We're moving to China.' And if you ask them why, in that case, you should subsidize them, they say, 'If you don't help us, we'll move to China faster.'"

Given how powerful Lockheed Martin is on Capitol Hill—the company even has the contract to maintain the server for the computers in Congress—the Lockheed vote was surprisingly easy. Maybe too easy. On the surface, it looked like traditional politics all the way, with Sanders applying his usual formula of securing as many Democratic votes as possible, then working to pry loose enough Republicans to get the vote through. In this case, the latter task proved not all that difficult, as Sanders had natural allies in each of those Republican representatives with targeted flight stations in their districts.

When the vote sailed through by a comfortable margin, however, Sanders didn't celebrate. Sometimes, he says, a vote like this one will pass easily in the House precisely because the leadership knows it will be able to kill it down the line.

"I don't want to accuse my fellow members of cynicism," he says, "but sometimes they'll vote for an amendment just so they can go back home and say they fought for this or that. In reality, they've been assured by the leadership that the measure will never make it through."

And if an offending bill somehow makes it through the House and the Senate, there's always the next and last step: the conference committee. Comprising bipartisan groups of conferees from the relevant House and Senate authorizing committees, these committees negotiate the final version of a bill. Like the Rules Committee, it has absolute power to make wholesale changes—which it usually does, safely out of the public's view.

With a measure like Sanders's Lockheed amendment, the chances were always going to be very slim that it would survive the whole process. Among other things, President Bush responded to the passage of the anti-Lockheed amendment by immediately threatening to veto the entire Transportation budget to which it was attached. (Bush made the same threat, incidentally, in response to the Ex-Im amendment, which was attached to the Foreign Operations budget.)

"Now the conference committee has political cover," Sanders says. "It's either take them out and restore that loan and that contract or the president vetoes an entire appropriations bill—and there's no funding for Foreign Operations or Transportation. There's really no choice."

In the case of the Lockheed amendment, however, things never get that far. Despite the amendment's comfortable victory in the House, weeks pass, and the Sanders staff cannot find a senator to sponsor the measure in the upper house. Though the staff still has hopes that a sponsor will be found, it's not always that easy to arrange. Especially when the president threatens a veto over the matter.

As for the Ex-Im amendment, the Sanders gambit against it perishes on that Tuesday afternoon, July 19, as the Senate wallops the Coburn version of the amendment, 62–37. According to Gunnels, the key vote ends up being cast by Democrat Harry Reid of Nevada.

"It was still close, around 24–23 or so, before Reid voted," he says. "It looked like a lot of Democrats were waiting to see which way he would go, him being the minority leader and all. As soon as he voted no, a whole slew of Democrats followed him and the amendment was dead."

Reid's predecessor as minority leader, Tom Daschle, was a marionette of the banking and credit-card industries whose public persona recalled a hopped-up suburban vacuum-cleaner salesman. In the wake of the Daschle experiment, Reid is the perfect inheritor of the Democratic leadership mantle: a dour, pro-life Mormon with a campaign chest full of casino money. Trying to figure out his motives on this vote proved no less difficult than figuring out what the Democratic Party stands for in general.

When I call Reid's office, spokesman Jim Manley initially refuses to offer an explanation for the senator's vote. He seems weirdly defensive about the issue, and we go back and forth on the matter for a while before he finally reads a statement explaining—or purporting to, anyway—his boss's vote on the China loan.

"As with questions raised about other transactions involving China, legitimate concerns are at issue," he reads. "But rather than Congress intervening in one transaction after another, what we really need is a coherent and comprehensive policy to address the emergence of China as an economic threat. This administration has failed to develop a China policy . . . and this utter failure has fueled congressional and public unease . . . Got that?"

"Um," I say, copying it down. "Sure. Wait—if the problem is that there's no comprehensive policy for China, why give them $5 billion to build nuclear plants? Why not give them, say, nothing at all?"

Silence on the other end of the line. Finally, Manley speaks.

"This administration has failed to develop a China policy," he repeats coldly. "And this utter failure has fueled congressional and public unease . . ."

In the end, after just a few weeks, every one of Sanders's victories was transformed into a defeat. He had won three major amendments and would likely have won a fourth, if the Rules Committee had permitted a vote on his Patriot Act measure. In each case, Sanders proved that his positions held wide support—even among a population as timid and corrupt as the U.S. Congress. Yet after passing his amendments by wide margins, he never really came close to converting popular will into law.

Sanders seems to take it strangely in stride. After a month of watching him and other members, I get the strong impression that even the idealists in Congress have learned to accept the body on its own terms. Congress isn't the steady assembly line of consensus policy ideas it's sold as but a kind of permanent emergency in which a majority of members work day and night to burgle the national treasure and burn the Constitution. A largely castrated minority tries, Alamo-style, to slow them down—but in the end spends most of its time beating calculated retreats and making loose plans to fight another day.

Taken all together, the whole thing is an ingenious system for inhibiting progress and the popular will. The deck is stacked just enough to make sure that nothing ever changes. But enough is left to chance to make sure that hope never completely dies out. Who knows, maybe it evolved that way for a reason.

"It's funny," Sanders says. "When I first came to Congress, I'd been mayor of Burlington, Vermont—a professional politician. And I didn't know any of this. I assumed that if you get majorities in both houses you win. I figured, it's democracy, right?"

Well, that's what they call it, anyway.

Bush vs. the Mother

On the president's doorstep—a dead soldier, an aggrieved housewife, and the start of something big

—

September 8, 2005

Crawford, the home of President George W. Bush, is a sun-scorched hole of a backwater Texas town—a single dreary railroad crossing surrounded on all sides by roasted earth the color of dried dog shit. There are scattered clumps of trees and brush, but all the foliage seems bent from the sun's rays and ready at any moment to burst into flames.

The moaning cattle along the lonely roads sound like they're begging for their lives. The downtown streets are empty. Just as the earth is home to natural bridges, this place is a natural dead end—the perfect place to drink a bottle of Lysol, wind up in a bad marriage, have your neck ripped out by a vulture.

It is a very unlikely place for a peace movement to be born. But that's exactly what happened a few weeks ago, when an aggrieved war mom named Cindy Sheehan set up camp along the road to the president's ranch and demanded a meeting with the commander in chief.

Sheehan's vigil began on Saturday, August 6, and was originally a solitary affair. Her twenty-four-year-old son, Casey Sheehan, was killed way back in April 2004, when he was one of eight marines struck down in an ambush in Baghdad's Sadr City.

Sheehan's demand was that Bush meet with her and explain to her what, exactly, her son had died for. The demand, and the accompanying solitary vigil, began as a simple, powerful, unequivocal political statement—the unarguably genuine protest of a single grieving individual. It was a quest that began on a moral territory almost beyond argument. How could anyone quibble with a mother who'd lost her son?

But Sheehan quickly became more than just the Next Big Media Thing, a successor to Kobe, Laci, and Michael. Her campsite became the epicenter of a national antiwar movement that until recently had been largely forgotten. By the end of a full week of media insanity, it seemed fit to ask if anything was left of that original simple message—or if something else had taken its place.

I arrived in Crawford early in the afternoon on Thursday, August 11, the sixth day of Sheehan's vigil. The campsite, dubbed "Camp Casey," was a small row of tents lining the side of a road cutting through a bleak stretch of singed ranch land, some three miles from the president's compound. There were about a hundred people there when I showed up, a large chunk of them reporters—whose presence, clearly, the protesters had already adjusted to. Along one row of tents, a small group of sunbathing young activists was trying out a new cheer for KCEN, the local NBC affiliate.

"C! I! N-D-Y! She deserves a reason why!"

On the other side of the camp was Sheehan herself, a tall, deliberate, sad-looking woman with sun-lightened hair and a face red from the afternoon heat. I didn't get within ten feet of her before I was intercepted by a pair of young women from the feminist antiwar organization CodePink. Alicia and Tiffany had apparently assumed the role of press secretaries; Sheehan was already operating on a rigid media schedule.

Throughout my stay in Texas I would run into a steady stream of young volunteers who seemed to consider it a great honor to be able to announce that "Cindy is too busy to talk with you right now." A solemn code of Cindy-reverence quickly became a leitmotif of the scene; preserving the sanctity of Sheehan's naps, meals, and Internet time became a principle that the whole compound worked together to uphold.

On my first night at the camp, a protester parked too close to a gully and her car slipped into a ditch. While a bunch of us tried to extricate it, pushing the car as its wheels spun, one protester leaned over to another.

"Blame George fucking Bush!" he said, pushing.

"I blame George fucking Bush for everything!" was the answer.

They were kidding, but we still didn't get the car out of the ditch that night. If the pre-Sheehan antiwar movement had a problem, it was stuff like this. The movement likes to think of itself as open and inclusive, but in practice it often comes off like a bunch of nerds whose favored recreation is coming up with clever passwords for their secret treehouse. The ostensible political purpose may be ending the war, but the immediate occupation for a sizable percentage of these people always seemed to be a kind of rolling adult tourist attraction called Hating George Bush. Marches become Hate Bush cruises; vigils, Hate Bush resorts. Hence the astonishingly wide variety of anti-Bush tees (Camp Casey featured a rare film-fantasy matched set, home at various times to BUSH IS SAURON and DARTH INVADER), and the unstoppable flow of Bush-themed folk songs. If you spend any amount of time involved with peace protests, as I have, you very quickly start to notice that Hating the President just seems like a little too much of a fun thing for too many of your brothers-in-arms.

Then again, here as in the rest of America, there's no shortage of folks who spend too much time sick with the opposite disease, Loving the President. In downtown Crawford, the two groups are separated by a Mason-Dixon line. While the anti-Bush protesters congregate at a Zonker Harris–style commune called the Crawford Peace House, the pro-Bush crowd has a meeting place in a giant gift shop called the Yellow Rose.

It's a striking visual scene. On one side of the railroad tracks running through town there's a creaky old house, bedecked with peace signs, that looks like the home of the Partridge family. A few hundred yards away, across the tracks, is the Yellow Rose—a patriotic storefront drenched in red, white, and blue whose entrance is obscured by a Liberty Bell, flanked by two huge stone tablets bearing the Ten Commandments. Together, the two places look like a pair of rides in a *Crossfire* theme park.

Early on my third day I was browsing in the hat section of the Yellow Rose when a clerk approached me.

"Excuse me," I said, holding up two Old Glory mesh hats. "Which of these do you think looks more American?"

She smiled and walked away. A friendly feeling welled up inside me. Within five minutes I was talking to store owner Bill Johnson, a fanatical Bush devotee with a striking resemblance to frozen-sausage king Jimmy Dean. I introduced myself as a Fox TV booker named Larry Weinblatt and told Bill I wanted to bring Sean Hannity down to do a whole show with Sean standing between the Ten Commandments tablets. Bill was all over the idea.

"We want to have that kind of godlike effect," I said.

"Right," Bill said, nodding.

"Secondly, Sean, when he travels," I said, "he brings his own Nautilus equipment. He pumps iron before he goes on."

"Does he really?"

"Yeah," I said. "We get a lot of demonstrators when Sean does his show, and so what he likes to do, when he finishes the broadcast, he takes his shirt off and flexes his muscles for the crowd. You know, *rrrr* . . ."

"Is he really built like that?"

"Oh, man, he's huge," I said.

We went on like this for a while. Fifteen minutes later, we wrapped up the negotiations.

"Again," I said, "we'd like to use the bell, the Ten Commandments, that backdrop, some horses, and if you have those good-looking Christian girls, we'll take them, too."

"Whatever you want, we'll do it," Bill said.

We shook hands. From there, I went to the inevitable conservative counterdemonstration, which was organized by Dallas right-wing talk-show reptile Darrell Ankarlo. Sheehan's transformation in the right-wing media from anonymous war mom to the great horned pinko Satan was unusually rapid, even by their standards.

The chief talking points were established within four days after her vigil had started. Sheehan was a fame-seeking narcissist, an anti-American traitor who dishonored her dead son (Bill O'Reilly questioned her motives and suggested people might see her actions as treasonous), and a stooge for Michael Moore. This Dallas jock Ankarlo chipped in with a claim that he'd received a series of death threats, some of which, he implied, had come from Sheehan's peaceniks.

There are times when American politics seems like little more than two groups in a fever to prevent each other from trespassing upon their respective soothing versions of unreality. At one point at Camp Casey, an informal poll taken around a campfire revealed that six out of a group of ten protesters, selected at random, believed that the United States government was directly involved in planning the 9/11 bombings. Flabbergasted, I tried to press the issue.

"Do you know how many people would have to be involved in that conspiracy?" I said. "I mean, start with the pilots . . ."

"The planes were flown by remote control," a girl sitting across from me snapped.

Things were no better at Ankarlo's counterdemonstration. Aaron Martin, thirty-one, had never heard the administration say that Iraq had nothing to do with 9/11, but Martin did remember one thing about Iraq that he said he'd heard "prior to 9/11."

"They had a fuselage," he said. "It was like a seven-forty-seven fuselage that they use for training purposes for terrorism."

Was there any other reason he believed Iraq was connected to 9/11?

"It's just a general feeling," he said.

Another group I spoke with asked me why I believed Iraq wasn't connected to 9/11. I answered that Saddam Hussein's secular government was a political enemy of the Islamic fundamentalists.

"Well," said Raymond Smith, forty-two, "the enemy of my enemy is my friend."

He laughed, and the group nodded at me triumphantly.

It was like a scene from *Spinal Tap*. Three seconds passed.

"But," I said finally, "that doesn't make any sense, does it?"

Everyone shrugged impatiently. Who gives a fuck? We believe what we believe—and fuck you if you don't like it. The Iraq war is like the sun: no one wants to stare at it too long.

By the time I finally sat down with Sheehan I was deeply frustrated with all of this, and I was ready to blame her for what had become, in my mind, a noisome exercise in blind chest-puffing on both sides. By the eighth day of her vigil, practically every anti-Bush movement under the sun had wiggled into Crawford to get a piece of the action, and it seemed to me that all had been lost and that Sheehan had allowed the illogic of a media hurricane—noise for noise's sake—to take over her protest. Particularly irritating was the sight of a giant school bus bearing the inscription "Free the Cuban Five" parked in front of the Peace House. Jesus, I thought. The Mumia people can't be far behind.

"What's the Cuban Five?" Sheehan asked when we finally sat down, alone.

"They're on the front lawn here . . ."

She shook her head helplessly. She had no idea who they were.

We met in a trailer parked outside the Peace House that someone had volunteered for her use. The trailer-sanctuary added to the movie-star vibe that followed Sheehan around everywhere in Crawford; I half expected to see a director's chair marked MS. SHEEHAN parked out front.

For all this, Sheehan seemed a very lonely woman. Tall, lanky, and clunkily built, with the most common and therefore most tragic of faces—the forgotten housewife whom life, with all its best joys, has long ago passed by—Sheehan had begun to move around the compound with a preternatural slowness, like a ghost. She floated, rather than walked, into the trailer. Following a week of media madness, she was like a superhero unable to return home after falling into a vat of disfiguring acid. Her past—the middle-class family life in Vacaville, California, with her four kids and the yellow station wagon they nicknamed the BananaMobile—all that was gone.

She had been through so much in the past week. In still more proof that red-blue politics often comes before family in this country, her in-laws had released a statement cruelly denouncing her. Her estranged husband, perhaps a coward and perhaps unable to handle the stress, filed for divorce. Revelations about her personal life were spilling into print, and all around the country, heartless creeps like Drudge and Ankarlo were casting themselves as friends and protectors of her fallen son and criticizing her for dishonoring him.

In return for all that, what Sheehan got was this: her own trailer, a couple of weeks' worth of airtime, and a bunch of people who called themselves her friends but were really just humping the latest cause. They would probably be moving on soon, and Sheehan would be left with nothing. Meeting her now, I was struck by one more thing. At the end, when it was all over, her son would still be gone. I felt very sorry for her.

"I never knew," she said, sighing. "Not only that I would become the face of the antiwar movement but also that I would become the sacrificial lamb of the antiwar movement."

I asked her if she was referring to all the personal attacks. She nodded.

"But I'd still do it again," she said. "Because it's so important."

Sheehan's political sincerity has been questioned, and in almost every case the charges against her have proved monstrous, calculating, and untrue. An example of the kind of thing that's been pinned to her: Matt Drudge blasted her for being a flip-flopper after digging up seemingly pro-Bush Sheehan quotes from a California newspaper after she and other war parents had met with the president.

Among those were "That was the gift the president gave us, the gift of happiness, of being together." Drudge implied that Sheehan was referring to the meeting with the president. In fact, what Sheehan was saying was that the real gift Bush gave the families was the opportunity to meet each other, not the president.

Things like this are what Sheehan's detractors are using to describe what they call "Cindy's political agenda," but I didn't observe any agenda from Sheehan, just a very tired woman. Like everyone else in antiwar circles, Sheehan does sometimes speak in the clubby language of Camp Bush Hater—but when she does this, she sounds like a follower, not a leader. In the end, the movement might overtake her, but while she is still at its center she seems genuinely to be trying to do the right thing.

"This thing," she said, "it's bigger than me now."

Sheehan believes that no matter what happens, one thing she accomplished was the returning of the Iraq war to its rightful place at the forefront of the national consciousness. She describes an experience earlier in the week when a TV producer offhandedly mentioned to her that her timing was perfect, that Sheehan had been lucky to hold her vigil on what was otherwise a slow news week.

"And I said to her, 'A slow news week? Didn't thirty soldiers die in the war this month?'" She shook her head. "It's crazy. Iraq should be the lead story every day."

Late that night, a car pulled up at the campsite. There was a woman at the wheel and she was crying.

She was a Bush supporter who lives in the area, but her son was about to be shipped off to Iraq. She had made a special trip out here to complain about the long row of white crosses the protesters had planted along the side of the road—each cross bearing the name of a fallen soldier. "Y'all are breaking my heart!" she cried. "My son hasn't gone yet, and I have to see those crosses every morning." She collected herself, wailed, and cried again, "You've broken one woman's heart!"

She drove off.

In the sixties, the antiwar movement was part of a cultural revolution. If you opposed Vietnam, you were also rejecting the whole rigid worldview that said life meant going to war, fighting the Commies, then coming back to work for the man, buying two cars, and dying with plenty of insurance. That life blueprint was the inflexible expectation of the time, and so ending the war of that era required a visionary movement.

Iraq isn't like that. Iraq is an insane blunder committed by a bunch of criminal incompetents who have managed so far to avoid the lash and the rack only because the machinery for avoiding reality is so advanced in this country. We don't watch the fighting, we don't see the bodies come home, and we don't hear anyone screaming when a house in Baghdad burns down or a child steps on a mine.

The only movement we're going to need to end this fiasco is a more regular exposure to consequence. It needs to feel its own pain. Cindy Sheehan didn't bring us folk songs but she did put pain on the front pages. And along a lonely Texas road late at night, I saw it spread.

Apocalypse There

A journey into the nightmare of New Orleans

—

October 6, 2005

It's a little before midnight on Friday, September 2, and I'm sitting in a hotel bar in Houston. Somewhere to the southeast, the worst natural disaster in American history is unfolding in the darkness, with an entire city shrouded in death, panic, and disease—and here we are, a bunch of half-drunk, affluent white people quaffing eleven-dollar foreign beers and planning what appears to be a paramilitary mission to rescue two cats and a maid in the wreckage of New Orleans.

I'm in the lounge of the Four Seasons with Sean Penn and other assorted media creatures, debating the merits of rescuing animals instead of humans in a disaster area. To my left is the eminent historian Douglas Brinkley, a friendly academic whose careful diction reminds me of Bob Woodward's. Brinkley is my contact in Houston. He's friends with Penn, and when he evacuated his home in New Orleans earlier in the week he left his cats and his maid behind in the flood zone. Now he and Penn are talking about commandeering private jets, helicopters, and weapons for a grand mission into hell that begins tomorrow.

I have no idea what the fuck is going on. At this point, five days into the disaster, I'm as clueless as President Bush. To those of us who didn't know any better, Katrina by her early satellite portrait looked like just another one of those watery curlicues that runs up the gulf from time to time, turning gap-toothed hayseeds out of their trailers on live television, titillating

Middle America just long enough to inspire the odd few days of canned-food drives or teddy-bear vigils.

But then Katrina snuck up on America, smashing it right in the breadbasket when not a soul anywhere was paying attention. For most of the country it was like going to bed one night with a mild toothache and waking up the next morning to find your balls smashed with a sledgehammer. Instead of leaving a little twisted timber and a few bodies behind, Katrina blew absolutely everything to shit and wiped an entire NFL market off the map. The standard television-entertainment formula for the meteorological catastrophe has been hopelessly disrupted, for in place of the Swift Government Reaction and the inevitable Inspirational Reconstruction and Recovery we have instead goodness knows what—some kind of gruesome existential horror story in which a mighty empire is transformed in a single night into a Hobbesian jungle, with taxpayers turned into wraiths and zombies, and not only no order but no clear idea of who is responsible for restoring it.

At the Four Seasons, Penn listens as a giggly Fox TV producer with big tits explains why she supports a mission, supposedly launched by Siegfried and Roy, to save the abandoned pets of New Orleans.

"I just have a soft spot for cats!" she gushes. "I can't stand to see them suffer—the little cuties!"

As she speaks, she tosses her hair back and brushes a tit against Penn's elbow. He shrugs.

"The way I see it," he says, "when in doubt, go human."

In the morning, Sean, Doug, and I fly in a small four-seater plane from Houston to Baton Rouge. The flight is without incident but also our last brush with normalcy.

The instant we land in Baton Rouge it is clear we are at the far edges of an extraordinary, cataclysmic event. The airport gates are clogged with military helicopters of every stripe, refueling and unloading, while the terminals and parking lots are spotted everywhere with stacks of food supplies and bottled water, a sight that will become increasingly familiar. There being no rental cars available, we hire what appears to be the last cab in Baton Rouge, an ancient minivan that lists badly to one side and makes knocking sounds at speeds over thirty-five miles per hour.

Actor, historian, and journalist pile into this ridiculous vehicle around noon on Saturday with no real concrete plans beyond a determination to find passage into New Orleans. We do have one definite order of business in Baton Rouge: visiting a black family that had just evacuated the city and is staying in a cramped room of a roadside hotel. Penn had seen the Browders on CNN and had called them to ask if he could help. They were hoping that he, being a celebrity, could get into New Orleans somehow and track down a lost relative.

Specifically, one Lillian Browder, the elderly mother of a frantic, gesticulating woman named Dorian Browder. Lillian had stayed behind to protect her home in a waterlogged neighborhood, and now the rest of the family doesn't know where she is.

"We can't get back to her, there's too much chaos," Dorian says, covering her eyes. "The last time I talked to her, the water was up to her waist . . ."

In her frenzied accounts of clashes with the rescue bureaucracy, Dorian describes an apparatus of police and National Guardsmen that is smug, callous, totally disorganized, given to lapsing into acronym-speak and military mumbo jumbo, and more focused on preserving their dubious situational authority than on using common sense. Even the only grown man in the room with us, who identifies himself as a New Orleans policeman, has been turned away, badge and all, in his attempt to reenter the city—the highly suspect reason being that he should not have left his jurisdiction in the first place.

Before this trip is over we'll hear a lot of complaints like this, and I'll see plenty of this kind of bureaucratic insanity myself, but the frantic scene at the hotel is the first place we encounter it.

"They're trying to keep it on the hush-hush," says Dorian. "But people are dying . . . People are dying all around you down there, and they're not doing anything about it."

The family gives us the address of Lillian's home, and when we leave everyone in the room embraces each of us in turn— even me, though I have done nothing but stand mute in the back of the room while Sean and Doug talk to Dorian. When Dorian hugs me there are tears in her eyes; she grasps me so hard I drop my notebook.

"God bless you!" she says. "You have to find her. Please!"

"Okay," I say, looking at Sean and Doug in a panic. Anyone who places her life-and-death hopes in the hands of a journalist is in a very desperate situation indeed. We all three of us seem to realize this, and we are all affected and even frightened by the raw fear and emotion in the room. There is no more talk about cats. Leaving the hotel, we each independently memorize the address of Lillian Jones—621 South Alexander. Reaching this place becomes the whole purpose of the trip.

We still have the problem of getting there though, and this is no simple matter. Our first thought is to simply hire the cab to drive all the way to New Orleans, but signs are posted on the interstate announcing the closure of all routes into the city. We spend the rest of the afternoon, almost until nightfall, searching out state and local agencies that might be charmed into giving us a ride into the city, before finally making it to the right place: the headquarters of the state Office of Emergency Preparedness, or the OEP.

Located across from the headquarters of the Louisiana State Police, the OEP headquarters has been transformed into a sort of chaotic intra-agency zoo, with uniformed personnel from every conceivable governmental agency—from the army to the police to the Department of Wildlife and Fisheries, which was handling boat convoys up the Mississippi River—rushing back and forth in a panic to acquire vehicles, weapons, and other "assets."

From the moment we arrive it is clear that the now famous bitter dispute between state and federal rescue agencies has already reached an advanced stage. What is even more evident (and more troubling) is that no one really knows who is in charge—not only of the New Orleans operation but of the OEP building itself. We are standing in the middle of a historic, and historically lethal, bureaucratic fuck-up.

Congressman Charlie Melancon, a Louisiana Democrat, is standing outside the entrance to the OEP building with a red face and gritted teeth, telling anyone who will listen that the federal government had senselessly dicked around for days after Governor Kathleen Blanco's original request for troops and aid. The federal response was so weak, Melancon says, that when he himself visited Plaquemines Parish (the New Orleans county that covers the mouth of the Mississippi) the day before, he was the first federal presence in the region since the day of the storm.

"The sheriff was not smiling when I got out of the car," he says.

He goes on to tell a story about standing with the sheriff shortly afterward and seeing a white car pull up.

"Two guys stepped out of the car and flipped up a badge, and they're like, 'We're from FEMA,'" Melancon says. "I don't want to say everyone burst out laughing but it was close."

Melancon is hot. He is in that rarest and most dangerous of states for a politician, when righteous anger overpowers calculation at the very moment a crowd of journalists has gathered.

"Look, this is a disaster," he hisses. "You shouldn't have to ask. They're treating this like a game of Mother May I. You ask for permission, but you can't move unless you say, 'May I?'"

Shortly after Melancon's aides finally pry him away from reporters, Republican Senator David Vitter emerges from the building. Normally Vitter looks like the quiet second dentist of a local family practice, but on this day he looks like the angriest family dentist in the world; in fact, he is wearing the same face as Melancon—that of a man who's just had his car stolen. I ask him if he agrees that the government response has been inadequate.

"In terms of the state bureaucracy and the federal bureaucracy, I would have to say yes, it was highly inadequate," he says. "And I promise you"—here he puts an index finger in my shoulder—"I promise you, there will be hearings about this."

Meanwhile, there are soldiers and cops rushing to and fro, all sighing and shaking their heads. The ones who have just come from New Orleans look wide-eyed and freaked out.

"It's like a war zone up there," says one guardsman.

"It's like nothing you've ever seen before," says another.

Throughout all this time, Doug and Sean have been rushing around the OEP looking for a way into the city. Brinkley in particular had been talking up every official on the property. The historian is one of the most relentlessly friendly people I've ever seen; it's beginning to freak me out. He is the kind of person who can secure a wedding invitation from a total stranger within four minutes. In any crowd situation he fans out in a fractal pattern, making friends as he goes along. At times you want him to cut it out, but he can't; he's friendly by nature, like a dolphin.

Doug is working on a National Guard official when Sean rushes out of the building and announces that the state police have agreed to give us a ride in. We pry Doug loose from his new friend, pile into a squad car, and head for the city, just beating the fall of darkness.

About a half hour out of the city, a terrible smell starts to waft in through the car's air vents. It is something like a cross between rotting milk and Elizabeth, New Jersey. From now until many decades hence any person who was in New Orleans during these weeks will recognize this horrific odor. "It gets worse as you get closer," our driver says.

For a person raised in civilization, it is a jarring thing to see a great city reduced to a wild state of nature. As we enter New Orleans, we note that buildings and houses are now just natural features, like cliffs and valleys. There is not a person in sight. After a harrowing drive through darkened streets blocked by downed trees and telephone poles, we make it to our destination for the evening—the private home of a Wealthy Local Attorney who is a friend of Brinkley's.

The place is a breathtaking manse in a still-dry section of town, a veritable palace of southern comfort and grace—with white columns, a manicured yard, and a stone wading pool obscured by lush hedges. It is an end-of-the-rainbow kind of home, a place one would fight to the death to defend, and this is exactly what the Wealthy Local Attorney is doing. He is holed up here with his own private army—a team of four seasoned ex-military specialists, Delta Force types who smile and apologetically refuse to answer when asked what branch of the army they graduated from. Tomorrow the attorney will welcome six more soldiers, only these will be from Israel.

Doug gets out of the car and shouts his name over the gates, thereby preventing us from being shot at. We'd made no arrangements in advance and instead were just hoping to be invited in once we arrived. After a pause, the gates open for Doug and a pair of soldiers come out to greet us. One points to the gigantic machine gun he is carrying.

"You see this?" he says. "This's called a street sweeper. This is what you need here."

I smile at him in a manly way, as if to say, yes, of course, I left mine at home by accident. He nods back. We are cool.

When Sean and I enter the house, the attorney is there to greet us. A big, bulky man with a barrel chest and a set of spindly legs poking out of baggy khaki shorts, he shakes our hands with one hand and keeps his other hand on his pistol.

The attorney's guards have transformed his elegant home into a floating military base. The interior has the feel of one of Saddam Hussein's commandeered palaces, with its portrait-lined corridors and stately sitting rooms now filled with weapons and supplies. An ostentatious vibe of rugged manliness pervades the whole compound; it is the kind of place where you can walk into any room at any hour and find groups of men either cleaning their weapons or munching something out of a can. When I enter my room to unpack, I find the team leader of the security guards—a young Special Forces type who not only calls himself "Johnny Fast" but insists that this is his real name—getting dressed after a bath. Stripped to the waist, muscles rippling and tattoos exposed, he regales me with tales of mysterious missions in the mountains of Afghanistan—places where he'd "done what he had to do" to "take the bad guys out."

"The most frustrating thing," he says, "is that most of the time, you don't get to do the job you've trained for. I'm not saying there's anything intrinsically satisfying about killing people, but . . . I mean, imagine practicing for a sport you never get to play."

Fast soon gets a chance to snap into action. The house has no running water, and when I go to use the facilities the toilet backs up. The attorney is summoned to the scene, and he interrogates me in great detail about how I had flushed. Then, satisfied with my answers, he considers the situation, scratching his chin.

"We've got to get a plunger," he says.

Since there is no plunger in the house, it is decided that an armed detail must be dispatched to procure one. A general alarm is sounded and the guards begin filing into the living room and grabbing shotguns off the floor. Sean immediately volunteers to go out on the mission as well and disappears into the living room with the rest of the team.

In general I've been very surprised by Penn. In every way he's been engaging, solicitous, and friendly. He seems deeply, almost neurotically, concerned with not coming off like a pretentious big-timer, and if he has one trait that stands out above all others, it is that he is always listening to what the other person has to say, which is actually a pretty rare quality. Basically he is a decent guy—normal, rational, easygoing.

That said, he has a thing about guns. In a previous life he was probably a cop or some jungle revolutionary's usefully paranoid bodyguard. Now, in the living room, he's admiring the barrel of an enormous shotgun.

"This thing loaded?" he asks.

"Yup," affirms one of the guards.

"All right," Penn says. "Let's go."

They rush out of the house. Doug, apparently not wanting to miss this, grabs a gun and comes along as well. In the end, six of us squeeze into a Jeep Cherokee—everyone but me armed with a shotgun. After a long search we finally stop at the home of a friend of the attorney. Sean and a guard secure the area while another of the mercenaries goes inside and locates a plunger, a box of Handi-Wipes, and a bottle of Clorox. The items are dumped on my lap as we speed back to the house. Here we are in the midst of the worst flood in the country's history and I am in the middle of an armed convoy, holding a plunger.

"Hey, guys," I say. "I think this might be the funniest thing I've ever been involved with."

"Shut up," says someone in the front seat.

Any country that enjoys fighting and bitching as a recreation as much as America does will always be, in some way or another, walking along a knife's edge. We're a nation that spends its afternoons watching white trash throw chairs at each other on *Jerry Springer,* its drive time listening to the partisan rantings of this or that hysterical political demagogue, and its late-night hours composing feverish blog entries full of anonymous screeds and denunciations. All of this shit is harmless enough so long as the power comes on every morning, fresh milk makes it to the shelves, there's a dial tone, and your front yard isn't underwater. But it becomes a problem when the magic grid goes down and suddenly there's no more machinery between you and whomever you happen to get off on hating.

Sunday, September 4, the first full day I spend in New Orleans, ends up being one of the most harrowing and unforgettable of my life. In many parts of the city, a full seven days after the storm, chaos still reigns. Rescue operations are mostly being left in the hands of ordinary people. We get our first hint of that early in the morning. On our way into town, we come across a small group of shirtless civilians tinkering with a couple of beat-up motorboats. They have the look of fishermen getting ready for a long day's work.

There are no firm shorelines to the flood zones. You'll be driving down a street in a dry area and you'll look down a side street and see water glimmering in the distance. In some places the flood is just a three-inch puddle stretching ten blocks; in other places you can launch a Boston whaler a few yards in from the water's edge. In this case, the men are launching their boats just a few blocks from the intersection of St. Charles and Napoleon, which is completely dry.

The boaters explain that they are ordinary city residents who have spent the last six consecutive days going out, pulling people out of their houses, and bringing them to dry land. At first they are civil and friendly, but when we ask where the police and National Guard boats are, they suddenly take on the character of an angry, pitchfork-wielding mob.

"Ain't nobody helping these people except us," says Ryan Asmussen, a young man with a shaved head and a workingman's deep tan. "All these people are dying and nobody's helping us with them. We're out here all day long."

"They fly overhead," adds Tim Thomas, a slightly older man with a mustache. "But they're not out there on the boats. What they do is fly overhead in the helicopters, and when they see someone trapped they hover. And then we've got to go fish 'em out."

"What about FEMA?" I ask.

The men erupt in snorts and derisive laughs. "If FEMA was here, people like us wouldn't be in a goddamn boat," Asmussen snaps. "They left it to us."

"It's a clusterfuck," says Thomas, shaking his head. "A total clusterfuck."

A phenomenon I notice throughout my stay in New Orleans is that a sort of unfriendly competition has broken out between civilians and the military when it comes to how many people they've rescued. People like Asmussen become furious when the radio reports some FEMA crew boasting about rescuing five or even ten people. The civilians measure their rescues in the dozens. Almost everyone you meet rescued sixty people yesterday and seventy the day before that, and the numbers get bigger each time you ask about them.

On the other hand, the military guys are pompously dismissive of any efforts made by civilians. I get the impression, in fact, that the military guys look at flood victims as prizes and seek to keep civilians off their turf so they can have more to themselves. "It's like they're after trophies, or heads to put on their walls," says one civilian, who was turned away from a particular neighborhood by the Coast Guard.

But there is no question that the civilians have done the bulk of the boat-rescue work in the crucial first week after the storm. A kind of society of volunteer rescuers has formed organically in places like this section of Napoleon Avenue; they are all over the city, and all have similar stories of being forced into action by the sheer incompetence of the authorities.

We end up inveigled in these activities by a curious route. Earlier in the morning we'd gone into the downtown area to look either for a boat of our own or for passage on an official rescue mission, the idea being to get to our original destination—621 South Alexander—and find Dorian Browder's mother. But that section of the city was blocked off by New Orleans police, who were conducting their own rescue operations there. We gave the authorities Browder's address—and that's when we ran into a black pastor named Willie Walker, who was running in between police airboats awaiting launch, telling anyone who will listen that there is a school on the other edge of town with hundreds of kids trapped inside. The police were blowing Walker off, but he quickly spotted us and next thing I knew he was sitting in the back of our pickup truck, giving us directions.

It is hard not to think that there is something serendipitous in our meeting with this Reverend Walker. The name of his congregation: the Noah's Ark Baptist Church.

At thirty-nine, Walker looks more like a club owner than a preacher. A former football star who once played wide receiver at Northwest Louisiana State, he says "dude" about five hundred times a day. He is brimming with grandiose thoughts and profound spiritual ruminations, and Katrina, with her biblical overtones—the high water, the ravaged earth, the judged city prostrate in its collective suffering—is the perfect setting for his passions. He has spent days racing across the city to rescue survivors, spending his nights wherever he finds himself at the end of the day (including, the night before, on a highway overpass) and getting up early again the next morning to start over. "This is my time," he tells us. "All of this is happening for a reason."

We follow his directions and soon find ourselves back at the intersection of St. Charles and Napoleon, where Ryan Asmussen, Tim Thomas, and the pack of civilians are running boats into the projects in search of survivors. Willie rounds up a few volunteers and persuades them to organize a mission to the school he knows about; everyone quickly agrees and a small armada is immediately put together.

We have managed to purloin a boat from a Famous Television Personality who knows Penn. His nervous British assistant doesn't want to let us take it, but the deal is sealed by another ex-preacher, a bombastic old white man named James Bundiff, who sends the frightened Brit scurrying away by impounding his vessel "in the name of the lieutenant governor of Louisiana."

I lean over to Willie. "Can he do that?" I whisper.

"Heck if I know, dude," he says and gets in the boat, now officially ours.

Thus the crew for the boat is settled: Willie, James, Sean, Doug, and me. The five of us will end up spending a very long day on the black water. With James, a longtime fisherman, at the helm and Willie giving directions, we head out onto the water.

Everyone by now has seen the video and knows what much of New Orleans looked like that week. But it's worse than it looks on television. What you miss on TV is the panoramic view, the dead stillness on the edges of the horizon in all directions, the whole sky filthy with helicopters. The vast scale of death and ruin is something that's impossible to grasp until you're in the middle of it. The black water sitting on top of New Orleans itself feels like a living thing, like a sci-fi creature that has swallowed a whole country and throbs faintly with malevolent life. It sends a chill up your spine to be out on top of it; it's as if you can feel it breathing.

We head down Napoleon Avenue to a neighborhood known as the Claiborne Avenue district, which happens to be not far from Willie's church. Not the worst ghetto in the city but a rough place nonetheless, with narrow streets full of warped wood houses stacked on top of one another and common areas filled with trash and cannibalized vehicles, chain link and barbed wire the main decorations. Like many neighborhoods in the city, this is a place where the local Winn-Dixie looks like the palace of Versailles.

The centers of the streets are mostly still; the edges ripple slightly with floating things. In all directions the houses and buildings are smashed and every nook and cranny is fouled with garbage, sewage, and debris. The first body we see is an older man facedown on the edge of a narrow street lined with crooked houses; we later see a woman bobbling in a parking lot, her skin bursting with huge gas bubbles. Most of the houses still contain the family dogs, who sit on the porches, keeping guard. This adds to the impression that these battered, broken-down neighborhoods have not been destroyed at all but have simply changed form, like an animal with two sets of skin—that these neglected, pissed-on city blocks have really looked like this underneath all along.

The stench is indescribable and everywhere. It will never go away. This city is gone, already dead, certain to be condemned and bulldozed to the ground—only not everyone knows it yet.

It turns out that another group of volunteers has already evacuated the school Willie heard about, and it is empty when we arrive. So we head off in a different direction, toward a series of apartment projects Willie knows about.

In our first hours on the water we come across dozens of people and encounter what I imagine is the full gamut of reasons they have for not coming to shore. There is the mechanic staying home to protect his tools from the looters who pass through the neighborhood in boats every night; the pair of Middle Eastern shop owners who appear leery of immigration authorities and choose to sleep in an exposed second-story bedroom over their store without walls or a ceiling; and the young man who's been hired by a landlord to watch over a housing project and is taking his job far too seriously.

There are plenty of young people caring for elderly relatives who won't move, and many of the people we see, according to

Willie, are drug dealers who have remained behind to protect their turf.

One very old man not far from Willie's church refuses to budge from his seat just inside his front door, which is one of those reinforced security doors with bars. Young people in the neighborhood pointed him out to us, saying he'd refused all entreaties to go. When we get there, Willie tries to tell him that the water is not subsiding and that he has to leave, for his own safety.

"No," says the old man. "Everything's fine. That's what they say on the news."

"What news?" Willie asks.

The old man gets up and, taking a full minute, walks two long steps over to the dead TV set across the room.

"This news," he says, pointing to the gray screen. "I been watching it."

"Jesus," I whisper.

Just then Penn wades over; he's been across the street, talking with one of the old man's neighbors.

"Is he coming?" Penn asks.

"Dude," Willie says. "He thinks his TV still works." Sean shakes his head. Together with one of the neighbors, a burly, soft-spoken builder named Willie Richardson who is staying in the area to protect his things, it is decided that they should try to remove the old man against his will. There is no one to take care of him, and he is too weak to move more than a few feet. Unless he is taken out of here soon, he has very little chance of getting out alive. So Willie the builder rips off the old man's barred window grate and tries to jump inside.

The old man responds by pulling out a machete and waving it out the window.

"You want to kill me, old man?" the builder shouts. "Come on, then, kill me!"

"I don't want to kill you!" cries the old man, practically in tears.

"Come on, Grandpa," the builder says gently, changing his tone. "Let us in, sir. We've got to get you out of here, do you understand? You've got to help us help you!"

"I ain't leaving!" he cries, still waving his machete out the window. "I ain't leaving!"

He starts crying. It is an awful scene. He won't budge, and in the end we have to leave him behind.

On the way back to the boat from the old man's place I wander up the adjacent block to check on a door. I thought I'd seen an old woman disappear into it a few minutes before. When I get there I find the front gate open but the door bolted. Whoever is here has ducked inside to hide. Only a few hours into the trip, I am already familiar with this routine. Folks just flat-out hide from anyone who comes by. I am standing outside the door calling out an offer to give a ride back to shore when suddenly a powerful wind appears out of nowhere and the water kicks up all around me.

The street turns into a wild black mist as an army helicopter, apparently having spotted me from afar, decides to swoop down to investigate. It was hard enough to jump into the filthy sludge up to my waist the first time. Now, with the helicopter hovering right overhead, my whole body is being soaked by this diseased water.

"I'm all right!" I call out. "You can go!"

A soldier in helmet and black goggles peers at me curiously, not offering so much as a thumbs-up sign.

"I'm okay, really!" I shout. "I'm press! You can go!"

No answer. He looks behind himself and seems to point me out to someone else in the chopper.

"Listen!" I scream. "Get out of here! *Fuck off!*"

Just then something lands with a loud splash right in front of me, sending even more water shooting up into my face. I look down and read

MEAL, READY TO EAT

CHEESE TORTELLINI IN TOMATO SAUCE

"Oh, for fuck's sake," I think.

I pick up the package and look back up at the helicopter. He whips another package at me; this one misses me by less than a foot. Then he signals to his pilot and the chopper peels out with a whoop and a whoosh, disappearing behind the row of houses.

I stand there in semi-amazement, drenched in black sludge and clutching my two MREs, digesting the situation. I look down the street; the old man has finally pulled his machete out of the open window. I guess he's gone back to watching TV.

In the end, we spend the whole day out on the water—until sundown, anyway—and bring nine or ten residents back to shore. One of our passengers is a schizophrenic whom Sean jumped in the water to save when the kick from the rotors of a hovering helicopter forced her underwater. Another passenger is a homeless man named Robert whom we found wading up to his chest in the filth-water with a huge smile on his face. He is carrying a giant pork roast wrapped in plastic that someone gave him, and once inside the boat he clutches the roast like it is a newborn baby. I notice he has a big open cut on his knee.

"Hey, Robert," I say. "You better get a shot, man. That knee is going to get infected."

"Heh, heh, it's fine," he says, smiling. "It's nothing. Just got to find somewheres to cook this meat."

"No, seriously," I say. "This water is diseased. It's gonna get in that cut and you're gonna be real sick." He laughs and rolls his eyes. "Heh, heh. No shit," he says. "Bet you're serious at that. Nope, it's fine."

Pastor Willie pipes in. "Hey, listen up," he says. "Man telling you you gonna be sick. Germs are going to get in that knee. All it takes is a little cut. You hear me?"

Robert looks up at Willie and his smile vanishes. "No shit?" he says.

"Yeah," Willie says. "We're taking you to a doctor." Robert frowns and clutches his roast. Willie looks up at me, shakes his head, and taps the black skin on the back of his own hand.

So here we are, heading back to shore with our passengers— one an outpatient who barely knows her name, the other a derelict about five minutes off from making love to a pork roast. All of us are soaked to the gills in death-bilge and smelling, with the possible exception of Robert, as badly as we will ever smell in our lives. And what happens? When we reach dry land, the boat is stopped by someone planting a shiny black boot heel on the bow. I look up to see a tall, jowly good-ol'-boy policeman in a gleaming blue uniform. Under the circumstances, with us pulling into an ad hoc weigh station where everybody coming in and out of boats is filth covered, a clean uniform is already a bit of an outrage. Then he opens his mouth.

"I'd like to question some of these people, if you don't mind," he says.

I look up at him. "Excuse me?"

"Some of these people you're bringing in—let's just say we know them pretty well," he says. "You know what I mean?"

"You mean these particular people?" I point at our two spaceshot passengers. Robert is rocking back and forth with his roast.

"No, not these particular ones," he says. "The general ones."

"Well, can we let these particular ones go?" I ask.

We argue for a moment. Finally he lets our two clearly infirm passengers waddle past.

Minutes later a different squad of police appears. It is a unit of five, dressed in khaki-colored paramilitary uniforms. I don't quite get what they are asking, but it has something to do with needing our boat to help catch car thieves, who are tearing through a hospital parking garage nearby. A humanitarian disaster is still going on less than a mile and a half away—and these guys have the balls to stand around in clean unis and try to drum up posses to stop property crime. New Orleans, I conclude, is one fucked-up city.

Many days later, after I'd followed evacuees back to Houston, I find people from this very neighborhood who tell very similar stories. Ollie Hull, a mother who was evacuated to the Astrodome, says she and her family had to make their own way out of her home on Claiborne and Martin Luther King Boulevard, as the police were too busy chasing thieves to help. "They was looking for looters," she says. "We dying and they looking for looters. We had to save ourselves, our children and babies."

"They were chickenshit motherfuckers," chimes in Pat Downs, an older woman who was one of the few white people in the Astrodome. "They were aiming guns at women and children."

Like many of the controversies borne by Katrina, this is an issue colored significantly by race. "We in the black community felt like the guardsmen were there to protect the property," says Phyllis Johnson, who spent most of the first week after the storm in the Superdome. "Nobody was helping us. They had empty trucks leaving the city while we were stuck in the Superdome. They were there to keep us from running loose in the streets of New Orleans."

When Johnson tried to escape—fleeing the disaster area on foot, in a stolen bottled-water truck and in a runaway city transit bus that had been commandeered by evacuees—the cops tried to prevent her from leaving. "In the water truck we made it as far as Westwego before we were stopped," she says. "The cops took us out of the truck and threw us facedown in the wet grass with the ants—including the children and the old people. Then they just took the truck and left us to fend for ourselves. Empty car after empty car drove by, and no one offered to help."

She pauses. "All you people who came down here and partied with us, who came to Bourbon Street to hang out with us, who got drunk with us, now you acting like you don't want to know us. Now, all of the sudden, you scared of us."

The flip side of that story, of course, is that New Orleans looters, once the lights went out, tried to steal everything that wasn't nailed to the floor. While Phyllis Johnson was moving from the inside of the Superdome to the ramp outside to escape the smell, forty-six-year-old Tim Johnson—one of just a few hundred whites who ended up in the stadium—was searching out safe places to sleep at night. I find Tim just a few dozen yards away from Phyllis at the Astrodome in Houston, sitting with a shell-shocked look on his face in a park outside the facility. He looks like a man who's just emerged from two weeks of electrical torture.

"They were animals," he whispers. His eyes darted back and forth as black residents of the Convention Center passed. "The animals came out. They broke into everything. They took what they want . . . I saw a guy getting his ass killed . . . and nobody would do nothing."

Stories I hear from both black and white evacuees who had been in the Superdome and the Convention Center suggest that both places turned into *Lord of the Flies*–like hellholes for days. I hear tales of gangsters jousting with hot-wired forklifts, New

Orleans Saints merchandise stores turned into brothels, ten-year-old boys selling cases of Absolut on the Superdome floor. When I see the Convention Center a week after the storm, it looks like Genghis Khan's army had put up there for a year. Piles of garbage six feet high clutter the outside; the inside is ruined to the very limit of human aggression, with every conceivable form of debris, from bloodstained curtains to putrid sides of beef to urine-soaked Coke machines to feces smeared on the walls.

Even now, days after the Superdome has been evacuated, the authorities seem unable to cope with the scale of the disaster. Earlier that morning, before we went out on the boats, the New Orleans police chief, W. J. Riley, announced that two officers had committed suicide. Moreover, he announced that an unspecified number of police had resigned. We found only one place in the city where there were a lot of cops: police headquarters. Under an awning at the Harrah's casino downtown, the police had formed a makeshift command center. We'd been there in the morning and found about 250 officers standing around, looking a lot happier than the ones we'd seen out in the city. The very moment we'd arrived, news chimed in over the police radios that cops had shot and killed five looters at a bridge somewhere outside town. The news was met with a high cheer ("That's right, motherfuckers!" was one cry), and the whole crowd was buzzed, like a bar after midnight.

While Sean and Doug plunged into the crowd to talk to someone about a boat, I wandered over to the food table and made the mistake of wrapping a few Krispy Kremes in a napkin.

"Hey," shouted a SWAT officer in a plaintive voice. "Don't take them all!"

"Sorry," I said, putting one of the doughnuts back. He frowned and went back to chatting with his crew.

The police in this city were on an island, fighting for their own survival. Saving people was never going to be their business.

At the end of the day, we find ourselves back at the inter- section of Napoleon and St. Charles. All of the people that we and the other volunteers have pulled out by boat are now huddled under a store awning—about fifty people total, the work of a half dozen boats. But the military and the police are not particularly interested in helping or processing anyone res- cued by private citizens, so the evacuees sit there under the sun—as buses and ambulances whiz past—waiting for the vol- unteers to take them to hospitals or shelters.

Not that there isn't plenty of available manpower. By the end of the day, word has gotten around that Sean Penn was out in a rescue boat, and a large contingent of the international press is waiting for us when we get back from our last run. One scene I'll never forget: a still photographer stepping over a sick one-legged black man lying on the ground in order to take a picture of Sean carrying a rifle. There have to be sixty or sev- enty reporters here, and of those only a reporter from the New York *Daily News* and a photographer from the *Village Voice* so much as offer to give any of the evacuees a ride to the hospital.

By the next morning—a full week after the storm—the au- thorities have finally taken control of the rescue operations. Sean and Doug decide to leave, but I stay on to spend a few more days with Willie, along with a pair of young New York newspaper reporters that he's picked up along the way. Willie has made arrangements with a friend of his, an air-conditioning salesman from the suburbs named John Ratcliffe, to take a boat out into the Ninth Ward—the worst neighborhood in the city. Ratcliffe has access to a much bigger boat than the one we'd been on the day before, a serious lake-fishing vessel, and he was to meet us early in the day and have Willie take us to the flooded areas.

But now that the state is in charge, they seem determined to stick it to the civilian rescuers. We are on our way to the East district when a Coast Guard roadblock stops John from driving through with his boat trailer. A young Coastie of about twenty, with the face of a constipated bureaucrat, leans into the driver's window of the truck, the whole time keeping his finger on the trigger of his weapon, which is pointed down at the ground.

"No, we don't need your help," he snaps. "We've got things under control."

Willie leans over and explains that he's been out running rescue boats for more than a week. The Coastie frowns and points at John's boat.

"These helicopters would flip that little thing in a second," he says. This, of course, is untrue; I'd seen Coast Guard helicopters flying over much smaller boats the previous day, to no effect. I point that out to the kid, explaining that we'd been under helicopters all day the day before.

"Yeah, those aviation guys are slammed," he says—as if the aviation guys, not the people still stuck out there, are the ones having the rough day.

Finally he orders us to turn back, explaining that the rescue is a "coordinated operation" and that no help is necessary. We are told the same thing in the nearby neighborhood of Gentilly, where Coast Guard officers repeat to us that they have the area under control. Fortunately, Willie and John ignore them and simply find another launch point.

When we head into the neighborhood—a middle-class area of one-story single-family homes with little yards set off by chain-link fences—we find many of the same things we'd seen the day before. The authorities have clearly decided not to pick up the bodies. At one intersection, a man who had handcuffed himself to the top of a STOP sign, apparently with the aim of not sinking below the water, hangs upside down, his eyes popping out of his head like baseballs. And once again there are plenty of residents who don't want to leave their homes—only in this case the reasons are different.

"I'd rather be a refugee here than sit with my thumb in my ass in Houston or wherever," says Steve Smith, a fifty-four-year-old white man who is sitting in an abandoned bar, drinking homemade whiskey. Like most of the people we come across, Steve has heard horror stories of people being evacuated to distant cities against their will, or of families being separated, or of the government otherwise fucking things up.

This particular neighborhood of Gentilly has been fairly heavily patrolled by Coast Guard boats for four or five days now—compared to the black neighborhood we'd been in yesterday, where the military had yet to appear in force. Here, the modus operandi is as follows: Coasties come out in little launches and offer to take people out. If the residents say yes, they are airlifted to the airport, where they join the cattle-car evacuee circus. In theory, evacuees can go wherever they want, but in practice . . . no one wants to take that chance.

John and Willie manage to persuade four people to leave Gentilly, promising to personally drive them to meet relatives in other parts of the state. "If you're going to go out and rescue people here, you have to have someone local to talk to them," John says. "It's just common sense." As we return to shore, sailors on the Coast Guard boats, all empty of passengers, glare angrily at us.

A lot of John and Willie's success has to do with attitude. Everywhere you go in New Orleans, the military imports strike the same pose. There is an unmistakable air of You Fucked Up

Badly Enough to Require Our Presence, So Now You're Going to Shut the Fuck Up and Let Us Do Our Job. At one point, Willie and I try to drive out of the city; we are stopped by a young National Guardsman. The guardsman has been told to reroute everyone whose home address on their driver's license includes a certain ZIP code. As it happens, Willie's license features that ZIP code, although he no longer lives there.

"You have to take the Jefferson Highway to 1-10 West, sir," the kid says.

"But I'm trying to leave—" Willie begins.

"Turn around, sir!" the kid barks.

Willie starts turning around, but traffic is backed up behind us. A few minutes later, Angry Guardsman returns. "Sir! You're leaving and not coming back?"

"Yes," Willie says.

"Then get the fuck out," the kid says, waving his arm frantically.

Willie hesitates.

"Take your crew and get the fuck out of here!" he repeats. We drive off.

Some eighty years ago, after the great Mississippi flood of 1927, white business leaders in New Orleans pressured the state to blow a levee, flooding mostly black areas in the Delta and forcing the rural poor into the cities. Thus part of what gave birth to the vast ghettos of black poor that Katrina wiped out was a man-made disaster in the distant past. Can something like this be remembered in the genes?

That night, no longer basking in the largess of Academy Award winner Sean Penn, I find myself homeless. Willie invites me to spend the night in his church. I am initially not enthused about the plan. I'd seen his church while out on the boats on Sunday. It is across the street from a gigantic cemetery where we'd seen numerous fresh graves—not exactly the kind of place you want to be wading around in waist-deep water, particularly at night. The longer you stay in New Orleans, the scarier that water seems. You start to imagine gangrene, tetanus, a life without legs, family members wheeling you around on your birthday. But Willie seems weirdly insistent about getting us out to his neighborhood that night, so I agree.

By the time we get there night has fallen. The good pastor is strapped, carrying a Rueger automatic. As we head deeper into the neighborhood, he actually draws his gun and carries it at his side as he walks.

Willie had been strangely quiet the entire time he'd been with us out in the boats for the past two days. Not that he wasn't sociable—he just didn't say much about the storm or talk much about anything serious. But now that he is back in his own territory he has some things to say.

Not far from his church we come upon a house full of elderly people who are sitting out on their porch. Their house is in only about three feet of water, but no police or guardsmen have come by to talk to them yet. Upon seeing Willie, Warren Champ and Jeannette Carter ask what the latest news is.

"Well, these reporters are here to see what y'all think about the storm," he says.

"You tell us, preacher," says Jeannette. "You're always reading the Bible and whatnot, doing all that reading."

"Well, you know this is all about bankruptcy," he says. "That levee? They letting it fail."

"Why would they do that?" Jeannette asks.

"All those years when they were stealing . . . all those failed schools, all those debts on the city rolls . . . it's all going to be washed away now. They're getting a clean slate, a brand-new slate."

Willie goes on to explain that most of these neighborhoods are going to be condemned, and that people will be asked to sell their properties: "They're getting all of y'all out of state, sending you to different parts of the country. And they're hoping you don't hold on to what you've got. They're hoping you take the money and move. And then they'll bring in the developers, and they'll make new neighborhoods, with a new tax base."

I am about to interrupt here, but white guilt slaps a hand over my mouth. What am I going to say—that white people aren't dastardly enough to blow a levee on purpose? This is the wrong audience for that joke. As for the rest of it, it rings unpleasantly true. Deep in my white heart I can appreciate the brutal logic of shipping 300,000 blacks out of town and hoping they stay away at a barbecue somewhere while you auction off their houses. I am definitely not going to argue with that part of it.

"But what is your advice for poor black people?" asks Carter.

"Hold on to your properties," he says. "Don't let them take what you've got. And you can listen to me. I'm not in it for the money. I'm in it for the blessings of God."

A few hours later, Willie and I sit in the office of the Noah's Ark Baptist Church, which is surrounded on all sides by water. It is a small church, with just a few pews and a little table full of pamphlets along one wall providing information about STDs and low-interest home loans.

Back in the office it is about a thousand degrees, and we are eating MREs—I am the only one hungry enough to try the tortellini—by the light of Sterno lamps and flashlights. Willie, who first checks to make sure everything is there ("I've had eighty-six break-ins"), talks about the neighborhood. He's never heard of gentrification, but this is what he is describing to us: parts of his community going to hell, vacant lots bought up by developers, the community slowly vanishing. It is his idea that the flood from Katrina will give him an opportunity to raise money to buy up the ruined lots himself—a process he's already started with a few adjoining partitions behind his church.

His thoughts are grand in scale, and at times he is unable to separate the hurricane and the bureaucratic response to it from the other forces that have helped bring ruin to his neighborhood over the years—drug dealers, venereal disease, bankruptcy, municipal corruption. Katrina offers him a final showdown with all of these forces.

"An empty cart makes a lot of noise," he says. "I don't have anyone paying me to be quiet. I'm going to save this neighborhood."

Eventually we fall asleep; I sack out on the floor, amid mice and various other creatures. We are all tired, and despite the heat and the mean conditions we are all deep asleep not long after midnight.

Sometime in the middle of the night Willie wakes us up.

"They're here," he shouts.

"What?" I say. "Who's here?"

"They're kicking the doors in," he says.

I get up. Willie is standing at the back door, his gun drawn. He is silhouetted by the light from a helicopter spotlight, which for some reason is trained on the swamp behind the church.

"They're coming. I knew it," he says.

"I don't think so, man," I say. "I think he's just hovering."

"If he comes," Willie says, "I'm shooting."

"I don't think he's coming," I repeat.

Finally the helicopter flies away. Willie puts the gun down and goes back to sleep. The next day, he goes back out on the water.

America is a country that has been skating for ages on its unparalleled ability to look marvelous on the outside. We've long had things arranged in such a way that our public exterior is always shimmering and clean—our airports, our food courts, our anchormen, our chain restaurants, our fleets of bombers, and our warehouses full of nick-free products in polymer-coated packaging. For most of the uglier things that are under the surface—the bitterness, the rancor, the greed, the selfishness, the loneliness, the isolation we feel from each other, our inability to communicate and empathize—we've found ways to keep these things out of sight. They can be heard, maybe, and read all over the Internet and elsewhere, but not seen—and in any case they have always been subordinate to our legend of supreme competence and efficiency. We may be many things, we Americans, but we always get the job done.

But what happens when we stop getting the job done? What are we left with then?

September 11, the first great paradigm-shifting event of our new century, was a disaster that the American psyche was prepared for. As horrible as it was, it spoke directly to our most deliciously satisfying persecution fantasies: it was *Independence Day, Deep Impact, War of the Worlds.* Stinky Klingons attack Manhattan; America straps it on and kicks ass. We knew the playbook for that one.

No one was ready for Katrina, though. He was ridiculed for saying it, but George Bush was absolutely right—painfully if unintentionally honest—when he said that "I don't think anyone anticipated" this disaster. New Orleans falls into the sea; whose ass do we kick now? When that isn't an option, we're left just staring at one another. And that's what really hurts.

Ms. America

Abu Ghraib irreparably damaged America's reputation, but Lynndie England's trial proved the nation will try to sweep anything under the rug

---

October 20, 2005

What a pathetic ending it was for Private Lynndie England, that little hillbilly twit with the rabbit cheeks and the upturned thumb who made the words "Abu Ghraib" infamous.

When she came out for her final curtain call last week—a dreary court-martial at Fort Hood, a hot little armpit in the middle of Texas—there was almost no one there. The court-room gallery, just three rows deep to begin with, was less than half full. Her mom was there, holding the seemingly normal-looking baby Lynndie managed to squeeze out after All That Terrible Stuff came out last year. There were a couple of ex-pert witnesses who came to say nice things at the sentencing hearing, a friend or two, and maybe a half dozen yawning reporters, all on standby for Hurricane Rita duty. And what they all turned up to watch, ultimately, was little Lynndie up on the stand, pulling a fifth-rate courtroom-beggar act like an immigrant personal-injury plaintiff in a neck brace.

Lynndie's whole trial strategy had centered around mock-retard Method acting of the *Sling Blade* or *My Left Foot* school—with the defendant staring off into space like a coma patient while her overmatched young military counsel tried to sell the five-member military jury on the idea that Lynndie was an "overly compliant personality" with "extraordinary deficits" who was not completely responsible for her actions in Iraq.

Accordingly, Lynndie spent most of the court-martial sitting with a stunned look, like she'd just been whacked in the face with a piece of plywood. The few times she did move, she'd pick up a piece of paper or a pen and stare at it quizzically for minutes, as though trying to figure out what it was.

When she finally took the stand, in the sentencing hearing, she spent most of her time trying to make the jury understand how hard life had been for a backward little dumb shit like herself.

Picked on by the other kids for being slow. Picked on for having a tomboy haircut. Picked on because she chewed funny in the school cafeteria. "The muscles in my jaw and my eyelids was different than other people, ma'am," she told her stammering attorney, Captain Katherine Krul, during testimony.

Finally, in a last plea for mercy, Lynndie reminded the jury that she was now a mother—she'd been knocked up in Iraq, after all, by fellow Abu Ghraib sadist Private Charles Graner. She was dumb from birth and didn't have none of that book lernin', but she did manage to get banged in a latrine somewhere in Iraq in between prisoner extractions, and now, backward as she was, she was at least in the society of mothers.

Watching Lynndie's defense team play the baby card in her sentencing hearing was like listening to a zoologist explain why Koko the gorilla can't be separated from her pet kitten. Even a crippled life-form such as this, they seemed to be saying, can experience strong maternal emotions. And in their very last appeal they swung for the fences, asking Lynndie to explain for the benefit of the jury a certain picture of little Carter.

"Why'd you pose him in front of the American flag?" Krul asked, holding up the photo and smiling in the jury's direction.

Lynndie looked at her lap. "I guess," she whispered, "I'm still patriotic, ma'am." Then she swallowed and went back to *I Am*

Sam land, drooping her eyes and fiddling with an imaginary something or other in her lap.

What bullshit, I thought. This girl goes off to fight a war but instead bangs some creep who she sees torturing people by the dozen every night. She's stupid enough to get her picture taken in the act of humiliating a whole race of people, inspiring an entire generation of martyrs for Allah and causing an international scandal—and now we're supposed to go easy on her because she wraps her demon love child in an American flag? As if!

The jury—a panel of five older male officers—apparently disagreed. They came back with a sentence: three years. The over/under in the press pool had been nine. It was a slap on the wrist.

It would have been an outrage, if anybody had been watching. But nobody was, of course.

The Abu Ghraib scandal hit America like the worst kind of surprise, like a long-dreaded psychosexual nightmare or closet phobia thrust suddenly into the open—like being caught in the office after hours jerking off to twink porn, or having to call an ambulance to get the proverbial frozen hot dog out of your snatch. This was the worst-case scenario come true, the gerbil-in-the-ass story—only it wasn't apocryphal at all, but cross-confirmed by a hundred sources in every newspaper and on every cable channel on earth.

At the center of the scandal was the discovery and release of scads of digital photos documenting the deeply twisted and oddly imaginative schemes of abuse of Iraqi prisoners by a squad of grinning hicks from the U.S. Army's 372nd Military Police Company. The two images that stuck most firmly in the public consciousness were the human pyramid of naked detainees and a beaming tomboy private named Lynndie England standing with a cigarette dangling out of her mouth, smugly pointing at the exposed balls of a naked Iraqi prisoner.

The pictures meant different things to different people, but their meaning was most clear to the Muslim world. Nothing could have been more horrible than the sight of a "liberated" American female—a frighteningly ugly beast with short hair, pants, and boots, not to mention a gun—forcing Muslim men to play the bottom role in smarmy leash-and-whip S&M scenes.

As a compendium of cultural insults, this was unmatched in its offensiveness, a sort of perfect storm of bad PR. An equivalent response might have included a gang of sheikhs putting a leash on the neck of the Virgin Mary and leading her to be violated by a camel . . . but even that, perhaps, wouldn't have inspired the outrage Lynndie England elicited in Muhammadan lands.

Non-Muslim foreigners saw in Lynndie another American prototype. With her "Get a load of me!" poses and her mania for picture taking, Lynndie reminded the whole world of the American tourist who stands holding a Schlitz in front of the Sistine Chapel. This was a new low, but also a sort of supreme achievement in Ugly Americanism: I COMMITED LOTS OF WAR CRIMES IN IRAQ AND ALL I GOT WAS THIS LOUSY T-SHIRT!

At home, Abu Ghraib in very short order turned into a comic pissing match between two sides dedicated to missing the point. The right spent months insisting that a human pyramid wasn't nearly as bad as a beheading, while the left just ate up the news without really knowing why. Both argued fiercely for half a year about how much play the pictures should get in the news and soon after forgot about them completely. In short, it was a textbook example of an American dialogue about a vital national problem.

Smells Like Dead Elephants

By the time this year's hurricane season rolled around, all that was left of the Abu Ghraib story was a formality. Sweep the last little bits of dirt under the rug. And they sure did a good job of it.

Why was Lynndie smiling in those pictures? Ask her expert witness! "American culture places a great emphasis on smiling," pronounced Dr. Stjepan Mestrovic, one of the experts the defense called to the stand. The renowned sociologist is a gloomy-looking foreigner, all droopy eyes and bulbous nose, who for a week has made no attempt to hide the fact that he considers almost everyone on this army base a barbarian.

"People here are forever smiling in pictures, they are saying the cheese," he goes on. "They see people smiling on the covers of magazines, on television shows. There is pressure always to be smiling . . . Put simply, Americans are smilers!"

The doctor folds his arms, thinking he has said something significant about Lynndie England's famous grin. He has, of course, but what he's mistaken about is in thinking anyone here gives a damn.

The court-martial of Lynndie England early on evolved into a kind of low-rent comic allegory about the American political scene, and Mestrovic played the role of the pointy-headed liberal who is too busy being right to see what a pain in the ass he is.

When he first took the stand, he spent five long minutes pompously detailing his various Ivy League degrees and didn't realize that by boasting of a guest lectureship at the Sorbonne to a bunch of Fort Hood army types, he might as well have confessed to buggering boys in sailor costumes.

The judge, an impatient blockhead named Colonel James Pohl, took an especial dislike to Mestrovic. His Honor looked like a man who takes his wife on dates to the Elks Club and yells at his children at barbecues; he winced visibly every time the effete foreigner opened his mouth.

Ostensibly the doctor was here to testify to the inevitability of the deviant behavior at Abu Ghraib, given the chaotic command structure and the army's failure to send clear messages to recruits about prisoner treatment. Mestrovic compared the army to an abusive parent who sends mixed messages to a child.

"The deviation was inevitable," he said.

Since Lynndie's guilt was never really in question ("She can't get off—she's in the dad-gum photographs!" was how a reporter from Texas put it to me), the court spent most of its time going in circles over this same idiotic liberal-arts argument. Was the individual to blame or was it society? Accusers and accused butted heads over this question for days on end, with the low point coming when Mestrovic described Abu Ghraib as a "state of anomie."

"A what?" Pohl snapped, frowning.

"A state of anomie," the doctor repeated.

Pohl shuddered and sipped his coffee, seeming to wonder whether such a word was even legal in Texas.

Few recall it now, but the original thrust of the exposés that brought Abu Ghraib out in the open was that such behaviors might have resulted from a conscious Pentagon policy, approved by Secretary of Defense Rumsfeld, of taking the gloves off with terror detainees. But every hint that the scandal might have been under the direction of military intelligence officers stationed at the prison was carefully expunged from the government's indictments and in the court-martial proceedings.

Sure, one of Lynndie's lawyers tried to call a certain Captain Ian Fishback to testify to other, similar abuses in Iraq; he claimed this witness would describe virtually identical behavior in other parts of Iraq, right down to another pyramid of naked detainees. But Pohl was having none of that crap. He disallowed Crisp's witness, saying, "There's basically no connections between the events," and, in the end, confined the trial to a silly little nature-nurture discussion, at the conclusion of which Lynndie got to knock a few years off her sentence by playing dumb-ass and claiming a bad childhood.

The real question buried in the Abu Ghraib mess, of course, was one that was never going to be answered in an army courtroom. No court-martial was ever going to be a referendum on the wisdom of fighting a war on the cheap, with post-invasion plans made up on the fly, placing the welfare of an entire population—a deeply religious population—in the hands of stupid, horny young Americans.

And no one anywhere was interested in wondering what kind of people we've become—completely devoid of morals and empathy but armed with digital cameras, ready to give that thumbs-up and "say the cheese."

Who needs that? We have hurricanes to worry about. Thanks for nothing, Lynndie. Leave the camera home next time.

Darwinian Warfare

In a Pennsylvania courtroom, America can't get the monkey off its back

___

November 3, 2005

As sequels go, it was a relatively bad one, barely reaching the level of *Grease 2* or *Alien: Resurrection*. But like most bad retreads it had at least one interesting moment . . .

The scene was *Kitzmiller et al. v. Dover Area School District et al.*, better known to the news-watching public as "Scopes II," the evolution-vs.-intelligent-design trial they're having in Harrisburg, Pennsylvania, these days. In a cavernous, poorly lit courtroom in the Pennsylvania capital, a distinguished-looking man with silver hair in a blue suit and a dark tie (speckled, amusingly, with missing-link skulls) submitted to the bumbling interrogation of a glum-looking Christian attorney named Robert J. Muise.

The two men were a study in contrasts, in both demeanor and diction. The former was Dr. Brian Alters, a Harvard man and professor of science education at McGill University in Montreal, who sat with his brow furrowed and a broad smile on his face—looking comfortable, even triumphant, on the witness stand.

He was here playing a by now familiar role in evolution trials, the very same role once played by his former colleague the late Stephen Jay Gould, at the 1982 case *McLean v. Arkansas Board of Education:* that of the learned progressive come to slay the dragon of fundamentalist ignorance.

89

Of course, in the first film of the monkey-trial franchise—*State of Tennessee v. John Thomas Scopes,* the sensational affair of 1925 that pitted evolution against religion in court for the first time— the side of science had not been allowed expert witnesses. But things had changed an awful lot in eighty years, as evidenced by Alters's sartorial dig at his reactionary inquisitors.

"It's *Homo habilis, Homo erectus,* and *Zinjanthropus boisei,*" he'd said during an earlier recess, looking down at his tie. "A student gave it to me."

Muise, meanwhile, looked like a line-drawn *Webster's* dictionary illustration of the word "loser." He was an unhappy-looking man, all forehead and sunken eyes, with the crudely wetted-down haircut and tight collar of a fourth-grader dressed by his mom. Throughout most of the trial he had sat mute and miserable in his chair at the defendants' table, like a boy watching an ice cream cone melt, not objecting even when his much-loathed American Civil Liberties Union counterpart across the room blatantly led his witnesses.

Muise was part of the legal team donated to the defense by a group bearing the impressively pretentious name of the Thomas More Law Center, a sort of Christian version of the ACLU. The group considers itself the vanguard of the anti-Darwinist movement—its understated slogan is "The Sword and Shield of People of Faith."

The lawyer had come to Harrisburg with these fellow knights-errant of the antievolution movement to defend one of the very stupidest concepts ever to get a hearing in an American courtroom: an alternative to evolution called Intelligent Design.

The theory, called ID for short, posits that life on earth was simply too complex to be explained by the random and undirected natural processes described in Darwin's theories.

The chief innovation of ID is that it did not call God by the name "God" but instead referred vaguely to an "intelligent designer."

The essence of its scientific claims was that biology was just too intense, dude, to be an accident. A local columnist mocked the theory as resembling a teenage stoner looking at the back of his hand and being too amazed to deal.

Muise was saddled with all of this—the bad haircut, the droopy face, the silly theory, the consciousness that everybody who's ever seen *Inherit the Wind* was going to consider him the bad guy at this trial. Worse, he was stuck with clients who were clearly on the wrong side of the law, and a case that, in an honest courtroom, even Johnnie Cochran couldn't win.

But Muise wasn't here to win. He was here to make a point, and he made it when he started asking Alters about statements made by certain prominent scientists.

"Dr. Alters," he said, "were you aware that Professor Steven Weinberg once said that 'I personally feel that the teaching of modern science is corrosive to religious belief, and I'm all for that!'"

"An unfortunate remark," said Alters, shaking his head and squirming. The look on his face said, "Can we move on?"

Muise didn't. He rattled off more quotes from prominent scientists, including one from Gould ("Before Darwin, we thought that a benevolent God had created us")—who, Muise noted with obvious pleasure, had once written a foreword to one of Alters's books. Alters shrugged it off, calmly sticking to his contention that evolution was not an indictment of religion.

As Alters gave his denials, Muise turned to the gallery and, for the first time that afternoon, evinced a small smile. That smile spoke volumes. It said, "At least my clients know when they're full of shit. But these eggheads . . ."

Muise had a point. His defendants and their ID theory had come under attack for an obvious reason: just because you say in a court of law that you're not creationists doesn't make it true.

Now Muise got to say the same thing to those superior-sounding intellectuals who flew into God's country and insisted, under oath, that they weren't enemies of religion. You can yell it at us till you're blue in the face, the lawyer seemed to be saying, but we who really believe know better.

To blue-state intellectuals like Alters, *Kitzmiller v. Dover* was just another clash with religious loonies of the same primitive sort found in the original Scopes trial, diehards determined for some incomprehensible reason to drag us back to the Stone Age.

But to the defendants in this case, *Kitzmiller* was a chance to turn Scopes on its head. If what Scopes's defense attorney Clarence Darrow accomplished eighty years ago was to expose the narrow-mindedness and anti-intellectualism of the Bible Belt, lawyers like Muise were out to show the opposite in *Kitzmiller*—that most scientists secretly hate God, laugh at his followers, and would like to stamp out both for all eternity, only they don't take Christians seriously enough to be straight with them about this.

Both sides were right, obviously, which made for the usual perfect comedy of American politics: two entrenched camps determined not to communicate, but still engaged in an extravagantly violent public waste of time and money, with no resolution visible, or even imaginable.

The reason for America's fascination with evolution trials isn't hard to figure. The Scopes monkey trial of 1925 was one of the great paradigmatic clashes of modern American history. The battle lines drawn in the punishing heat of that Tennessee courtroom vividly described, for the first time, the basic political divisions that would end up dominating modern American society.

The first skirmish in the war between red states and blue states was held there, in Dayton, where smartass ice heathens from the north descended upon small-town America to laugh at the superstitious but numerically superior yokels of the heartland. In a breathtakingly accurate preview of things to come, the yokels actually won the trial, but history judged them the losers—thanks mainly to the flamboyant propaganda of a godless misanthrope named H. L. Mencken, the brilliant Darwinian ancestor of the modern liberal media.

The same basic conflict has persisted to this day. If anything, the political echo from the Dayton courtroom has grown exponentially louder. The modern right-left, Bush/anti-Bush, red-blue, Hannity-v.-Air America paradigm more than ever mirrors the courtroom geography of the Dayton trial, which pitted the urbane, Europe-loving intellectual of the north against the defiant God-fearing patriot of the south.

Both sides still define themselves in terms of that story, with red-staters especially still smarting from the same underlying intolerable insult: being told how to live by silver-tongued out-of-towners.

The urge to throw off that invading infidel has been the force driving conservative-talk-radio ratings into the stratosphere for nearly two decades. Eighty years later, Rush Limbaugh's act is really no different at all from that of Scopes's inquisitor William Jennings Bryan, another fat man with a loud voice who seized power by warning that the devil was leaving the campuses of the north and headed your way.

Kitzmiller v. Dover looked like Scopes in reverse. Instead of a single schoolteacher trying to buck the law by teaching evolution in the intractable heart of the Bible Belt, this case involved a single school board trying to buck the law by slipping a teaspoonful of God into a continent-size, thoroughly secularized school system.

Like Scopes, this case began as a minor political disagreement in a small town that self-consciously grew into a national controversy. Making a long story short, *Kitzmiller v. Dover* boiled down to a few unusually pious individuals on the school board of a little Pennsylvania town unilaterally voting, in October 2004, to insert a four-paragraph statement about "Intelligent Design" into the local high school's curriculum. Immediately a coalition of parents filed a federal lawsuit against the renegade school board.

The basis of the plaintiffs' suit was found in the 1987 Supreme Court case *Edwards v. Aguillard,* in which the court ruled that the teaching of "scientific creationism" in Louisiana public schools violated the establishment clause of the Constitution. The crux of the plaintiffs' case in *Kitzmiller* was that "Intelligent Design"—the theory backed by the school board—was just creationism in disguise. If it was, then the Dover school officials would be guilty of the same First Amendment offense described in *Aguillard*.

Again, this was Scopes, but backward. The religious side was at the defendants' table, and this time it was religion and conservatism that would have to struggle to get a public hearing for its newfangled theory.

More important, however, the prognosis this time imagined religion as the legal loser but the practical winner, instead of the other way around.

Playing the role of Clarence Darrow in this case was an ACLU lawyer named Witold "Vic" Walczak, a well-spoken, witty

Bruce Springsteen fanatic with a distant but significantly less thuggish resemblance to Armand Assante. For Walczak (pronounced Wall-check), the question of the underlying meaning of *Kitzmiller* was a lot less important than its immediate legal import.

"It is difficult to sugarcoat the implications of a loss," he said, conceding that the meaning of a win would be harder to define. "If the court rules that ID can be taught, it's gonna be like mushrooms in the forest after a summer rain. They'll be teaching ID everywhere."

But the trial quickly unfolded into a blowout, with ID proponents experiencing a fresh slaughter in each successive day of the proceedings. The most damaging testimony came from a philosophy professor named Barbara Forrest, who testified that in early versions of *Of Pandas and People*—the pro-ID textbook offered to the children of the Dover school district—the word "creationism" had been used in places where the text now reads "intelligent design."

Much of the trial continued in this fashion, with the defense of the Thomas More lawyers amounting to little more than tiresome exercises in semantic hairsplitting—as when Muise asked Alters if intelligent design ever overtly named God as the "intelligent designer," or if he even knew of any instance in which any of the Dover children had even read *Of Pandas and People* (a Clintonian line of defense if there ever was one: yes, we put an ID book in the library, but nobody read it).

Yet the real victory of the defense was in forcing men like Alters to insist with a straight face that Darwinism is not incompatible with religion. Technically this was true, of course, but it is striking that it was exactly the same kind of feeble technicality as the contention that ID has no literal connection to God or the Bible. A technicality like Clinton not sleeping with Monica Lewinsky, like John Kerry owning a rifle. Technically true—but fooling no one.

Intelligent design may very well have been conceived as an end run around the Supreme Court, and in a matter of weeks it will likely be exposed as such, when the Honorable Judge John E. Jones III rules in favor of Kitzmiller et al. in the Dover case.

ID is also revealing itself here in Pennsylvania in another form. It's having a coming-out party as a deliberate satirical echo of the great liberal lie of the modern age: the idea that progressive science and religion can coexist.

For a century or so since Nietzsche, popular culture in the West has operated according to an uneasy truce, in which God both is and is not dead. We teach our children the evidence-based materialism of science and tell them they can believe in God and a faith-based morality in their spare time if they like.

And in some parts of the country, we celebrate Scopes as a victory over ignorance, while still insisting that we do not also celebrate it as a victory over religion. What these endless Scopes sequels tell us is that somewhere many years from now we're going to hit a fork in the road, beyond which this have-it-both-ways philosophy isn't going to fly anymore. Is God dead or isn't he? Are we believers or not? They know what we think. They just want us to come out and say it.

The End of the Party

In the House, Bush is a liability, the Hammer's been indicted, and the once-united GOP juggernaut stumbles toward an ugly divorce

—

December 15, 2005

The first hint I had that something was wrong—that the karmic balance of the U.S. House of Representatives had shifted irrevocably—came at about the twenty-two-minute mark of what was supposed to be a routine fifteen-minute vote on a labor appropriations bill. Republicans weren't supposed to lose this bill—H.R. 3010, a relatively uncontroversial Fiscal Year 2006 Appropriations Act for the Departments of Labor, Health and Human Services, and Education. It wasn't even supposed to be in play. The big challenge was supposed to be later that evening, in a heavily politicked budget-reconciliation package that threatened to be the toughest fight a wounded Republican Party had faced since the Gingrich years.

The press section was unusually crowded and buzzing with anticipation over that bill. But no one gave a shit about H.R. 3010. Few observers even knew what was in it. It was just another bill that would send a huge hunk of money rolling off the presses into nowhere, like hundreds of others that had sailed out of Congress unmolested in the first five Bush years.

I closed my eyes to take a nap in the gallery when H.R. 3010 went to the floor for a vote. I woke up about twenty minutes later, looked at the electronic scoreboard over the majority side of the floor, and saw the following stat line:

YEAS 200 NAYS 220 TIME 0:00

The time limit had expired and the Democrats were ahead by twenty votes. For anyone who has spent any time watching the Tom DeLay Congress, where there is only one outcome, this was a visual non sequitur—a logical impossibility, like a car parked on one wheel.

On the floor, the stand-in speaker, the bespectacled, pasty-faced Nebraska Republican Lee Terry, was looking frantically in all directions, like a man who has lost a child in an airport. On the majority side of the floor, Republicans were huddled in clumps all over the place, screeching like zoo macaques and intermittently whipping their heads up to check the board.

In one section toward the rear, a very weird foursome had gathered. The notorious Bakersfield, California, congressman Bill Thomas—the vicious Ways and Means Committee chair and the first congressman to have been found in bed with the pharmaceutical industry (he got caught having an affair with a female lobbyist from the group Pharma)—was gesticulating wildly while being advanced upon by a trio of the heaviest hitters on the Hill.

That trio represented the remaining congressional power core of the once-unstoppable Bush-Rove loyalists: Speaker Dennis Hastert, interim Majority Leader Roy Blunt, and Rules Committee chair David Dreier.

Thomas had a red mark next to his name on the display listing the members and their votes. Nay. So Bill Thomas, one of the vilest scumbags in all of Washington and normally a Bush loyalist of Himmler-esque dependability, was betraying the president and party at the eleventh hour of what was shaping up to be a losing appropriations vote. What the hell was going on?

Terry, the panicked speaker, stalled for another minute or two, then shockingly struck his gavel and ended the vote. The final tally: 224–209 against.

"The nays have it!" the green-faced Terry shouted.

The majority side of the floor collectively slumped in its chairs and stared forward, open-mouthed. Their half of Congress looked like a bar on Landsdowne Street after Bill Buckner. It was the Republicans' first loss on an appropriations vote since 1995, ending one of the longest political winning streaks in the country's history—and the beginning of what was looking more and more like the bloody collapse of Republican rule in Washington.

The backdrop for the vote on the bill—known colloquially as "Labor H"—involved a compound fracture within a Republican Party badly wounded by legal woes and the declining poll numbers of George Bush.

The latter fact became a pressing issue in Congress on the election night of November 8, when Republicans suffered defeats in two critical states, losing the governorships of both New Jersey and Virginia.

But in the most telling November 8 result, incumbent St. Paul, Minnesota, mayor Randy Kelly, a Democrat who endorsed Bush, was whipped by another Democrat, Chris Coleman, who won by almost 70 percent; polls showed that nearly two-thirds of voters wanted to punish Kelly for his support of the president.

Once everyone saw that Bush could not be counted on to deliver coattail victories, Hill lawmakers began scrambling to distance themselves from the more unpopular aspects of Bush's agenda. In the House, this resulted in a three-way split within the Republican Party.

On the one hand, there suddenly appeared to be a dissenting group of socially liberal Republicans—most hailing from northern states with significant minority and organized-labor presences—who were hostile to Bush's tax cuts, to the war, and to some cuts in social spending. This bunch, called the moderates or the "Tuesday group" (an incorrect nickname; they actually meet on Wednesdays), includes Republicans such as New York's Sherwood Boehlert, Connecticut's Rob Simmons, and Iowa's Jim Leach.

Then there were the hard-liners, also called the "true conservatives," who organized in opposition to the Bush administration's long record of unchecked spending. This group, which on the whole opposes social expenditure of any kind and would like to see programs such as Medicaid eliminated, has wide support and a strong organization in the House. Calling itself the Republican Study Committee, the group is led by the unsmiling, pencil-necked congressman from Indiana Mike Pence, and it has forced a showdown with the old Republican leadership of the House over spending for the Hurricane Katrina disaster.

The RSC has unveiled a plan called Operation Offset, which would pay for Katrina by making commensurate "offsets" in House spending through cuts in social programming. In a bucking of superficial unity that would have been unthinkable a year ago, the RSC publicly threatened to force a vote on the House leadership seats if Operation Offset were not instituted.

The latter issue is the last key factor in the Republican troubles, for the third group in the new three-sided Republican Party—the Bush-loyalist old guard still nominally in charge—is in complete disarray. Majority Leader Tom DeLay is under indictment and has been forced to step down temporarily. His interim replacement, Missouri's Roy Blunt, looks like he will be sucked into the Jack Abramoff scandal and Speaker Hastert has his own Abramoff problems.

Therefore, the Bush coterie in the House is battered and staggering and, as a result, has been scrambling in recent weeks to pull off the difficult task of satisfying both dissident factions within its ranks. With regard to the Labor H bill, the Republican leadership bowed to pressure from the conservative wing and not only implemented widespread spending offsets but agreed, no doubt with a significant measure of physical agony, to an across-the-board ban on earmarks—those tossed-in local pork projects, stuffed in the anus of appropriations bills, that are the staple of the congressional political diet.

While the last-minute spending cuts were largely what doomed the bill, with most of the "moderates" voting nay— Arizona's Rick Renzi rejected the bill because of cuts in rural-education funding—the party also lost a few Bush loyalists who couldn't swallow the loss of their beloved earmarks. One of those was Thomas, the Ways and Means chairman. What he couldn't swallow was a last-minute change in the law that moved up a ban on the use of Medicaid funds to pay for erectile-dysfunction drugs—a step that would result in a $90 million offset.

Thomas—who besides having his fling with a Pharma lobbyist received $112,619 in campaign funds from the pharmaceutical industry in the 2004 cycle—couldn't brook passage of a bill forbidding the state to pay for ED drugs.

In other words, Thomas couldn't vote without Viagra. If there is a better metaphor for the Republican troubles, I haven't heard it.

But the Republicans would return to form late that same night with the passage of their controversial budget-reconciliation package.

The victory had all the trappings of a DeLay win in a major vote. One, it was conducted in the middle of the night, so that the smarmy process could be viewed by the minimum number of people and/or reporters. Two, it was a narrow win: 217–215.

The one- or two-vote victory has been a hallmark of the DeLay method: compromise as little as possible on your pork and your social cuts, fuck 'em if they don't like it, and win by one vote if you have to, holding the floor open for three hours if needed.

Third, the bill was an Orwellian monstrosity in the classically DeLay-ian mold. The shepherd of such hilariously named bills as the Clear Skies Act (for a bill partially repealing Clean Air) and the Healthy Forests Act (easing restrictions on commercial logging) this time had come up with the Deficit Reduction Act of 2006, a bill that added $20 billion to the deficit. Even in this desperate time for the party, and with the budget already heavily burdened by spending on the Iraq war and Katrina, the DeLay leadership team is still clinging to a plan to implement $70 billion in new tax breaks, with more than half being extended to citizens with incomes over $1 million. To pay for that $70 billion in new shortfalls, DeLay and Co. came up with this Deficit Reduction Act, which cut funding from programs for the very poorest citizens—mainly from Medicaid, food stamps, and student loans.

It took tremendous balls for DeLay to push this bill, given his situation, but he had an ace in the hole: himself. For the night vote, DeLay returned to the chamber to play the role of floor assassin, replacing Blunt and Dreier and Hastert, who'd failed that same assignment earlier in the day.

Watching DeLay wade through a crowd of his own party members during a critical vote is an awesome thing, a nature show worthy of Sir David Attenborough. DeLay moves through the aisles like some kind of balding incubus, and as he passes Republican members instinctively turn their backs on him, not wanting to be caught in the Gorgon's gaze (or, more to the point, be threatened with the loss of a chairmanship or reelection funding).

The Democrats had this vote won—until DeLay approached a pair of Republicans who had voted nay: Steven LaTourette of Ohio and Maryland's Wayne Gilchrest. DeLay leaned over and spoke for a few minutes into both sets of ears. I looked up at the board and watched Gilchrest's red mark turn green; then I saw DeLay walking away from LaTourette, with the latter sighing and pulling out a vote-changing form.

"They broke his arm!" a reporter in the gallery shouted. "They broke his arm!"

A few minutes later the gavel struck and the Republicans had won. But it was a hollow victory. DeLay and his goons were still on top, still together—but they were headed for a nasty divorce.

It has gotten so bad for Republicans around Washington that even their usual trump play—the dirty kick in the balls—has abandoned them. It wasn't long ago that Republicans could pull a Roy Cohn and pin the scarlet letter even on legless war heroes like Max Cleland and get away with parading them through the public arena as commies and traitors. But when they tried the same thing in Congress on the day after the budget bill, trotting out feckless freshman Representative Jean Schmidt (a wrinkly, witchlike woman with a penchant for dressing like a harbor buoy) to denounce war critic and Vietnam veteran Representative John Murtha as an unpatriotic coward, the ploy blew up in their faces almost immediately. The whole country reacted with an audible collective retching sound, "Mean Jean" was savaged on *SNL,* and she had to spend three days hiding from reporters; meanwhile, Murtha spent the weekend getting fellated by Tim Russert and other media heavies, who feted the Democrat as though he were a cross between Audie Murphy and the pope. Overnight, it seemed, Republicans had lost a yard off their fastball.

The party has been riding a terrific formula for political success in the past five years: don't compromise, crush your enemies, ruthlessly enforce discipline, and then keep the soldiers happy by handing out campaign money and George Bush largess at election time. While everyone was winning, the internal contradictions were kept well hidden. Even the hard-line deficit hawks and Goldwaterites didn't seem to mind racking up $3 trillion in new debt over five years, just as long as Georgie could produce a W for them by making a few appearances before the polls opened.

Now Bush is stumbling around Washington with spears sticking out of him, and his soldiers are running for the hills, looking for a fresh horse to ride. The old days of everyone in the party getting laid and paid are over. The fatal hidden paradox of Bush's political success has finally come back to bite him, exposing this damning riddle. How do you give away the entire national treasure and also keep the fiscal conservatives in your party happy? It should always have been impossible; now it really is.

In a meeting last week, the conservative RSC showed the finale of *The Bridge on the River Kwai* to celebrate the defeat of the $230 million Alaskan "Bridge to Nowhere" pork project rammed into a highway bill over the summer. When the bridge over the Kwai exploded at the movie's end, the crowd of GOP congressmen cheered. Republicans celebrating the death of a Republican bridge.

Could any Republican, much less one hundred of them, have pulled a stunt like that in public a year ago?

No way. The party's over, George.

The Magical Victory Tour
While Iraq burns, the president keeps playing the same old song
▬

December 29, 2005

December 7, 10:44 a.m., the sixty-fourth anniversary of Pearl Harbor day. I've just woken up with a line of drool on my face in the back row of a ballroom at the Omni Shoreham Hotel in Washington, D.C., where any minute now President George W. Bush will give the second address of his barnburning four-speech "National Strategy for Victory in Iraq" tour.

There are no T-shirts for this concert tour, but if there were the venue list on the back would make for one of the weirder souvenirs in rock 'n' roll history. U.S. Naval Academy in Annapolis, Maryland, November 30, no advance publicity, closed audience: check. Here at the Omni, December 7, again no advance warning, handpicked audience, ten reporters max (no one else knew about it), with even the cashiers in the hotel's coffee shop unaware of the president's presence: check. Dates three and four, venues and dates unknown for security reasons: check and check.

This is how President Bush takes his message to the people these days: in furtive sneak-attack addresses to closed audiences of elite friendlies at weird early-morning hours. If you want to catch Bush's act in person during this tour, you have to stalk him for days and keep both ears open for last-minute changes of plan; I actually missed the Annapolis speech when I made the mistake of briefly taking my eye off him the day before.

Here at the Omni I showed up early, determined not to repeat my mistake. I was not going to miss the National Strategy for Victory in Iraq, no sir. But for all my preparations I did almost screw it up again. I fell asleep an hour before the event and awoke only in the middle of the introductory remarks by Richard N. Haass, the president of the Council on Foreign Relations, the stodgy, status quo think tank hosting the event. I pried my eyes open just in time to see Bush, looking spooked and shrunken, take the stage.

Bush in person always strikes me as the kind of guy who would ask a woman for a hand job at the end of a first date. He has days where he looks like she said yes, and days where the answer was no.

Today was one of his no days. He frowned, looking wronged, and grabbed the microphone. I pulled out my notebook . . .

A few minutes later I felt like a hooker who's just blinked under a blanket with a prep-school virgin. Was that it? Is it over? It seemed to be; Bush was off the podium and slipping down the first line of the crowd, pumping hands for a minute and then promptly Snagglepussing toward the left exit. By the time I made it five rows into the crowd he had vanished into a sea of Secret Servicemen, who whisked him away, presumably to return him posthaste to his formaldehyde tank.

I looked down at my notes. They indicated that Bush had opened his remarks by comparing the Iraq war to World War II ("We liberated millions, we aided the rise of democracy in Europe and Asia. . . ."). From there we learned that we were fighting an enemy without conscience, but all was not lost, because the entrepreneurial spirit is alive and well in Iraq. Of course there had been setbacks, because in the past after we took a city, we left it and the terrorists would just take it back again. But we've stopped doing that now and so things are better. In conclusion, Senator Joe Lieberman visited Iraq four times in the past seventeen months and, goddamn it, he liked what he saw.

In the Obey Your Thirst/Image Is Everything era of American politics, Bush's National Victory campaign is a creepy innovation. It features the president thumping a document—the "National Strategy for Victory in Iraq"—that was largely written not by diplomats or generals but by a pair of academics from Duke University named Peter Feaver and Christopher Gelpi. Essentially a PR document, the paper is basically a living political experiment, designed to prove that Americans will more readily accept military casualties if the word "victory" is repeated a great many times in public.

"This is not really a strategy document from the Pentagon about fighting the insurgency," Gelpi told the *New York Times*. "The document is clearly targeted at American public opinion."

In other words, this was really a National Strategy for Victory at Home. It was classic Bush-think. Instead of bombing the insurgency off the map, he bombs the map—in lieu of actually fighting the war, a bold strategy, to be sure. But would it work?

Both the record and my notes indicate that the audience applauded on two occasions. The first came after the line "And now the terrorists think they can make America run in Iraq, and that is not going to happen so long as I'm the commander in chief." My notes say, "Scattered but by no means unanimous applause." The second time came at the end of the speech, after the last line, "May God continue to bless our country." This time the reaction was more enthusiastic, but at least one person—me—was clapping because it was over.

The Council on Foreign Relations was good enough to pass out a list of the expected attendees at the speech. Here are some of the names that one could find in Bush's audience: Frank Finelli, the Carlyle Group; Adam Fromm, office of Representative Dennis Hastert; Robert W. Haines, ExxonMobil Corp.;

Paul W. Butler, Akin Gump Strauss Hauer and Feld LLP; Robert Bremer, Lockheed Martin Corp.; Scott Sendek, Eli Lilly and Co.; James H. Lambright, Export-Import Bank of the United States.

The point is obvious; Bush's audience was like a guest list for a Monster's Ball of the military-industrial establishment. And even in this crowd full of corporate lawyers, investment bankers, weapons makers, ex-spooks, and, for Christ's sake, lobbyists, the president of the United States couldn't cook up more than two tepid applause lines for his Iraq policy—and one of those was because he was finishing up and, one guesses, freeing the audience to go call their brokers.

God bless George Bush. The Middle East is in flames and how does he answer the call? He rolls up to the side entrance of a four-star Washington hotel, slips unobserved into a select gathering of the richest fatheads in his dad's Rolodex, spends a few tortured minutes exposing his half-assed policies like a campus flasher, and then ducks back into his rabbit hole while he waits for his next speech to be written by paid liars.

If that isn't leadership, what is?

Not many people in the Omni audience hung around to be interviewed when it was over. The few who did make themselves available tried to put a brave face on the situation.

"Well, he did the best he could under, uh, difficult circumstances," said council member Jeffrey Pryce.

Did he detect anything new in the new strategy?

"No," he said, shrugging. "But he's in a tough spot."

I'd been following the national tour for more than a week. If the reception at the Omni was stale, that was nothing compared to how it was going over in the White House briefing room. On the day before the Omni speech, I actually worried that gopher-faced administration spokescreature Scott McClellan might be physically attacked by reporters, who appeared ready to give official notice of having had Enough of This Bullshit.

In fact the room at one point seemed on the verge of a *Blazing Saddles*–style chair-throwing brawl when McClellan refused to answer the cheeky question of why, if we weren't planning on torturing war-on-terror detainees in foreign prisons, we couldn't just bring them back to be incarcerated in the United States.

"I think the American people understand," McClellan said, "the importance of protecting sources and methods, and not compromising ongoing efforts in the war on terrorism . . ."

When a contingent of audibly groaning reporters pressed, McClellan shrugged and tried a new tack. "I'm not going to talk further about intelligence matters of this nature," he said.

A reporter next to me threw his head back in disgust. "Oh, fuckin' A . . ." he whispered. The room broke out into hoots and howls; even the usually dignified Bill Plante of CBS started openly calling McClellan out. "The question you're currently evading is not about an intelligence matter," he hissed.

I looked around. "Man," I thought. "This place sure looks better on television." On TV, the whole package—the deep-blue curtains, the solemn great seal—suggests majesty, power, drama. For years I'd dreamed of coming here, the Graceland of politics.

In real life, however, the White House briefing room is a grimy little closet that's peeling and cracking in every corner and looks like it hasn't seen a bottle of Windex in ten years. The first chair in the fifth row is broken; the fold-up seat doesn't fold up and in fact dangles on its hinge, so that you'd slide off if you tried to sit on it. No science exists that could determine the original color of these hideous carpets. Reporters throw their coats and coffee cups wherever. The place is a fucking sty.

It's a raggedy-ass old stage, and the act that plays on it isn't getting any fresher, either. All partisan sniping aside, this latest counteroffensive from the White House says just about everything you need to know about George Bush and the men who work for him.

Up until now this president's solution to everything has been to stare into the cameras, lie, and keep on lying until such time as the political problem disappears. And now, unable to comprehend that while political crises may wilt in the face of such tactics real crises do not, he and his team are responding to this first serious feet-to-the-fire Iraq emergency in the same way they always have—with a fusillade of silly, easily disprovable bullshit. Bush and his mouthpieces continue to try to obfuscate and cloud the issue of why we're in Iraq, and they do so not only selectively but constantly, compulsively, like mental patients who can't stop jacking off in public. They don't know the difference between a real problem and a political problem, because to them there is no difference. What could possibly be worse than bad poll numbers?

On this particular day in the briefing room, it's just more of the same disease. McClellan, a cringing yes-man type who tries to soften the effect of his nonanswers by projecting an air of being just as out of the loop as you are, starts pimping lies and crap the moment he enters the room. He's the cheapest kind of political hack, a greedy little bum making a living by throwing his hat on the ground and juggling lemons for pennies.

Putting his hat out for the Strategy for Victory, he says nothing new—there is no real strategy, remember, just words—and it quickly becomes clear that the whole purpose of this campaign is not to offer new information but to reinforce the administration's most shameless and irresponsible myths about the war:

that we invaded to liberate Iraq, that Saddam Hussein was behind 9/11, and so on. McClellan does this even in the context of
responding to angry denunciations of this very tactic.

For instance, when a reporter asked why the administration
still insists on giving the impression that Saddam Hussein was
behind the 9/11 attacks, McClellan answered, "I don't think
that [it] does. But I think what you have to understand about
September eleventh is that September eleventh taught us some
important lessons: one, that we need to take the fight to the
enemy and engage them abroad . . ."

Implying, in other words, that the enemy who attacked us
was in Iraq. Same old shit.

After hearing McClellan talk for what seemed like the thir-
tieth time about our continuing efforts to spread democracy, I
finally felt insulted. Giving in to the same basic instinct that
leads people to buy lottery tickets I raised my hand. I figured
I'd ask nicely, just give him a chance to come clean. C'mon,
man, we know you're lying, why not just leave it alone? I asked
him if he couldn't just admit, once and for all, that we didn't
go to Iraq to spread democracy, that maybe it was time to re-
tire that line, at least.

"Well," he said, "we set out the reasons we went to Iraq, and
I would encourage you to go back and look at that. We have
liberated twenty-five million people in Iraq and twenty-five
million people in Afghanistan . . ."

"But that wasn't the reason we went—"

"Spreading freedom and democracy," he said, ignoring me.
"Well, we're not going to relitigate why we went into Iraq.
We've made very clear what the reasons were. And no, I don't
think you define them accurately by being so selective in the
question . . . that's important for spreading hope and opportunity in the broader Middle East . . ."

"Just to be clear," I said, exasperated, "that's a different argument than was made to the American people before the war."

"Our arguments are very public," he said. "You can go look at what the arguments are. That's not what I was talking about."

He smiled at me. There's your strategy for victory in Iraq: Fuck all of you—we're sticking to our story.

The Harder They Fall
Republicans are scrambling to clean their House—but the dirt won't wash off

February 9, 2006

"The Republicans are now and always have been the party of reform," said a grinning David Dreier, surveying the crowd of journalists in the congressional radio and TV gallery.

The nattily dressed House Rules Committee chairman then paused, as if to give someone in the crowd a chance to chuck a bottle at his head. No one did. So he went on. "I see this," he said, "as a wonderful new opportunity for us . . ."

Again, he paused. No bottles, no rotten tomatoes, no clouds of flying dog shit landing with a *slap!* on his receding forehead. Given what the Republican leadership might have expected, at a press conference unveiling a "lobby reform" package in the wake of the Jack Abramoff scandal (what Dreier meant by "this"), the event was a smashing success.

Standing next to Dreier, nodding with mild approval but also scanning the crowd cautiously, was the boarlike House speaker, Dennis Hastert. Hastert had kicked off this presser with similarly inspired oratory—the highlight of which, according to my notes, was this line: "It's not acceptable to, uh, break the rules or the law."

Now he was standing there next to Dreier, motionless and mute, with the nervous, half-bored look of a man with a commuter train to catch. It was a lonely picture: an exhausted fat man playing his last political card and an effete Californian in a too-orange tie, standing alone behind a plywood podium in a dank congressional closet, putting a brave face on The End. In the wake of the Abramoff scandal, they were all that was left of the once-vaunted Republican leadership. It was like a *Star Trek* script gone hopelessly wrong, with Kirk and Spock beheaded in the first two minutes, and no one left to man the bridge but Scotty and maybe that blond nurse of McCoy's, the one in the blue minidress.

The Dreier-Hastert press conference felt in every way like the very last act in the desperate black comedy known as the Tom DeLay era of Republican rule in Washington. What will follow is a new play, a gruesome tragedy in all likelihood, whose main characters will be Abramoff, an enraged public, and a succession of grandstanding criminal prosecutors. But lonely and desperate as it was, this last event had all the wit and spirit of an inspired farce—the chutzpah, the arrogance, the spit-in-your-eye rhetoric, the maddening cloud of impunity hanging over it all.

Just consider: At this critical moment in the party's history, when survival required some kind of dramatic public gesture toward self-policing, the GOP needed an innocent, someone with clean hands, to lead the "anti-corruption" drive. The Democrats, who a day later would announce their own reform bill, would do just that—elevating relative political virgins Representative Louise Slaughter and Senator Barack Obama to starring roles in their own "Clean House" movement.

But the Republicans who ran this town like a dictatorship for most of the past five years apparently looked around and could not find a single plausible virgin for the part of their Mr. Clean.

Of the two leading candidates for the recently vacated House majority leader seat, one (acting leader Roy Blunt) had attempted to slip tobacco-friendly language into a Homeland Security authorization bill while having an extramarital affair with a Philip Morris lobbyist, and the other (John Boehner) had once been caught handing out checks from tobacco interests to members of Congress on the floor of the House.

Elsewhere, the Commerce Committee chairman (Joe Barton) had inserted a provision into an energy bill on behalf of a company that had paid $56,000 to a PAC to "get a seat at the table," and the names of the House deputy whip (Eric Cantor), the House conference secretary (John Doolittle), and the House Appropriations chair (Jerry Lewis) were all floating around in various sordid Abramoff tales involving golf junkets, Indian tribes, and floating casinos. The only Republican names not burning putrid holes in the front pages of the *Washington Post* were the ones who at that very minute were busy forming alliances and gearing up for a factional challenge to the DeLay/Hastert/Bush–backed congressional leadership.

So in the end to whom did the Republicans turn to be their white knight? David Dreier, a man whose very first act in last year's Congress was to write a Rules package that not only sought to rewrite the congressional rules to allow the majority leader to continue service while under indictment for a felony but also castrated the Ethics Committee, changing its structure in such a way that the Republicans could unilaterally quash any further investigations of DeLay.

As chair of the Rules Committee—a murky body whose chairman has the power to rewrite bills entirely before they are voted on—Dreier moreover was presumably the gatekeeper to much of the midnight shenanigans involving earmarks and last-minute insertions of paid-for corporate goodies in big pieces of legislation. Perhaps more than any other Republican, Dreier was a symbol of the institutional corruption that allowed DeLay to almost single-handedly manipulate Congress like a marionette for the Abramoffs of the world. As one Democratic staffer said to me, "Putting Dreier in charge of this is the biggest fucking joke you can possibly imagine."

Which made it all the more beautiful that when Dreier brazen performance worthy of the best and most confident days of the in-your-face DeLay regime. Grinning and fingering his tangerine-colored tie (Dreier's inappropriately cheery Crayola tie collection is a source of many dark jokes in Congress), Dreier explained that when he'd called to wish Hastert a Happy New Year, the latter had surprised him by asking him to take up lobby reform.

"And I thought," said Dreier, raising his hands to his chest, "'My gosh, is this something more that I want to take on?'"

The "my gosh" inspired a muffled groan on my side of the room. Dreier smiled and went on. "Yesterday, we marked the birthday of Dr. Martin Luther King . . ."

Reporters shot each other looks, all thinking the same thing: In this dire situation, with Jack Abramoff babbling strings of names and account numbers into an inquisitor's mike somewhere, would even a Tom DeLay Republican have the balls to defile the corpse of Martin Luther King? The answer came quickly, as Dreier quoted MLK to explain his attitude toward lobbyist reform:

"I thought about one of his letters," he began. "'We should always be careful about the tranquilizing drug of gradualism . . .'"

He smiled and surveyed the crowd, a hand still pressed to his breast. Gradualism! It was a breathtaking show of balls—a cynical display of Mozartian virtuosity. Well, I thought, they're not dead yet. Or if they are, what a way to go out!

Washington is a different place since January 3, a date that will go down in infamy for this Republican regime. It was on that quiet day at the tail end of the New Year hangover that the superlobbyist Abramoff announced his intention to cop a plea—an announcement that sent half of Washington in search of good criminal representation.

Since that day, the Republicans in this town can often be seen staggering down the halls of Congress, faces caked with debris and still deaf from the impact of the Abramoff nuclear shit-bomb. Complicating matters is the fact that the party has been forced to return to congressional business very early in the winter recess to conduct elections for the House majority leadership seat, which of course was recently vacated by Tom DeLay, himself now headed for Texas to meet with the Hand of Fate.

There are three candidates for the leadership spot, who represent three distinct strategies for dealing with the current crisis. The front-runner is the acting leader, Blunt, who pointedly represents a strategy of doing nothing at all. Blunt's biography is brimming with the kind of pornographic devotion to money and corporate privilege that was a prerequisite for political success in the good old days.

The Missouri congressman three years ago ditched his wife for a Philip Morris lobbyist named Abigail Perlman, whom he subsequently married; it's been a profitable marriage, as Philip Morris (now called Altria) has donated more than $270,000 to committees tied to Blunt. Meanwhile, Blunt's son Andrew is also an Altria lobbyist, and Blunt's other son, Matt, is governor of his home state—elected, conveniently, with the help of funds from Altria. One gets the impression that the whole family spends its holidays sitting in a circle, two-fistedly smoking Chesterfields while handing each other wads of hundred-dollar bills.

Blunt's hands are also wet with the blood of the Abramoff scandal; as party whip he cosigned (with DeLay) letters on behalf of a Louisiana Indian tribe represented by Abramoff. Meanwhile, Abramoff is one of the first names on the list of 2004 individual donors to Blunt's PAC, the sickeningly named Rely on Your Beliefs fund.

Blunt appears to be the choice for majority leader in the event that the party concludes that it still has a chance to get away with absolutely everything, Abramoff trial be damned. But the next choice, Ohio long-timer John Boehner, appears to be the cosmetic fallback position should the party conclude that business can go back to operating as usual only after a few carefully chosen heads are rendered unto Caesar—whomever Abramoff decides to give up.

On the surface, Boehner would seem a brilliant choice; he has game-show-host looks, no shame, and has never been indicted for anything. Although his own sugary-titled PAC, the Freedom Project, has accepted some $31,000 from Abramoff clients over the years, there are as yet no allegations that Boehner has ever traded favors with the Evil One.

Still, folks around the House describe the long-serving Boehner—who was kicked out of party leadership once before (he was House Republican Conference chairman in the 104th and 105th Congresses but lost his seat when his mentor, Newt Gingrich, was ousted)—as having an off-putting, semi-delusional, almost Kerry-esque sense of entitlement about the leadership post.

Boehner's zeal for the leadership post is such that he issued a thirty-seven-page PowerPoint presentation to campaign for the job. The document is a towering monument to political cliché, wrapping quotations of Reagan, Churchill, and John Paul II around paeans to the virtues of change, light, hope, "big goals," and hitting the accelerator while others stay stuck in neutral.

For all his sterling qualifications, though, Boehner can hardly be described as someone who lived outside the K Street/DeLay universe. If anyone in this race can claim that distinction, it could only be the third and last candidate, John Shadegg of Arizona, another Gingrich protégé, who kicked off his campaign by bragging on national television that his "level of taint" was, if not entirely absent, at least "decidedly lower" than that of his opponents. A late entry into the race, Shadegg menacingly represents the prayer-and-belt-tightening future of the Republican Party, should Abramoff sink the Rove-DeLay-Hastert-Norquist rampaging corporate-money machine that took over the party in 1999.

While those Republicans spent the years since treating Washington like their own personal *Girls Gone Wild* video— drinking champagne out of bra cups at lavish corporate fundraisers and turning Congress into one big turnstile, passing any and every law that anyone with a dollar felt like paying for— there were other Republicans with actual ideological convictions who just went along with it all in a codependent fashion.

These were the true believers, the deficit hawks, and the Bible thumpers, who bit their lips and voted the party line even as the government exploded in size in the first five years of the Bush presidency. They had blind faith, but now they're organizing to take the party back. This process began last fall with the ascendancy of the uber-conservative Republican Study Group, which mounted a brazen factional challenge to new acting leader Blunt over emergency spending for Hurricane Katrina. It continues now with the leadership candidacy of the humorless Shadegg, whose conservative bona fides include a father who managed the 1952 Senate campaign of Barry Goldwater.

Shadegg's run coincides unpleasantly—almost audibly, like fingernails on a blackboard—with the unsolicited reappearance on the public scene of his mentor Gingrich. The latter keeps showing up in newspapers with the description "presidential hopeful" violently attached to his person, shaking his head in anguish over this whole Abramoff business and acting as though someone asked for his advice.

That Gingrich has somehow managed to position himself as a pre-Abramoff Republican champion shows how dangerous a moment this is not only for the Republicans but for the country in general. All but forgotten now is the fact that Gingrich more or less invented the K Street Project—a Republican scheme to freeze out Democratic lobbyists—and that Abramoff was a bridge between K Street and Gingrich as long as a dozen years ago.

The raging shit-fire that is the Abramoff scandal exposed Washington as a veritable inferno of crushed values and boundless activist cynicism. It eloquently revealed an America whose system of government had finally mutated to fit the vapidity and anything-for-money morality of the culture as a whole. In a country where people eat bugs for money on national television, how surprising is a congressman who sells his vote or a Congress run like a Wal-Mart?

Barring a sudden and unforeseen flowering of affirmative values in the depraved whorehouse that is our nation's capital, money is still going to remain a hell of an effective substitute for political principle in this town, meaning all manner of frauds—from Gingrich on down—will be moving in not to do anything different but to take over the old dealer's territory. The Democrats, whose innocence in the crimes of the past five years to date corresponds exactly to their lack of opportunities for corruption, may now get a chance at the helm. But it won't take much exposure to cheap stunts like a beaming Harry Reid and Nancy Pelosi signing a "Declaration of Honest Leadership" before people begin to remember how much the other guys can suck, too.

Bush haters are celebrating this week as old villains descend to the death chamber, but they should be careful what they wish for. Trusting Washington to fix itself is a whole new kind of torture.

Generation Enron

In George Bush's America, the only crime is being poor

February 23, 2006

Tuesday morning, January 31, Houston. I'm in the press listening room of the Enron trial, trying to keep track of prosecutor John Hueston's opening statement. The bespectacled inquisitor is trying, vainly, it seems, to explain to the jury an Enron investment vehicle called Raptor.

"Now imagine that you've driven a brand-new truck worth $30,000 into sort of a big barrel," he says. "The truck drives around in that barrel for a while, then finally crashes and burns and ends up in a heap. Now the truck is only worth $5,000, but Enron is still saying it's worth $30,000. That's Raptor . . ."

I sigh and write in my notebook:

Enron: Big rubber barrel full of trucks

Trucks = shitty investments

"You will hear," Hueston continues, "that they were able to put almost anything in that barrel . . ."

I look back at my notes. Less than fifteen minutes ago, in another prosecutorial scenario, Raptor was a cookie jar. Now I'm wondering: Was it a rubber cookie jar? Were there cookies in the barrel? If so, what size were the cookies, relative to the trucks? Covering the Enron trial is like being trapped in the world's longest Thomas Friedman column, a Salvador Dalí landscape of violently mixed nightmare metaphors. I shudder, my pie rising.

It was inevitable that the Enron trial would devolve into a verbal jumble. For the defense, obfuscation would be necessary;

in order to keep the jury away from the facts, there had to be a lot of talk about steady hands at the helm, sheep running from wolves, and other such self-serving, incoherent bullshit. Therefore, in their opening statements, the defense counsel wasted no time in blinding the jury with crap imagery like "You might think of the admiral of the navy as the CEO . . . An economic storm was raging . . ."

The prosecution had the opposite rhetorical challenge. On the one hand, it had to present to the jury an easily digestible tale of corporate fraud and insider dealing, and indeed it focused heavily on evidence that defendants Ken Lay and Jeffrey Skilling had dumped millions in company shares just before Enron's meltdown.

On the other hand, it had to illuminate the fantastic tale of a major public corporation that hid assets and losses in hundred-million-dollar shell companies named after Chewbacca from *Star Wars,* did side deals with phantom companies registered in the name of an officer's gay lover, and made billion-dollar bets on the Brazilian energy market without remembering to figure in the exchange rate in its calculations. Describing the corruption of Enron is like describing distances in the universe: impossible to express in rational numbers. Hence the barrels and trucks and cookie jars.

All of which set the stage for the Houston trial: two judicial contestants, both speaking in riddles, taking turns trying to explain one of the biggest piles of bullshit in human history.

By all rights, the trial of former Enron chiefs Ken Lay and Jeffrey Skilling ought to be a benchmark moment in this particular era of America's history, the cathartic burning at the stake of two infamous villains who together flamboyantly represented the tragic character flaw of our fallen society at the turn of the century.

And that's exactly what it might have been, if this trial had taken place a few years ago, at the peak of public outrage, when the sensational show trial and legal mauling of any close friend of George Bush's seemed a remote and unlikely possibility. In the first year or so after the coinciding events of 9/11 and the Enron meltdown, the Bush-Cheney-Rove clan seemed unstoppable, with poll numbers through the roof and plans for an insane new war marching inexorably toward realization. It seemed like we would never get our hands on the likes of a Lay and Skilling; *the bastards will get off* was the prevailing wisdom of anyone who felt himself to be on the wrong side of flag-waving, Clear Channel America.

Some three years have passed since then, and a funny thing has happened in the meantime. Lay and Skilling are finally ascending to the gallows, but no one cares, because the brazen impunity of their particular class of wheeler-dealer con artist is no longer a shock. In fact, in the past three years the national tableau has become positively filthy with wreckage from the high-speed flameouts of similarly hyperenterprising liars and cheaters. The corporate captains, the Rigases and the Kozlowskis, went down first, but then there were others, representing other fields: Jayson Blair and Judy Miller headlined an unpleasantly teeming bunch of lying-ass journalists, and then came Jack Abramoff, and Tom DeLay, and Karl Rove himself, and Scooter Libby, and Bob Ney, and that asshole memoirist Frey . . . and by now who even cares who else?

The theme of all these stories was almost exactly the same: the sociopathic pursuit of naked, narrow self-interest, executed not only without any regard for any broader consequences but without any understanding that such consequences might exist. The thread linking Lay and Skilling with Abramoff and DeLay and Miller and even Michael Jackson was their failure to see or admit, even after being caught red-handed, that they had done anything wrong.

They were just doing what any of us would do, given the opportunity: taking as much money or fame or power or influence or little boys plied with Jesus juice or whatever as they could get, and fuck everyone else, because that's the name of the game. Outwit, outplay, outlast—and cheat if you have to, because it's a jungle out there. Anyone who says otherwise is just a sore loser, whining about not being let into the club.

When Daniel Petrocelli, Skilling's grating and pompous solicitor, made his "my client is just a simple caveman" pitch to the jury, he argued with a straight face that rich people are more perfect and less prone to temptation than the rest of us.

"In 1999, [Skilling] had more money than he ever dreamed of having," he said. Indeed, Skilling and Lay walked away with $150 million and $220 million, respectively. "So why would he do it? What is Jeff Skilling's motive?"

There was silence for a moment, and I kept waiting for some enraged citizen to leap out of the jury box, tackle Petrocelli, start pulling ligature out of his neck. The obscenity of the lawyer's argument defied description, but it also expressed the mind-set that led to Enron. In Skilling's world, being poor was the only real crime; at any rate, being poor made you more suspect than someone with $150 million.

The Enron scandal, from the very beginning, was always about men not being satisfied with mere riches. The Lay and Skilling story is the story of a company with a simple, comprehensible, and highly successful pipeline business that was hijacked by economic revolutionaries desperate to break free of the old reins of traditional business. Their innovation was a

125

gibberish algorithm that allowed them to will themselves to vast riches simply by saying they had them. The idea that there should be any limits offended these people; they wanted to be gods, with limitless wealth, and not subject to the rules of the market but actually being the market themselves. Petrocelli himself reiterated this in his opening.

"[Skilling] didn't lead any conspiracy," he said, his voice rising with a Dr. Frankensteinian manic tinge. "What he led was a transformation in the energy industry!"

It was the same infantile dream of omniscience, impunity, and unbounded indulgence that would eventually become the hallmark of the George Bush era. Exercising power isn't enough; the important thing is to exercise power without having to ask for permission or compromise, à la DeLay in Congress or Bush in Iraq. And like all such revolutionaries, Skilling and Lay would go to the firing squad professing True Belief; it was clear that the righteous cause was their whole defense.

"This is not a case of 'hear no evil, see no evil,'" said Petrocelli. "This is a case of there was no evil at all!"

Before the trial, there was much discussion of how the two defense teams—in whom the defendants are said to have invested some $38 million to date—would interact. Rumors spread that there was friction between the Skilling team, led by the fat-faced, heavily moussed Californian Petrocelli, and the Lay team, led by the legendary Texas criminal lawyer Mike Ramsey, a likable character with a homespun-hayseed demeanor. The two teams had clashed over how much to blame Enron's collapse on already convicted ex-CFO Andy Fastow, and how much ignorance the defendants should plead about the affairs of the corporation they ruled.

As it turned out, the two basically divvied up the work right down the middle, each articulating half of the defendants' psychotic formula for self-apology. Petrocelli spent most of his time arguing that Lay and Skilling were too rich to break the law and that Enron, far from being a criminal enterprise and a cheap Ponzi scheme in a $10,000 suit, was a brilliant and innovative company that was a gift to the world until it wasn't.

Ramsey, meanwhile, handled the negatives, explaining Enron's collapse as a freak accident brought on by a stock-market phenomenon identical in its unforeseeability to a whole city full of people flushing their toilets at the same time. He then provided an unseemly window into the conscience of the rich by making shameless repeated mention of the large amount of money Lay gave to charity ("$25 million, ladies and gentlemen, $25 million!"), as if this somehow justified his and Skilling's gluttonous pursuit, using all manner of lies and bluster, of every last dollar on Wall Street.

But it was in a seemingly offhand comment in the middle of Ramsey's oddly lyrical address that the defense made its bravest admission. While Petrocelli's speech was nothing but a bald and unrepentant "We didn't fucking do it," Ramsey's speech from the beginning promised to answer the jury's inevitable questions and suspicions that something, indeed, was rotten at Enron. The lawyer seemed to understand that the public craved some evidence of introspection and self-examination on the part of the Enron heads, and he gave it in a quiet line at the start of his address.

"Failure," he said, "is not a crime."

He paused. It was a big deal, psychologically, for high-rolling lifetime winners like Lay and Skilling to admit to being failures. But that was all they were willing to admit, and they certainly wouldn't admit to doing anything wrong. Moreover, Ramsey sabotaged his own line about failure with a "joke" that was clearly designed to show he didn't really mean what he'd just said.

"Failure is not a crime," he repeated. "If it was, we'd have to turn all of Oklahoma back into a penal colony—heh, heh."

The courtroom didn't laugh with him, not a peep from anywhere in the room. This is how Ken Lay asks for forgiveness—by calling all of Oklahoma a bunch of losers?

Just a few hours after counsel finished their statements, President Bush strapped it on for the State of the Union address. Five years ago, Enron emerged out of the ashes of a worldwide market meltdown, an economic storm that shook out the ugly truth. Now Bush is himself holding on for dear life in the middle of a comparable political catastrophe: disaster abroad, indictments pending, whole sections of his administration burning with investigatory fires. The latest nightmare involves an NSA eavesdropping program in which the president's defense is going to be the limitless authority of the chief executive in times of war. In his speech, a clearly pissed-off Bush addressed the issue.

"Previous presidents have used the same constitutional authority I have and federal courts have approved the use of that authority," he said. "Appropriate members of Congress have been kept informed . . ."

The dream of unlimited power dies hard—if it dies at all—in an America with nothing else to live for.

How to Be a Lobbyist Without Trying

A personal journey into Washington's culture of greed

———

April 6, 2006

In January, I was in Washington, D.C., interviewing an activist from a political watchdog group about Abramoff-related stuff.

"I'll tell you who's got a lot of balls," he said to me. "Senator Conrad Burns. He talked about his lobby-reform plan today, but check it out, he's throwing a thousand-buck-a-plate birthday party for himself tomorrow night. I'm surprised he didn't show up on the Hill today in a fucking Hamburglar costume."

The activist handed me a printout with the details: "Please join us for Senator Burns's Birthday!!!" It was $1,000 a ticket for organizations, $500 for individuals. RSVP Amy Miller, the Bellwether Group.

It sure would be interesting to go to that party, I thought.

"So go to the party!" said my Friend in Politics. "Just say you're a lobbyist and go. Who's stopping you?"

We hashed out a plan. All I needed to do, he said, was print out a few business cards, and maybe—for just-in-case verisimilitude—type out a jazzy-looking fact sheet with a plan for some bogus project my "clients" would be pushing. "But make it as ridiculous as possible," my Friend insisted. "The magic words are: 'My clients will be seeking some regulatory relief' and 'Our project has an energy-independent profile.' Trust me, a guy like Conrad Burns will pop a boner in ten seconds flat."

Jack Abramoff would later tell reporters that he and his team got "every appropriation we wanted" from the staff of Senator Conrad Burns, who sat on a number of important committees, including Indian Affairs and Energy and Natural Resources. Overall, Abramoff gave more to Burns than to any other politician. Though Abramoff would later claim that he himself was the "softest touch in town," in reality he probably meant he was the second-softest, after the wrinkly senator from Montana. Burns, a mean-spirited dipshit, is one of dozens of craven morons whose presence has only recently been detected, with the aid of the Abramoff scandal. Among other things, reporters combing through his record found that he once answered "[It's] a hell of a challenge" to a Montanan supporter who asked how he could live in Washington with "all those niggers."

My fact sheet was headlined crude oil in grand canyon national park. It had a nice picture of the Grand Canyon on it. I was going to be Matthew Taibbi, Government Relations adviser for Dosko, a fictional Russian firm representing various energy interests, including a fictional oil company called PerDuNefteGaz that wanted to drill for oil in the Grand Canyon. My friend ratified the plan as the perfect lobbyist's pitch: shady foreign company seeking to violate, with a long metal phallus, America's most sacred natural landmark. I'd be welcomed with open arms, he said.

I called the Bellwether Group to reserve a spot at the party. A girl named Monica swallowed my introduction but added a warning.

"We're expecting some protesters tonight," she said. "I thought you should know." "Protesters?" I said. "Gosh, what for?"

"It's a long story," she said. "We're expecting . . . two people in Jack Abramoff costumes."

"Oh, that's ridiculous," I said. "People have to grow up."

"I know, it's silly," she said. "Well, see you tonight."

By the time I showed up at the small reception hall, the angry mob that had been there at the reception had dwindled to a few sorry individuals shivering in the cold weather. I slithered past them unnoticed.

The schmoozefest was on. There were about fifty people present, all in suits and all with name tags representing everyone from the NRA to Motorola to the White House; they all started furiously shaking one another's hands and gaping at one another's name tags, like dogs sniffing each other in a Central Park run. I accosted a young girl named Kristin, who was wearing a Burns name tag, and explained who I was and what I wanted, stammering out the phrase "seeking regulatory relief" and mentioning oil in the Grand Canyon.

"You need to talk to Chris Heggem," she said.

She led me across the room and passed me off to an early-fortyish woman with dirty-blond hair who was busily engaged with three other suits. "This is the person to talk to," Kristin whispered. "She handles all of the energy and commerce and . . . the energy and commerce and, uh . . . environment."

When Heggem was finally free, I introduced myself. "I work for Dosko-Konsult," I said. "We're a Russian company. We represent a number of Russian energy companies. Specifically I work with a company called PerDuNefteGaz."

"What?" she said, leaning over.

"PerDuNefteGaz," I said. "It's a Russian oil company . . ."

"Oh, yeah," she said. "Yeah, of course."

I suppressed a laugh. My Friend in Politics had told me that everyone I met at the party would pretend to know the company I worked for. "PerDuNefteGaz" translates roughly as "FartOilGas."

I pressed on, stammering through a researched speech about my client's discovery of an "abiogenic theory of petroleum recovery" and some new surveys we'd been conducting. A sharp woman, Heggem was right there with me, even when I stopped making sense. "Basically you're using new technology, new recovery methods," she said.

"Exactly," I said. Then I laid it on her. "We're pursuing a number of projects," I said. "Including one that would involve some exploratory drilling in Grand Canyon National Park. Now, obviously this is complicated but . . . at some point in time I was hoping we could sit down and I could tell you a little more about our company and our energy-independent project."

"Okay," she said. She gave me her information and told me to call her anytime. We shook hands. For a few minutes more we stood there chatting. I asked what the protesters were there for, pleading ignorance—I'd just flown in from Moscow.

"It's all of that Abramoff stuff," she said.

"It's funny," I said. "In Russia, they can't understand . . ."

"They don't understand why this is even a big deal with Abramoff, right?" she cut in.

"Exactly," I said.

We parted; I moved through the crowd in the direction of Burns. Up close, the senator looks like little more than a big exhausted lump—like a sack of potatoes with a mushy, half-caved-in pineapple on top.

"Senator!" I said, extending a hand. "Matt Taibbi, Dosko-Konsult. Happy birthday, sir . . ."

"Yeah," he snorted, half-assedly shaking my hand and quickly ditching me in favor of a crowd of telecom suits.

Jilted, I stood there guzzling a beer for a moment. A friendly lobbyist/advertising guy came up and struck up a conversation. We talked about Abramoff.

"I don't know if everything he did was illegal, exactly," he said. "But it was just too excessive, in bad taste."

"My clients want to drill for oil in the Grand Canyon," I blurted out.

"Well, as long as you've got the environmental-impact research, that won't be too bad," he said.

"Our research shows that less than eleven percent of marine life will be affected," I said, misquoting my own fact sheet.

"Yeah, well . . ." he said.

A few minutes later I was talking to a lobbyist and her schoolteacher husband, who were hanging around the periphery of the party. I spilled a very long spiel about our Grand Canyon project, railing against government regulation. The husband joined me in being angry about the obstacles.

"The thing is, you come up with something like that, the first thing they'll say is [*here he changed his voice to a high-pitched whine*], 'Oh, the animals, the animals!' Fucking New York liberals."

"Yeah," I said. "It's like the spotted owl and all that shit."

"Totally," he said.

Later on, I met my Friend in Politics, who said, "Well, at least you learned something: it costs five hundred dollars for a meeting." He paused. "And you're an utter tool, too."

"I guess it would be a lot easier for a professional like Abramoff," I said.

"Yeah," my friend said. "And he had a lot more than five hundred bucks. A lot more."

Meet Mr. Republican
The secret history of the most corrupt man in Washington

April 6, 2006

So this is it, finally. By the time this magazine hits the news-stands, Jack Abramoff—right-wing megalobbyist and great feck-less shitwad of our new American century—will be but a tick of the geological clock away from The End. There will be no rack, no stoning, no scorpion-filled sand pit, no bucket of fire ants. Just a sanitary plea agreement and a single blow of the gavel, and "Casino Jack" Abramoff will disappear for a few years of weight lifting and Talmudic study.

En route to his day of reckoning, Abramoff really did travel each and every right-wing highway, from Jo-burg in the old days to the Bush White House. But he's being sentenced for only the last few miles of that trip. It's almost an insult to a criminal of Abramoff's caliber that the charge he'll go to jail for is a low-rent wire-fraud scheme committed in a pickpocket capital like Miami Beach. In that one, Jack and his cronies claimed to have $23 million in assets when he didn't have a dime, and he persuaded financial backers to purchase a $147.5 million cruise-ship casino empire. A nice score for a Gotti child, maybe, but a bit gauche for the wizard of the Republi-can fast lane.

The other charges are a little more respectable. He took tens of millions from Indian tribes that sought relief from Wash-ington on gaming-industry questions, illegally pocketed mil-lions in lobbying fees, and evaded taxes on his ill-gotten gains. He also used their money to provide, in exchange for favors, a "stream of things of value" to elected officials, including golf junkets to Scotland, free meals, and other swag.

It's that last bit that made Abramoff a national celebrity, the poster boy for the way the Bush administration does business and the most feared name around in a Washington political society that is still waiting with bated lizard breath for the other shoe to drop. To most Americans, Jack Abramoff is the bloodsucking bogeyman with a wad of bills in his teeth who came through the window in the middle of the night and stole their voice in government. But he was much more than that. Abramoff was as much a symbol of his generation's Republican Party as Ronald Reagan or Barry Goldwater were of theirs.

He was an amazingly ubiquitous figure, a sort of Zelig of the political right—you could find him somewhere, in the foreground or the background, in almost every Republican political scandal of the past twenty-five years. He carried water for the racist government of Pretoria during the apartheid days and whispered in the ear of those Republican congressmen who infamously voted against antiapartheid resolutions. He organized rallies in support of the Grenada invasion, showed up in Ollie North's offices during Iran-Contra, palled around with Mobutu Sese Seko, Jonas Savimbi, and the Afghan mujahedin.

All along, Abramoff was buying journalists, creating tax-exempt organizations to fund campaign activities, and using charities to fund foreign conflicts. He spent the past twenty years doing business with everyone from James Dobson to the Gambino family, from Ralph Reed to Grover Norquist to Karl Rove to White House procurements chief David Safavian. He is even lurking in the background of the 2004 Ohio voting-irregularities scandal, having worked with the Diebold voting-machine company to defeat requirements for a paper trail in elections.

He is a living museum of corruption, and in a way it is altogether too bad that he is about to disappear from public scrutiny. In a hilariously tardy attempt to attend to his moral self-image, he lately has been repackaging himself as a fallen prophet, a humbled super-Jew who was guilty only of going too far to serve God. He was the "softest touch in town," he has said, a sucker for causes who "incorrectly didn't follow the mitzvah of giving away at most twenty percent." Then he shows up a few weeks before sentencing with his cock wedged in the mouth of an adoring *Vanity Fair* reporter, claiming with a straight face that his problems came from trying to "save the world."

There is no evidence yet that anyone is going to call him on any of this bullshit, and we can see where all of this is going. He'll go away now for his Martha Stewart fitness tour, and a few years from now he'll slide straight into his own prime-time family show for cable's inevitable Orthodox Channel and a $14 million deal from HarperCollins for his 290-page illustrated manual of marriage and intimacy for devout Jewish couples.

No other outcome is really possible, given the logic of the American celebrity world. What is unknown, as yet, is whether America will learn any lessons from the here-and-now of the Jack Abramoff story. For that to happen, we would all have to take a good, hard look at the remarkable life story he is now temporarily leaving us to consider.

Abramoff is a man defined by his connections. As an individual—as a lone dot on a schematic diagram, an intersection of crossed strands in a web—Jack Abramoff is a nobody, just another pompous Washington greedhead distinguished only by the world's silliest Boris Badenov fedora. ("That was between me and God," Abramoff now says of the infamous hat.) But let him loose in society and magic happens. Jack Abramoff's instinctive political talent was for first locating and then inveigling himself into the disreputable backroom deal of the hour. He was a walking cut corner, a thumb on the scale of American history.

The story about Jack Abramoff and the elementary school election, the one first reported by the *Los Angeles Times,* is true. It only seems like apocryphal bullshit. Born in Atlantic City to Frank Abramoff, an affluent Diner's Club executive who would go on to represent golfer Arnold Palmer, Jack moved with his family to Beverly Hills as a boy and grew up attending one of the more prestigious elementary schools in the country, the Hawthorne School. And it was here, at this same fancy-pants school that would one day be home to a chubby girl named Monica Lewinsky, that Jack got his start in politics by being disqualified from a race for student-body president for cheating.

"Jack was a very, very, very smart boy with a straight-A average," recalls Milton Rowen, the then-principal of the school. "We had certain rules about the amount of money that could be spent, and there was no electioneering outside of the school . . . He had his mother come up with hot dogs in her car and give them out to the kids.

"He was a very nice boy," the eighty-seven-year-old now says, laughing. "But he hot-dogged it."

Still, even with that setback, Abramoff was already off and running on a course that would lead him straight to the political underworld. Like Watergate vets Donald Segretti, Dwight Chapin, Gordon Strachan, and Ron Ziegler before him, Abramoff throughout his youth would be drawn to student politics, running (and losing) again for student-body president at Beverly Hills High before becoming head of the Massachusetts College Republicans while at Brandeis University in the Boston suburb of Waltham.

Abramoff was part of the first wave of young people who came back to the Republican Party en masse during the so-called Reagan Revolution. The year 1980 was a time of resurgence for a party that just four years before had been in a post-Watergate death spiral; the Moral Majority had just been founded, and new-right prophets such as Howard Phillips, Paul Weyrich, and Richard Viguerie were attracting a fresh generation of young people to the brash, piss-in-your-face, fuck-the-poor ideas emanating from places like the Heritage Foundation and Bill Buckley's Young Americans for Freedom. Among their other converts at this time were Grover Norquist and Ralph Reed, a pair of ambitious students from Harvard and Emory University, respectively.

After Reagan's 1980 landslide win, those two, along with Abramoff, would work together at the College Republicans National Committee, and when Abramoff succeeded Norquist as CRNC chief he would win a national reputation as a hardliner with his Lenin-esque pronouncement that it wasn't the job of young Republicans to "seek peaceful coexistence with the left." The take-no-prisoners stance of the twentysomething student leader: "Our job is to remove them from power permanently."

All accounts point to Abramoff as the prototypically humorless *Animal House* campus villain. A thick-necked champion weight lifter (he still holds the Beverly Hills High bench-press record) with a square jaw and exquisite hygiene, the man-child Abramoff also had the kind of sadistic jock temperament that impresses coaches and corporate recruiters alike. "The football coach was always afraid that Jack was going to kill somebody if he hit him head-on," Rowen says. By the time he went away to Brandeis, he'd already undergone a conversion to Orthodox Judaism, having found religion at the Sinai Temple in Los Angeles (after seeing *Fiddler on the Roof* as a youngster, Abramoff says), and so he arrived in 1970s Massachusetts the rarest of East Coast campus creatures: a moralizing weight lifter with short hair and a passion for Republican politics.

The Abramoff story, in fact, confirms in the most dramatic way every vicious popular stereotype about campus conservatives. Kids who get involved with lefty politics on campus almost always graduate straight into some degrading state of semi-employment—the defining characteristic of lefty student movements is how few doors they open for you. Another defining characteristic of the student left is its persistent, unquenchable, and irrational suspicion that the campus Republicans hold their meetings in the offices of someplace like the Rand Corporation, where they have their buttocks branded with Sumerian symbols in secret ceremonies that upon graduation will gain all of them entrance to the upper ranks of corporate and governmental privilege.

That was Jack Abramoff. Like those famed USC student "ratfuckers" who went on to hold the ultimate panty raid in the Watergate Hotel, Abramoff and his close friends Norquist and Ralph Reed (the onetime head of the Georgia College Republicans used to sleep on Abramoff's couch) never really abandoned the laughable training-wheel secrecy and capture-the-flag gamesmanship of student politics. His buttocks freshly branded, Abramoff in 1983 traveled to Johannesburg on behalf of the CRNC and immediately parlayed his student experience into a real job as a sort of frontman for South African intelligence services. He was the young progressive's paranoid nightmare come shockingly true: absurd campus Republican proto-geek effortlessly transformed at graduation into flesh-and-blood neo-Nazi spook.

139

It is not easy to find anyone who actually encountered Abramoff during his South Africa experiences, although one source who was involved with South African right-wing student politics recalled "Casino Jack" as a "blue-eyed boy" who rubbed people the wrong way with his arrogant demeanor. On his first trip to Johannesburg in 1983, Abramoff met with leaders from the archconservative, pro-apartheid National Students Federation, which itself is alleged to have been created by South Africa's notorious Bureau of Security Services. Together with NSF member Russel Crystal—today a prominent South African politician in the Democratic Alliance, an anti–African National Congress party—Abramoff subsequently, in 1986, chaired the head of a conservative think tank called the International Freedom Foundation.

The creation of the IFF officially marked the beginning of the silly phase of Abramoff's career. According to testimony before Democratic South Africa's Truth and Reconciliation Commission in 1995, the IFF was not a conservative think tank but actually a front for the South African army. Testimony in sealed TRC hearings reportedly reveals that the IFF was known by the nickname "Pacman" in the South African army and that its activities were part of a larger plan called "Operation Babushka," designed to use propaganda to discredit the ANC and Nelson Mandela at home and abroad. Among other things, Abramoff managed during this time to funnel funds and support from the IFF to a variety of stalwart congressmen and senators, including Representative Dan Burton and Senator Jesse Helms, all of whom consistently opposed congressional resolutions against apartheid. These members of Congress would deny knowing that the IFF's money came from the South African government, because that, of course, would have been illegal; Abramoff himself denied it too, although he has been largely quiet on the subject since the TRC testimony in 1995.

In a hilarious convergence of ordinary workaday incompetence and pointlessly secretive cloak-and-dagger horseshit, Operation Babushka's grand opus would ultimately turn out to be the production of the 1989 Dolph Lundgren vehicle *Red Scorpion,* in which American moviegoers were invited to care about an anticommunist revolutionary targeted for execution by a sweat-drenched jungle version of Lundgren's overacting Ivan Drago persona. The film, which Abramoff wrote and produced, was instantly derided by critics around the world as one of the stupidest movies ever made.

Veteran character actor Carmen Argenziano, who played the heavy, Colonel Zayas, in *Red Scorpion,* recalls the "Cimino-esque" film shoot in Namibia as one of the most surreal experiences of his career. "It was pretty weird," he says. "What was going on was fishy, and then in the middle of production the word spread that there was some kind of weird South African/ CIA connection. And that bummed everyone out."

Argenziano, whom history will likely absolve for being, with Lundgren, one half of the film's only memorable scene, which also perhaps represents the apex of Jack Abramoff's literary career (Argenziano: "Are you out of your mind?" Lundgren: "No. Just out of bullets"), laughs almost nonstop as he recalls his Namibia experiences.

"We were all staying in this hotel called the Kalahari Sands in Windhoek, the capital," he says. "There was this huge new escalator in the hotel. I guess it was the only one in the country, because little African kids kept coming in to stare at it. But the South Africans we had on the shoot [Abramoff was reportedly provided free labor by the South African army] kept shooing them away, literally pushing kids off the escalator, shouting these racist words at them. Wasn't exactly good for morale."

The eighties show Abramoff involved in a series of almost comic backroom escapades, the most famous being the organization of a sort of trade convention for anticommunist rebel leaders in Jamba, Angola. There are not many facts on the record about this incident, but what is known smacks of an articulate young Darth Vader putting out scones and lemonade at a sand-planet meeting of the leading bounty-hunter scum in the universe. Under the auspices of the Citizens for America, a group founded by Rite Aid drugstore magnate and onetime New York gubernatorial candidate Lewis Lehrman at the request of Ronald Reagan, Abramoff helped organize a meeting of anticommunist rebels that included Angolan UNITA fighters, Afghan mujahedin, Laotian guerrillas, and Nicaraguan Contras.

Some reports speculate that the meeting was convened so that one of the Americans—perhaps Abramoff or Lehrman—could pass along a message of support from the White House. But it's more likely that this will be just another Abramoff episode to remain shrouded in mystery. Twenty-one years later, Lehrman won't say what it was all about, noting that "I do not recall if there was a White House message discussion" and adding only that "there were very many anticommunist individuals present in Jamba."

Abramoff's CFA experience was extensive enough, however, to make him a character in the Iran-Contra scandal. His ostensible role was to raise support for the Contras through the CFA. "Abramoff was a bit player in Iran-Contra," says Jack Blum, a Washington lawyer who served as a special counsel to the Senate Foreign Relations Committee during the Iran-

Contra investigation. "That's where he learned that the money wasn't in the ideological skulduggery world. It was in the go-buy-the-government world." But, Blum adds, Abramoff's experiences with various conservative foundations and nonprofits during this period proved valuable later on. "This is when he made all his connections," he says. "It was through them that he learned that it was much more lucrative to work in the commercial end of politics."

Abramoff, Norquist, and Reed were all in their mid- to late twenties, and all were experiencing paradigmatic life changes. While Abramoff was joining such groups as the Council for National Policy, the CFA, and the United States of America Foundation, Norquist was founding Americans for Tax Reform, the organization he would later ride to prominence as a fat, hygienically deficient tax-policy oracle. Reed, meanwhile, was recovering from the trauma of an April 1983 incident in which he was reportedly caught plagiarizing for his student newspaper a *Commentary* article denouncing Mohandas Gandhi. A few months after that setback, however, Reed found Jesus in a phone booth outside the Bullfeathers pub in Washington—and by 1985 he, too, had found his calling, terrorizing abortion clinics with the Students for America, a sort of pale precursor to the Christian Coalition.

There is a common thread running through almost all of Abramoff's activities during this tadpole period of his in the eighties. Suggested in his every action is an utter contempt for legal governmental processes; he behaves as if ordinary regulations are for suckers and the uncommitted. If the government won't step up to the plate and sign off on support for the Contras, you go through channels and do it yourself. If you really want to win an election, you find ways around finance laws and spending limits. And if you want to oppose a national antiapartheid movement on the country's campuses, don't waste time building from the ground up; go straight to Pretoria and bring home a few million dollars in a bag.

One of the ugliest developments in American culture since Abramoff's obscure Cold Warrior days in the eighties has been the raging but highly temporary success of various "smart guys" who upon closer examination aren't all that smart. There was BALCO steroid scum Victor Conte ("The smartest son of a bitch I ever met in my life," said one Olympian client), Enron's "smartest guys in the room" Jeff Skilling and Ken Lay, and, finally, "ingenious dealmaker" Jack Abramoff. Somewhere along the line, in the years since the Cold War, Americans as a whole became such craven, bum-licking, self-absorbed fat cats that they were willing to listen to these fifth-rate prophets who pretended that the idea that rules could be broken was some kind of earth-shattering revelation—as though they had fucking invented fraud and cheating. To a man, however, they all turned out to be dumb, incompetent fuckups, destined to bring us all down with them—not even good at being criminals.

All of Abramoff's late-career capers—the inner-city youth charity that actually bought sniper scopes for Israeli settlers, the academic think tank that turned out to be a lifeguard in a shack on Rehoboth Beach, the "check's in the mail" fleecing of his own tailor out of a bill for suits—they all exude the same infuriating "Check out the brains on us!" vibe.

Take the infamous Naftasib scheme of 1997–98. The short version of this story is that Abramoff and Tom DeLay met with a bunch of shady Russian oil executives in 1997; the Russians then sent $1 million to a British law firm called James and Sarch; James and Sarch then sent a million to the pompously named nonprofit "U.S. Family Network," which in turn sent money to numerous destinations. It went to a lobbyist agency called the Alexander Strategy Group that was run by DeLay's ex–chief of staff Edwin Buckham; the agency would subsequently hire DeLay's wife at a salary of $3,200 a month. It went toward the purchase of a luxury D.C. town house that DeLay would use to raise money. And it went toward the purchase of a luxury box at FedExField, which Abramoff used to watch the Redskins. If you follow the loop all the way around, the quid pro quo probably involved DeLay's 1998 decision to support an IMF loan to Russia, whose economy collapsed that year and would rely on an IMF bailout to survive. A Maryland pastor named Christopher Geeslin, who briefly served as the U.S. Family Network's president, would later say that Buckham told him that the $1 million from the Russians was intended to influence DeLay's decision regarding funding for the IMF. DeLay ended up voting to replenish IMF funds in September of that year, right at the time of the bailout.

Is this smart? Sure, if you're fucking ten years old. If your idea of smart is turning an IMF loan into Redskins tickets, then, yeah, this is smart. But another way to look at it is that these assholes got themselves Redskins tickets by giving $18 billion to one of the most corrupt governments on earth. I'd call that buying at a premium.

That's the most striking characteristic of Abramoff and his crew of ex–student leaders; nearly thirty years out of college, no longer young at all, the whole bunch of them are still Dean Wormer's sneaky little shits, high-fiving one another for executing the brilliant theft and predawn public hanging of the rival college's stuffed-bear mascot. That whole adolescent vibe permeates the confiscated Abramoff e-mails, the best example of which being this exchange between Jack and his "evil elf" aide Michael Scanlon regarding their lobbying fees for the Coushatta Indian tribe:

Scanlon: Coushatta is an absolute cake walk. Your cut on the project as proposed is at least 800k.

Abramoff: How can I say this strongly enough: YOU IZ DA MAN.

Again, these assholes affirm every stereotype about campus conservatives. They don't spend enough time being kids when they're supposed to, so they do it when they're balding, middle-aged men with handles and back hair—using Washington and Congress as their own personal sandbox.

They figured out how to beat everything. Everything about the Abramoff story suggests that, at some point, he and his buddies Norquist, Reed, and DeLay took a long, hard look at the American system, war-gamed it, and came up with a master plan to strike hard at its weakest points. In the end, almost all of the Abramoff scams revolved around the vulnerability of the national legislature to outside manipulation. Once Abramoff and his cabal figured out how to beat Congress, everything else fell into place.

Case in point: Abramoff's remarkable success in defeating H.R. 521, a 2001 House bill that would place the Guam Superior Court under the control of a federally controlled Supreme Court. Led by Judge Alberto Lamorena, Guam Superior Court justices hired the lobbyist to defeat the bill, which would have unseated them as the chief judicial authorities of the island. It says something for Abramoff's ability to bring out the worst in people that he managed to get a group of sitting judges to pay him $324,000 in public funds in $9,000 installments so as to avoid detection.

Despite the $324,000 fee, Abramoff could not prevent the House Resources committee from unanimously recommending

H.R. 521 for passage. Would the superlobbyist finally fail? No, of course not. Given what we know about Abramoff's tactics, we'd be naive not to conclude that he could lean on DeLay and then-Whip Roy Blunt to stall the bill in the congressional machinery. On May 27, 2002, just five days after the Resources Committee made its recommendation, an Abramoff-linked PAC wrote two checks for $5,000—one to Blunt, one to DeLay. H.R. 521 never reached the floor.

The Guam incident certainly shows how easily the whole Congress was controlled by a small gang. The DeLay Republicans, along with Abramoff, were apparently the first to recognize the opportunities for corruption presented by the House leadership's dictatorial control over key committees, in particular the Rules Committee. Now, a single call to a lone Tom DeLay could decide the fate of any piece of legislation, pushing it through to a vote or gumming it up in the works as needed. The other 430-odd congressmen were window dressing.

I asked Representative Louise Slaughter if the Guam case, which showed that just two men could quash a bill, proved that Congress was especially vulnerable to manipulation by the likes of Abramoff.

"Absolutely," she said. "And the thing is, we have no idea how many incidents like that there were. What else didn't get to the floor? We have no idea. No way of knowing."

Even more ominously, Abramoff would eventually come under fire in Guam following the mysterious removal of Guam Attorney General Frederick Black, who had seen the fate of H.R. 521 and decided to investigate Abramoff's role in it.

"The thing that really worries me about Guam is the prosecutor who was plucked off the case," says Slaughter, a New York Democrat who has spearheaded her party's lobby-reform drive. "It makes you wonder what really went on there."

At the very least, Abramoff's relationship with White House procurements officer David Safavian shows that he made at least some inroads into the world of White House patronage. Abramoff took Safavian on one of his famous Scotland golfing junkets and reportedly was receiving help from Safavian in leasing government property. Safavian was working on the distribution of millions in federal aid to Katrina-affected regions when he was arrested, which raises all kinds of questions about what else might have been going on.

"There were so many contracts, from Katrina to Iraq—God knows what really went on in there," says Slaughter.

Once Congress was conquered, Abramoff, Norquist et al. apparently discovered a means for turning it into a pure engine for profit. The game they may have discovered worked like this: One lobbyist (Abramoff, say) represents one group of interests—for example, the Malaysian government. Then, a lobbyist friend of Abramoff's (say, Norquist) represents an antagonist to Abramoff's client, in this case, let's say dissident leader Anwar Ibrahim. Ibrahim asks Norquist to press his case against the Malaysian state in Washington; Norquist complies and uses his contacts to raise a stink on the Hill. Abramoff's client, unnerved, turns to Abramoff to make the problem go away. Abramoff dutifully goes to the same friends Norquist applied to in the first place, and the problem does indeed go away. In the end, everyone is happy and both lobbyists have performed and gotten paid. Abramoff apparently pulled this kind of double-dealing scheme more than once, as he and Ralph Reed appear to have run a similar con on the Coushatta and Tigua Indian tribes, who were on opposite sides of a gaming dispute.

An idiot might call a scheme like this clever. But that's only true if you don't consider what really happened here. Dozens of people conspiring to reduce the U.S. Congress to the level of a Belarussian rubber stamp for the sake of . . . what? A few million dollars in lobbying fees? And not even a few million dollars apiece but a few million dollars split several ways. Shit, even *Paris Hilton* can make a million dollars in this country without blowing up two hundred years of democracy. How smart can these guys be?

Everyone sold themselves on the cheap. They apparently got Representative Bob Ney (R-Ohio), and many others in the House, to lie back and open their legs all the way for a few thousand dollars in campaign contributions. In the Third World, corrupt politicians at least get something for selling out the people—boats, mansions, villas in the south of France. If you offered the lowest, most drunken ex-mobster in the Russian Duma $5,000, $10,000, $15,000 in soft money for his vote, he would laugh in your face; he might even be insulted enough to shoot you. But Jack Abramoff apparently got any number of congressmen to play ball for the same kind of money.

They paid journalists to change their opinions; as it turns out, the right to free speech is worth about $2,000 a column to America's journalists like Doug Bandow of Copley News Service. And now it comes out that Diebold, the notorious voting-machine company, paid some $275,000 to Abramoff's firm, Greenberg Traurig, with the apparent aim of keeping legislation requiring paper trails in the voting process from getting into the Help America Vote Act. Conveniently, Abramoff pal Bob Ney, one of the HAVA architects, blocked every attempt to put paper trails into law, even after the controversial electoral debacles of 2000 and 2004.

They targeted Congress, the courts, the integrity of elections, and the free press, and in every corner they found willing partners who could be had for a few bucks and a package of golf tees. That doesn't mean Jack Abramoff was so very smart. No, what that says is that America is no longer trying very hard. And when Jack Abramoff hears his sentence, ours will certainly be made plain soon after. Jack Abramoff was the Patient Zero of Washington corruption. He's the girl at school that everyone got a piece of, including two janitors in their forties. It strains all credulity to think that he's been talking to the Department of Justice for months and yet prosecutors still have to "encircle" a lone congressman, Bob Ney, as has been reported. If Ney is the big target the government made a deal with Abramoff for, we'll know we've been had again.

"If you're venal and cunning enough, like him, you can do it," says Slaughter, when asked if the American system has become easy to beat. "But he had a lot of help."

How to Steal a Coastline

The Gulf is still in ruins—but Bush has opened the door
for the casinos and carpetbaggers, and now there's
a cutthroat race to the high ground

April 20, 2006

New Orleans, Ninth Ward, near the infamous levee, the last
Tuesday in March. I'm in the passenger seat of a spiffy black
Volkswagen, staring out my window in shock. Only one word
comes to mind: Hiroshima. Houses all sideways and blown
to bits, cars flipped over, ground covered with glass and wire
and dismembered dolls' heads. No water, no electricity, no
civilization.

Katrina might as well have hit yesterday. Almost nobody has
come back. Goateed white college volunteers living in tents
seem to outnumber actual residents ten-to-one. On any given
street, anything moving is probably either a rat or a CUNY
sophomore. The death smell still hangs everywhere.

The VW stops and I'm staring at a nearby car crushed under
a house. Next to it is a half-crumpled shack with a message
written in spray paint: "Possible child body inside."

"Holy shit," I whisper.

"You ain't seen nothing yet, dude," says the man beside me.

I last saw the Reverend Willie Walker when we went out in
rescue boats together just after the storm. The affable black
pastor's cell phone and BlackBerry are constantly buzzing; he's
always making new contacts, trying to get something organized.
The good reverend is a hustler for God. I like Willie a lot. He's
sincere without being a bore. And another thing. When he's

my tour guide, I always seem to end up interviewing a lot of pretty girls.

Back in September, Willie had told me while standing in his ruined church, the fatefully named Noah's Ark Baptist, that he feared what lay ahead.

"They're going to take it all," he had said. "They're going to bring in the developers, and this neighborhood is going to be gone."

Willie foresaw that some combination of post-disaster zoning, forced property condemnations, infrastructural inattention, and carpetbagging real estate vultures would turn Katrina into one giant gentrification project. "They're hoping that you take the money and move," he had told people on the street.

Now Willie is leading me on a tour of the ruined city. Willie is usually a chatty guy, but now, here in the Ninth Ward, neither of us is talking. New Orleans is not a conversation. It's an image. You have to see it in person to comprehend it. It's a Grand Canyon of continuing misery and failure.

"Jesus," I say, staring at the wreckage. "What the hell have they been doing all this time?"

Willie laughs morbidly. "Nothing, dude," he says. "Absolutely nothing."

The wreckage on the ground is, pointedly, the only thing about New Orleans that hasn't changed since the storm. Without actually fixing much, everyone seems to have done a lot of moving on. On a national level, the city's official return to normalcy has been preposterously celebrated with the triumphant return of the NBA's Hornets. Even Mike Brown, the disgraced ex-FEMA chief, is enjoying an improbable Leslie Nielsen–esque career recycling, recently making a revoltingly self-flagellating appearance on *The Colbert Report*. Only in America can you destroy a major city and within six months be using your own incompetence to launch a second career in self-parody.

Here in New Orleans, Mayor Ray Nagin has been playing Hamlet, only without the intellect and eloquence. His first plan was to recommend turning some of these ruined black neighborhoods into parks, but then he quickly changed his mind when residents responded with impassioned calls for his oblong head. In the current vacuum of leadership, no one really knows what the plan is. Sitting in the Ninth Ward, I find it hard to believe that there's any plan.

"All this is a test," says Willie, waving his hand in front of the wreckage of the Ninth Ward. "We're being tested. If we keep this up, in a few years there won't be any America left at all."

One part of that test comes in the next few weeks, when the federal disaster agency FEMA is expected to settle on its new flood-zone guidelines for fallen New Orleans. Behind this seemingly innocuous decision lurks a hornets' nest of vicious racial politics that could be the final undoing of Mayor Nagin's "chocolate city." It's a drama that's already played out—to catastrophic results—in other parts of the Gulf Coast.

While its wreckage lacks the Dresden-esque feel of the Ninth Ward, the ruined Gulf Coast city of Biloxi, Mississippi, is creepy in its own way. The sand-blown streets of what was once a bustling tourist trap recall *Planet of the Apes,* or one of Hitler's watercolors—people all gone, somewhere. A wind-battered sign for a beachfront Waffle House blown out to sea hints that this was the capital of some mighty cracker empire gone suddenly and tragically extinct.

I came down here to investigate reports of immigrant recovery workers who'd been laid off, left unpaid, and mistreated by various scoundrelous villains of the industrial elite—Halliburton and such ilk. In light of other news reports to surface about the Katrina recovery effort—including recent revelations by the General Accounting Office that millions upon millions of dollars handed out in no-bid federal contracts had vanished down a budgetary rabbit hole of dubious reconstruction projects and inflated "aid" efforts—I thought it would be prudent to see what this corruption looked like on the business end of it.

But when I got to East Biloxi, the storm-tossed ghetto that Mississippians are quick to call "our Ninth Ward," what I heard at first was a familiar rundown of paranoid-sounding complaints about preferential treatment supposedly given to white hurricane victims. I had meetings with black activists and storm victims in which agencies such as FEMA and the Red Cross were described as being involved in a sweeping conspiracy to turn the Katrina disaster area into a sort of secret Club Med resort for white people, complete with shuffleboard, back rubs, and fancy dinners. "Bags of chicken," says Ruby Campbell, an East Biloxi native. "They was giving out bags of chicken in the white neighborhoods."

"We learned that the Red Cross is basically a paramilitary organization," says Jaribu Hill, founder of the Mississippi Workers' Center, "subsidized by the government."

It struck me suddenly that being an effete, overeducated, basketball-playing New Yorker who read *Soul on Ice* six times in college did not require me to endorse any of this paranoid bullshit. The next hurricane, I knew, could touch ground in my bedroom and nobody from the government was going to give me anything, much less a bag of fucking chicken.

The problem with racial politics in the Katrina story is that a lot of the real ugliness is buried far under the surface of this same petty and mostly infuriating he said–she said historical argument about Who Got What in the first days after the storm.

When I was in New Orleans after Katrina, I saw white cops in clean, crisp uniforms lazing at the edges of the flood lines while civilians of both races went out in boats into the black neighborhoods to rescue people. I also had grown black men in the Houston Astrodome complain to me that their free amusement-park privileges (some evacuees were given passes to Six Flags in the first weeks after the storm) had been cut off.

In between those two poles there is an argument to have, and those who want to can have it. My own feeling is that accusations of chicken-hoarding are an insult to white invidiousness everywhere. Institutional racism has always aimed a lot higher than chicken. And the Katrina reconstruction effort has been one of the all-time masterpieces of bloodless institutional racism, a resounding tribute to America's unparalleled ability to fuck the poor under pressure.

Biloxi has been one of the earlier test cases of the post-Katrina racial dynamic. Before the hurricane, the city had been a booming casino and vacation territory, crammed along the coastline with glitzy gaming palaces, hotels, and restaurants, while remaining geographically segregated in the interior— mostly white on the west side, mostly black and Vietnamese on the east side. Home to the state's first legal casinos after the passage of the 1990 Mississippi Gaming Control Act, Biloxi had become something of a showcase city for a new Republican ethos of vice-funded political power in an era of vanishing manufacturing revenues, as symbolized by the rise of biped swine like Jack Abramoff. This was the new America: tourism, shopping, fast food, and poker, fueled by transient traffic. The old communities parked behind the casinos were the anachronism.

What's happening now is that legal processes have been instituted that are all but guaranteed to cause a rapid outflow of those poor blacks from the eastern interior, while at the same time a new wave of commercial developers will float in on a cloud of government largesse. The mechanism here is an uneven application of new safety guidelines for residential home owners, passed quietly alongside a colossal tax break for commercial investors. It's a high-stakes hand of real estate poker, and the casinos, the condo developers, and contractors such as Halliburton are the ones drawing extra cards.

The scam in East Biloxi centers around flood maps, and it mirrors what is likely to be a similar fiasco in New Orleans. New guidelines called Advisory Base Flood Elevations, or ABFEs, issued quietly and unilaterally by FEMA in late 2005, place the average suggested elevation above sea level for house construction in most of peninsular East Biloxi at eighteen feet. In order to qualify for any federal assistance in rebuilding your home, you must rebuild according to these guidelines.

Currently, most houses in the neighborhood are at about nine feet or less.

"Now you've got to build your house on stilts, so to speak," says city councilman Bill Stallworth, who represents the sunken, screwed portion of East Biloxi. Well over six feet tall, with a religious man's equanimity and a wry smile brought on by what appears to be extreme exhaustion, Stallworth holds his hand high above his head. "Here's where your floor has to be now."

Stallworth says the ABFE regulations add an average of $30,000 in new costs to those returnees who want to rebuild their homes—homes that are mostly worth no more than $110,000.

And that's not all. According to Stallworth, regulations for handicapped-access ramps require ten inches of run for every inch of rise. "So what that means," he says, "is that if you have to raise your house up twelve feet, you need a hundred-and-twenty-foot ramp. You're starting your ramp three houses down."

Stallworth says that when he approached a FEMA rep about the dilemma for the elderly (Biloxi has a high percentage of retirees), the FEMA official told him, in a line straight out of Marie Antoinette, "They can build an elevator."

Like the Ninth Ward and many other New Orleans neighborhoods, East Biloxi is located on much lower ground than the surrounding white neighborhoods. Therefore, while the ABFEs in places like North Biloxi might be listed at the same levels as the East Biloxi ABFEs, the reality is that they are meaningless to North Biloxi residents whose houses already sit at those levels but are quite consequential to those in East Biloxi. Think about it. Would you bother to rebuild a house if you had to walk up ten feet just to get to the ground floor?

"I asked the FEMA guy, 'Do you understand what you're telling me?'" says Stallworth. "People will get a picture in their mind: 'You can't live here.'"

Compounding the ABFE dilemma are the usual array of bureaucratic stupidities and leprechaun tricks designed to separate the poor individual from public money. For instance, the federal government did issue a $4 billion grant for reconstruction aid under the auspices of the Department of Housing and Urban Development, through which individuals are entitled to "up to" $150,000. But, according to Stallworth, the fine print indicates that applicants are eligible to receive only the difference between the value of their insurance policies and the value of their settlements. If you have no insurance you get nothing. If you received a $20,000 settlement on a $30,000 policy, you can't get any more than $10,000.

You can also get up to $26,500 for housing from FEMA, but in order to get the money you have to jump through a dizzying array of bureaucratic hoops. For one thing, you can't even apply for FEMA money until you get rejected for a loan from the Small Business Administration. Why a sixty-year-old personal home owner should have to apply to the SBA is not a question that anyone has a good answer for, but it's the rule. Even getting that rejection letter can take months (many in East Biloxi are still waiting), but it's almost worse for you if the SBA accepts your application—then the money is not a gift but a loan, a loan you probably didn't want in the first place.

"We have at least ten elderly clients who have actually been approved for SBA loans," says Teresa Manley, vice president of Urban Life Ministries, a relief organization that has been one of the most effective aid agencies in East Biloxi. "We don't think it's right that seventy-year-old people should be saddled with thirty-year commercial loans. But they had no choice."

Then, in another trick that smacks of the chicanery-filled good old days before the Voting Rights Act, nearly all applicants for FEMA aid get a slippery bit of misdirection in the mail early on in the process.

"What we've found out is that FEMA automatically sends you a turn-down letter," says Stallworth. "At the top, it says, 'You are not eligible.' Only at the bottom does it say that you can reapply. If you have no experience with these things, you just think you're not eligible."

Of course, the way around all of this is to skip government aid entirely and rebuild your home with your own private funding, in which case the old zoning guidelines still apply. (Local officials expect a hideous patchwork of high-built and low-built houses at the end of reconstruction.) Here is where the true face of American capitalism—protection for the seller, risk for the individual consumer—shows itself. According to Stallworth, 82 percent of East Biloxi residents did not have flood insurance. I must have met more than a dozen families who had been paying home owner's premiums for decades but got either nothing at all or a negligible settlement after the storm. The insurance companies didn't even show up on the field of play for this one. To the last, they classified most all Katrina damage as flood damage, even when the water only washed away houses already destroyed by wind and rain.

"You had people who were standing in their houses when the wind blew it down," says Marvin Koury, a real estate adviser in Gulfport, Mississippi, "and the insurance companies were trying to tell them it was flood."

Then there's the flip side. The Bush administration opened the door for big corporate developers by offering huge tax incentives. And they're jumping on it. According to residents, within a month of the storm much of East Biloxi was papered with little pink flyers that read: IF YOU OWN LAND IN EAST BILOXI AND WOULD LIKE TO SELL YOUR LAND TO A CASINO/DEVELOPER, CALL (228) 239-xxxx

Around the time that FEMA was issuing its ABFEs for East Biloxi, Congress was passing the Gulf Opportunity Zone Act of 2005, colloquially known as the GoZone Act. When President Bush signed the law on December 21, he made it sound like a relief program for the little guy. "It's a step forward to fulfill this country's commitment to help rebuild," he said. "It's going to help small businesses, is what it's going to do."

Well, not exactly. GoZone does an important thing. It provides a first-year bonus depreciation of 50 percent for commercial real estate investors within the designated areas, which include East Biloxi and most of the lower parts of Mississippi, Louisiana, and western Alabama. What this means, essentially, is that investors who bought into large projects after August 28, 2005, will pay a fraction of the usual taxes in the first year of the investment.

The GoZone law is just another hand job for the rich, of the sort that has become a staple of the Bush administration's post-Katrina strategy. If the strategy for keeping public money from reaching the poor is to force people to first stand upside down and sing "Come On Eileen" backward and blindfolded, the strategy for giving money to the rich is a little more subtle. First, you give them tax breaks for indulging in the same activity you told the poor was dangerous, then you issue aid packages that find their way down to needy recipients only long after the value has been torn from the package's spine by a string of rapacious subcontractors, each taking its cut, who of course never had to enter into a competitive bid for their trouble. Carrying charges, my boy, carrying charges!

"The labor starts off at twenty-seven, thirty bucks [a yard], and by the time it gets down to me, it's five or seven dollars," says Richard Rispoli, a gregarious Georgian contractor who came to East Biloxi to work after the storm. In Rispoli's case, the chain started at a local construction company and passed down through three subcontractors on the way to Rispoli, who ended up not being paid at all by the last subcontractor, who simply split with the money. (The common thief who steals the last exposed bits of the public-aid package is a recurring character in the Katrina story.) Living now in a trailer in East Biloxi while he awaits payment for his work ("If the trailer's a-rockin', don't come a knockin'!" says his girlfriend Diane),

Rispoli is now faced with the prospect of selling his equipment in order to raise money for the trip back to Georgia.

Rispoli was one of the lucky ones, relatively. Vicky Cintra of the Mississippi Immigrant Rights Alliance has been compiling cases of undocumented migrant workers in the area who have been hired for recovery work—and left unpaid—by subcontractors of KBR, a subsidiary of Halliburton. Some of them live in squalid trailer parks and tent cities on the outskirts of Gulfport. (KBR/Halliburton has denied using undocumented workers in their operations.)

"Latino workers are being invited to New Orleans and the South without the proper conditions to protect them," Cintra says.

Forget bags of chicken. This is the kind of thing that made white people famous around the world—charging the government sixty-five bucks an hour for labor, then hiring illegals to do the same work for free.

The Katrina story is just the same old story of all of earth's history, only in concentrated form. Big fish eating little fish. Little fish eating smaller fish. And the smallest fish being told they have to build plank houses on fucking stilts. And wait to be eaten.

The story here will probably end with East Biloxi slowly disappearing against a steady advance of condo developments and curio shops; sometime around 2010, the last black resident, a poor grandmother who bought her home for 60K in the fifties, will finally sell after her property-tax bill, reflecting a new assessment, shoots past her annual Social Security disbursement.

By then, Mississippi governor Haley Barbour will be running for president, and his Gulf Coast will be a showpiece microcosm of an ideal America—plenty of condo space, casinos on every block, no abortions, and no darkies. Thank you, Hurricane Katrina!

Not long after I arrived in Biloxi, I read about a storm-damaged black church in Saraland, Alabama, where the image of Christ had appeared in a piece of drywall. As any godless northern journalist would in that situation, I quickly raced over there in search of what I thought would be a good laugh. My carpet-bagging vampire heart pumping malevolently, I went inside, put on a solemn face, and tried not to burst out laughing at the sight of the "Christ"—an incoherent ripple that looked more like a sideways version of a waterlogged Houston Texans logo than the prophet.

But when I decided to stay awhile, I watched in shock as dozens upon dozens of people came to kneel and weep before the image. Suddenly, I felt very guilty. "Man," I thought. "How rough must your life be if you're praying to a piece of freaking drywall?"

Then, one of the ministers, a woman named Marlette Holt, leaned over to me. "Folks," she said, "have had it tough."

Thank You, Tom DeLay

You were the Hammer—the most brutal and feared
of all Republican leaders—but only your rank
incompetence saved us from your revolution

———

May 4, 2006

The halls of Congress already feel different. Under the old House majority leader, the Rayburn Building had the Kubrickian feel of the *Full Metal Jacket* barracks—heels audibly clicking, something evil hissing in the background. Now it just feels like a building.

I ran into a Democratic staffer friend. "Admit it," I said. "You're going to miss Tom DeLay."

He frowned at me. "Taibbi, you ever have a hemorrhoid?"

I shrugged. "Sure," I said.

"You miss it?" he asked, then walked away not waiting for my answer.

There are some people out there who think that Tom DeLay is too easy a target, that it's cheap to hit him now, while he's down. It makes sense on the surface. DeLay is a short guy with a paunch and an ass-crack face who spent most of his precongressional life cutting rat bait and growing the state of Texas's silliest set of sideburns. He was ugly outside and in. His religious conversion came while watching a videotaped James Dobson sermon, which means that the most important moment of his spiritual life occurred as he sat in front of a television. In a hilarious example of petty capitalist parasitism, he bought his pest control company, Albo, in order to feed off the dubious largesse of the Alpo dog food company. Like our current president, he's an ex-drunk (he claims he used to suck down twelve martinis a night) given to preposterous rhetorical excesses (he once compared the Audubon Society to the Klan), making him a sort of cartoon version of a shameless, pig-hearted right-wing hypocrite.

He was, moreover, all of these things, always, without ever for a second exhibiting any countermanding positive qualities. Tom DeLay was never handsome, never eloquent, never profound, never engaging, and certainly never funny. Chicks did not dig DeLay. There is no secondary career as an adored, turtlenecked, coed-ogling poli-sci professor awaiting him. No bar back home full of tough guys is waiting to serve him up a congratulatory cold one, nobody at NASA will name the next comet after him, and he will not be a candidate for the next commissioner of the NFL. The only people left to honor his name will be a bunch of dingbat Christian dispensationalists with big ears and sky-blue suits eager to reward him for his undeniable role in speeding humanity toward the Apocalypse.

No, without his hands on the levers of power, DeLay is a total zero, a loser, two hundred–odd pounds of the world's purest pussy repellent, and with his resignation many out there will be tempted to revel in that fact without considering the larger picture.

And the larger picture is this: Tom DeLay was the Stalin of the Republican revolution. The difference is we caught him in time.

The right-wing revolution started out as all revolutions start out: as a piece of upper-class political theater that used the unwashed masses as a stage prop, a pair of crossed pistols on the wall. It was always absurd, this idea of a savage campaign against "elites" being led by a poofy wordsmith like Rush Limbaugh, a Harvard fatty like Grover Norquist, a dickless academic like Newt Gingrich, and a diaper-dumping oligarch like George W. Bush. They were just another band of mischievous aristocrats who played at being the voice of the common man—these new wingers sold themselves as the champions of the fucked-over little guy, in this case the terminally frustrated boobus Americanus, who for decades had been made to sit idly by while ethnics stole his job, evil liberals mocked his religion and his simple way of life, and media "elitists" shut out his views and sent porn and married queers into his living room via the television set.

What made Tom DeLay different is that Tom DeLay was a little guy. He had more in common with Bill Clinton (whom not surprisingly he despised, probably precisely for this reason) than with Gingrich or Norquist or Bush. He came from the dirt of the South, with a drunken reprobate for a father and nothing but white trash in his family tree. Unlike Clinton, however, DeLay was not blessed with personal gifts—looks, brains, charm. Instead of Oxford and Yale, DeLay dropped out of Baylor after being inveigled in a childish campus-vandalism scandal. His pre-politics career as a rat and bug killer was marked by a continual failure that has to be considered shocking in a state so teeming with vermin. An exterminator failing in southeast Texas is like a pimp failing in Bangkok during tourist season.

Gingrich and Limbaugh only played at being an American loser; Tom DeLay atually was one. In his first big move as congressman, when he took on the sinful National Endowment for Arts, DeLay said, "I don't know of one dollar in this whole budget that feeds anybody or clothes anybody or helps anybody, other than a bunch of rich people in Houston." That would be absurd coming from a Norquist or a Bush, but DeLay really meant it.

In the Russian Revolution, Stalin was the penniless, crude, tongue-tied seminary dropout kept in the movement as a hanger-on by brilliant, swashbuckling orators and theorists such as Trotsky, Lenin, and Bukharin, who all cynically pretended at fellowship with their darkish brute ethnic comrade. Stalin knew better, and by the time he solidified his grip on power it was those same handsome intellectuals who ended up crawling on the floors of Moscow garages with bullets in their livers. The famously vengeful DeLay was on the way to remaking his party in the same way, disdaining charismatic talkers like Gingrich and Bob Livingston and replacing their type in the apparatus of Washington—not only in Congress but in the lobbies and the think tanks, who were often forced to comply with his litmus-test hiring preferences—with his faceless, dependable, snake-mean Christian cronies.

What was terrifying about DeLay was that he was the barking voice of that afternoon talk-radio caller given full reign of Washington. He was that same angry lout, not invoked and used by clever academics and con men, but actually in charge: a narrow, selfish, envious, mean-spirited prick who had the whole capital on its knees. What kind of man was he? He went into national politics in the first place only because the federal government had banned a potentially carcinogenic pesticide called Mirex that DeLay had used to kill ants. That was his idea of injustice. He invoked God and counseled a business owner in Saipan to "resist evil" when the "evil" was a set of worker protections designed to prevent atrocities like forced abortions. He nearly overthrew the government over a blow job. And for all that, DeLay now exits politics with surely only one regret: that he was once described as a "moderate" by the *Washington Times*.

No, I guess I'm not going to miss Tom DeLay either.

Fort Apache, Iraq

Travel the bloody roads with GIs, meet the carpetbaggers,
go inside Abu Ghraib, and witness the catastrophic nature
of the American conquest

July 13, 2006

I. THE GANG THAT DIDN'T GET HIT

The 158th Field Artillery had been in country since January
and had never been hit. They were never going to get hit. You
could just feel it. They were a security detail of good-natured
Oklahoma boys, guardsmen from Fort Sill back home, traveling all over the country as they ferried a hotshot California
colonel around to inspect Iraqi police facilities.

Back in Baghdad they'd thrown me in the back of the third
of four Humvees in the convoy, a truck code-named Juliet.

"Juliet is like cock and ready to rock," said Sergeant Stephen
Wilkerson as we roared out of the motor pool in Camp Victory
to the exit of the base, headed on a six-day journey across
northern Iraq, the first stage of my five-week stay in the war
zone.

To understand the war in Iraq, you first have to understand
the people who are fighting it. And the way to do that isn't to
burst in with your head in a point, bitching about WMDs and
croaking passages from Arab history books. Jump in the truck
and shut your mouth; get on board, literally and figuratively.
In America, everyone has an opinion about Iraq, even me—but
if you're going to take the step of actually going there you've
got to give it a chance.

Our route was north 225 miles to the city of Mosul, site of numerous bomb attacks in recent months, then on to Tal Afar— same situation there—and then back to Mosul before veering east to Irbil in free and peaceful Kurdistan and then south toward Baghdad again. When I arrived, there was news about a new prime minister, and Abu Musab al-Zarqawi was about a month from getting killed in an airstrike. And maybe some of al-Zarqawi's men were hiding behind car wrecks, watching us through the cross hairs, but nobody was worried about that here. We were never going to get hit. The real problem was lunch—rumor had it that it was to be meals ready to eat, or MREs, on this first leg of the trip. Fuck al-Zarqawi. When do we get hot food?

"Hey, look up ahead," said the driver, Specialist Kevin Spicer.

Spicer isn't that tall, but his head is shaved shiny bald and he can bench-press about 9,000 pounds. His physique suggests something out of *The X-Men,* but underneath it all he is a softy who has a weakness for schlock soaps like *The O.C.* He pointed at a kid on the side of the road with a dirt-covered face.

"There," he said. "Cute kid."

The kid came into focus. Mud-streaked, in rags, standing in a trash pile. Roadside Iraqis were seemingly always doing two things: peeing and standing on trash piles.

"Scrawny-ass little boy," muttered Wilkerson, the team commander, sitting behind a big navigational console in the passenger seat. Wilkerson has an outstanding tattoo on his foot, an arrow pointing to his big toe that reads TAG GOES HERE. Back home in Oklahoma he'd been one half of the inspiration for an underground comic book called *Split-Dick and Stretch-Nuts.* Which half? Wilkerson could pull his nut sack so far out of his zipper that he could balance a sixteen-ounce can of Heineken on the outstretched membrane tray. It was a trick the whole squad referred to, with reverent awe, as "the Grandmother's Tongue." "I just have stretchy skin, I guess," he said.

Wilkerson has close-cropped dark hair and keeps his helmet shoved down just above his eyeline; he speaks with a twang thick enough to scare the banjo guy from *Deliverance*. Taking a second look at the kid on the horizon, he lurched forward suddenly.

"Oh, shit!" he said. "He just gave us the thumbs-down!"

"Well, fuck him and his Tonka truck," Spicer shot back.

Wilkerson shook his head in mock despair. "You know," he said, "we're over here doing who knows what, and he's giving us the thumbs-down." With great pathos he sighed into the vehicle intercom system. "Shit," he said. "If we weren't in this country, his mommy and daddy wouldn't be getting paid to blow us up."

"That's just ungrateful," said Spicer. "Sad, really."

Above us, the team's truck gunner, a languid ex-cop, Sergeant Dustin Hames, who had been following the conversation on the VIC but apparently had not been sufficiently impressed to participate, ended the debate by tossing the kid a Beanie Baby from the gun bay in the Humvee ceiling. Somebody at home donated the Beanie Babies in massive numbers, and we donated the ones that we didn't give to female MPs ("Can I have your moose?" one had asked us) to kids on the side of the road. Thankfully, this one fell wide right. Earlier in the day Hames had thrown a blue furry animal at a little girl and bonked her square in the forehead. Since then we had been debating the need for Hames to draw silhouettes on the side of the Hummer for every kid he nailed with a Beanie Baby.

"Damn," said Wilkerson. "Some guys are worried about how many insurgents they kill. We're worried about how many kids we hit with Beanie Babies. Shit, man. Wow."

We rolled on. We were somewhere on a road headed north out of Baghdad, just beyond a notorious stretch of highway that was hit so frequently by improvised explosive devices, or IEDs, that most squads trembled at the thought of driving on it—most squads except this group from the 158th, which was never going to get hit. The highway was a flat road ringed with sun-cooked brush. As is always the case in Iraq, the road was littered everywhere with war-zone hazards: unsmiling young men tinkering with broken-down vehicles, animal carcasses, unnatural-looking piles of stones, potholes, mysterious trash formations. All the classic warning signs of IEDs. We roared right past them.

"If we stopped to check out every last thing," said Wilkerson, "we'd never get anywhere."

Toward nightfall we reached the base at Mosul. Along with Tal Afar, it was a favorite stronghold of foreign fighters, particularly from Syria. A police training academy here had been blown up twice. Even the cafeteria at the FOB (forward operating base) we were visiting later that night had been blown to bits once. The place we were planning to eat dinner!

"This looks like Ireland," said Wilkerson philosophically, surveying the fields just outside the city.

"They even got sheep," noted Spicer.

"That's what I mean," Wilkerson agreed. "You see Ireland in the movies, you always get motherfuckers herding sheep in this green-ass pasture and stuff."

We stayed overnight at the FOB in Mosul. Like all FOBs, it was an otherworldly suburban expanse of mud, gravel, white-paneled trailers, and ad hoc fast-food joints carved incongruously into the ancient landscape of Iraq like giant, teeming anthills of Americana. The FOB in Iraq is often absurdly luxurious, with an array of Middle American comforts like

Popeyes, Burger King, and Cinnabon at the soldiers' disposal and most of the services (from food to laundry to shuttle buses to the rec centers) maintained with peak capitalist efficiency by the Halliburton subsidiary Kellogg Brown and Root, which goes so far as to leave customer-survey forms almost everywhere you go.

These preposterous Tell Us How U Like Our War!–esque survey sheets ("Please give your overall level of satisfaction for services provided by KBR . . .") provided a stark contrast to the idea of customer service just beyond the FOB wall, where gangs of Islamic extremists might put a bullet in your brain for buying the wrong thing—blue jeans, cigarettes; there were parts of Baghdad, it was said, where Sunni insurgents were killing civilians for making ice, ice of course being unholy since it wasn't around in Mohammad's time. (There weren't Kalashnikovs, either, but who's counting?)

In the morning, Wilkerson stood on the trunk of the Humvee and cleverly emptied the melted ice in the water cooler in such a way that it looked, from the side, like he was peeing first on the forehead of Specialist Matt Adamson and then on the scalp of the bespectacled medic Specialist Aaron "Doc" Gray, who opened his mouth and let the "pee" run down his throat. The photos came out great. Adamson's girlfriend was about to have a baby back home, but Doc's wife was the more immediate concern in the squad because she had sent Doc a picture of herself naked except for a few strategically placed rose petals. The production values of the picture were tremendous—hence the concern.

"Somebody, somebody took nekkid pictures of Doc's wife," said Steve. "And he claims it was her. He claims it was her."

"How could it be her?" I asked, the investigative journalist in me taking over. "She's got rose petals all over her."

"My wife finished third in her high school class," said Doc defiantly. "She's a very smart girl."

"That's why you'll never find out who he is," snapped Spicer.

We rolled out of the FOB—our objective on the first day had been just to reach Mosul, but now we had actual business in the province—steamed through the city, and roared forty-six miles to Tal Afar. During our brief stay in Mosul, an American soldier from another unit had been killed by a bomb just outside the wall of the FOB, and an Iraqi policewoman had also been shot to death—but that was never going to happen to us; it just wasn't possible.

We had a better shot at action in Tal Afar, a place lately beset by IED bombings and foreign-fighter attacks after a period of relative quiet. Not long ago, President Bush himself had given a speech in Cleveland and declared Tal Afar—an ancient-looking city near the Syrian border where foreign fighters had been slipping into the country—safe ground. Bush said that Tal Afar was "today a free city that gives reason for hope for a free Iraq." Not surprisingly, the insurgents had responded by bombing the living fuck out of the place, so much so that by the time we got there we found the mayor and most of the rest of the municipal government huddled up back-to-back in a heavily guarded castle on a hill like the last trembling teenagers in one of the *Halloween* movies.

"I love the president, he's my commander in chief," said one of the sergeants in our convoy. "But sometimes I wish he'd keep his fucking mouth shut."

Our cargo, Colonel Donald Currier, a stately, silver-mustached officer who, dressed in anything but camouflage, would look very much like an English professor, was in charge of inspecting Iraqi police efforts around the country and also helping administer and coordinate American aid to said stations. A former deputy cabinet secretary to California governor Arnold Schwarzenegger, Currier was a soft-spoken intellectual who believed implicitly in the ultimate success of the American mission in Iraq. He worked tirelessly toward that end, seemingly visiting every police station in the country in search of weak links in the chain.

In Tal Afar, a place where the police stations were under constant siege, the bureaucratic life preserver he represented was clearly needed. We met with the city's mayor, the lean, nervous-looking bureaucrat Najim Abdullah al-Jubori, who first asked for money and equipment and then presented Currier with the good news that "the people no longer call the insurgents mujahedin. They call them terrorists." That was enough good news to keep the ball rolling, so we moved out of the castle keep and inspected a few scattered police stations in town, including one where a small gang of miserable-looking American MPs were holed up on guard duty, four of them occupying a closet-size room on the second floor of the precinct house, where they lived seemingly around the clock, joylessly consuming MREs and playing Halo. Those MPs saw a lot of action. They not only had to fend off constant insurgent attacks against the police station, occasionally they had to break up violent struggles between local Iraqi army units (IAs, as we call them) and the Iraqi police (IPs). While the Iraqi army traditionally has had a closer relationship with U.S. forces, Iraqi police have often been more independent and have been known to fall prey to infiltration by various extremist groups.

"Our guys will go out and catch somebody who attacked us," said Specialist Dan Mulford. "Then the IAs will roll in and say, 'How come you took this guy? He's a good guy.' And we'll say, 'No, he's a bad guy.'" He shook his head. "Next thing you know, the IAs and the IPs are going at it. We'll fire a round in the air to disperse them."

The 158th had better luck—it was nothing but blue sky, empty roads, and happy children waving at us as we roared down Iraq's third world streets in our monstrous Space Age machines, spitting Beanie Babies in all directions. We stormed out of the city back toward Mosul. A week later, Tal Afar would be the site of a horrific suicide bombing that would kill twenty-four and wound dozens more, but of course we were long gone by then.

As we pulled out of town the sides of the road were lined for miles and miles with IPs loyal to Colonel Wathiq Ali, chief of police for the province. The show of force by Wathiq was probably a means of heightening his prestige in Currier's eyes, but getting that many men to stand up in public with the United States in today's Iraq was no small achievement. The police saluted as we drove by, and the line went on seemingly forever, or at least for most of the whole road back to Mosul. It was an impressive show of force and, my eyes fixed on the passing desert behind cool wraparound sunglasses, I allowed myself to be seduced by it.

That's right, motherfuckers, keep those hands up. America is driving by!

The conventional wisdom about Iraq these days is that this war was and is a colossal blunder, a classic crime of hubris that has metastasized into a disaster rapidly spinning far beyond our control. And, well, who knows, that may be true—but only a goddamn Canadian can fail to appreciate the dream of omnipotence roaring along these Middle Eastern highways.

At home we deride every American soldier as a potential war criminal, we label them committers of massacres, we call them

175

dumb, and when we're really being nice we say they're just dupes, field hands for the rich frat boys who got high on punch and drove us into this mess. But there's something beautiful about the way you can pluck fifteen American kids from the parking lots of the Midwest, drop them anywhere in the world, and you'll get the same thing every time: dip, dick jokes, and 50,000 pounds of finely tuned convoy rumbling at top speed. Our kids may not be the best educated, they may not read many books, but in a fair fight they will kick your ass.

Whether or not this is a fair fight is another question. But you can see why the army is still convinced we can win this thing. The army thinks it can do anything. The army looks at Iraq like a drooling six-foot-six-inch bully would, staring in at home plate with an arm full of ninety-nine-mph heaters. To that kid the game is never over. They almost all think like that over here. God forbid they should ever stop thinking like that.

It was a drive of several hours back to the FOB in Mosul that night, and after we made it without incident we sacked out for the night. While we were sleeping, another soldier got shot outside the wall, but he wasn't with us. Moreover, word filtered back the next day that the first police station we'd visited in Tal Afar the day before had been shot up with AK fire. When we gassed the vehicles before leaving the FOB, we ran into another squad that had been hit; I talked to a twenty-year-old Californian named Anthony Matthews who was just coming back from medical leave after taking an IED in the face. Matthews looked just barely old enough to have a beard and reminded me of someone I'd see pumping Slurpees in a Georgia truck stop, but his face was already lightly scarred from the bomb fragments. Like most of the Iraq casualties of late, he was a gunner.

"What happened? I got blowed up," said Matthews, who told me right up front that he disliked the media. "I blew up at this one reporter," he snarled. "She was like, 'So you saw an IED?' And I was like, 'Motherfucker, I *touched* an IED.' I got six pieces of shrapnel in my face, so don't talk to me about *seeing*."

The guys in the squad listened vaguely to the story, then jumped in their vehicles and drove off, past the spot where the sniper had picked off one of ours the night before, past the spot where the other MP had caught shrapnel in his chest two nights ago, and then finally out of town and due north. If the enemy was watching, we didn't know it; not even a cat crossed our path all day long. Eventually we made it to a Kurdish city called Irbil, where everybody loved us and we got to stay in a hotel and eat pizza and watch shitty American soap operas on a giant projection television in the hotel lobby, where we lolled around with our feet up on the furniture like cows sleeping in high grass.

Kurdistan is paradise for American troops. "If only they were all Kurds" is something you'll hear said often by soldiers. Oppressed for centuries by Arabs of all stripes—Sunni, Shia, Syrian, Iraqi—the Kurds have been legitimately worshipful of American troops. This raw countryside with low, rolling mountains and smiling dark-haired men and women in Western dress provides a stark contrast to the rest of Iraq, covered in garbage and full of people who sneer in the best-case scenario.

The rumor in Kurdistan is that the local Kurdish militia— the formerly anti-Saddam guerrillas, the Peshmerga—will kill ten civilians for every American killed, which means you can walk the streets here. So we walked the streets, with their old markets of hanging clothes and cheap gold chains and big baskets of nuts and fruits, bought ice cream, winked at girls, and snapped pictures of ruins. Conquering heroes. We were Donald Rumsfeld's wet dream.

But later that night, after we visited an Iraqi police target-shooting range, a somber mood fell over the squad. Who knows what it was. Maybe it was because it didn't really feel right being here, if you weren't getting shot at. "I'd just like to feel like I was participating," said Corporal Jimmy Shepard, an affable weight lifter. The lot of us were crammed into a pair of civilian SUVs run by the MPs up there—they have no need to drive in armor all the time in Kurdistan—and on the way home from the range, everyone's head was hanging as the sun went down on another incident-free day. The 158th is a wonder when it's loose and working; it doesn't do too well with silence.

Just then something horrible befouled the air. One of the guys had farted, breaking up the somber moment. It was the perfect response to the overserious "war is hell" vibe threatening the atmosphere.

"That shit just ain't right," Spicer protested.

"That's as wrong as two boys fucking," agreed Wilkerson.

Then the group broke out singing a song called "Gay Factory Worker from the South" and the mood was restored. The trip ended a few days later without incident. The 158th was never going to get hit.

II. THE BIG SCORE

Porkfest in the Desert

Iraq is many things—a horrifically dangerous war zone, a crumbling nation-state, a lousy place to buy a blintz. It is also a privateer's paradise, a macro version of one of those department-store contests where the contestant gets to run up and down the aisles cramming as much shit as possible into his shopping cart. Except the time period is ten years, not ten minutes.

By the time we reached a Kurdish city called Sulimaniyah, less than a week into my trip, the euphoria I'd felt in my first days with the 158th was rapidly giving way to more predictable feelings of paranoia and self-recrimination. As a journalist in Iraq, you can't help but start to feel like what you are, which is a vermin and an outsider. In many ways, being embedded with U.S. troops in the liberal-media/Michael Moore age is sort of like being asked to march into Sunday services in a Lexington, Kentucky, megachurch wearing an assless biker-dominatrix costume: one is conscious of having been the subject of many past sermons. In the army mind-set, the relative success and failure of the Iraq War is all a matter of perception, and if you follow that calculus far enough, which a certain unmistakable minority of soldiers will, all of the bombings are actually the media's fault.

Any journalist in Iraq who does not regularly feel the urge to puke his guts out from conscience-sickness is probably not in the right line of work, because increasingly almost anything he does here is a gruesome betrayal of someone or other—the soldiers and their mission if he tells too much of the truth, himself and the public if he does not.

I was already beginning to feel weighed down by that issue when we reached Sulimaniyah, having seen things that I knew would fall under the category of "not helpful" if they appeared in print. The job in Suli was a visit/inspection by Currier of the Sulimaniyah Police Academy, a training facility built by the Americans and maintained by a pair of steely-eyed, sun-beaten Las Vegans whom I will call Bob and Ray. As the conduits to American funding of the school and, indirectly, the region, Bob and Ray clearly enjoyed the status of local emirs of the *Man Who Would Be King* genus, suckling languidly at the teat of the war effort and cheerfully overseeing various budget-devouring construction initiatives. When I arrived, they were in the middle of building a full-size "mock police station," complete with every conceivable bell and whistle for use in teaching recruits, while also training police recruits of various stripes and enthusiasms—some had been rejected when portraits of Saddam Hussein were discovered in their shirt pockets.

The whole setup reeked of some idle midwestern retired police officer's ultimate leisure fantasy: a tit job, a nice fat income, an endlessly replicating budget kept thousands of miles and a war zone away from any scrutiny by Washington, a huge staff of mute, mustachioed subordinates to build cabinets and sweep floors, a pool table, a satellite TV, and a big yard full of rocks and desert plants to pump a few rounds into when things get slow. Yes, they lived in grim, modular trailers, but that seemed like a fair trade-off for a honey life. I could barely contain my jealousy.

Bob and Ray clearly had a plan in place for Currier's visit: to beg shamelessly for $4 million more to expand the facility. They had already gotten $4.8 million, but who knows what the final cost would end up being. Private contractors play an intimate role in almost every aspect of the Iraq War operation, performing a whole range of tasks traditionally handled by the military—driving convoy trucks, providing security for government officials and other important personages, even "sucking shit," as the soldiers call cleaning out sewage. The profits can be astronomical, and there is plenty of evidence that costs to the taxpayer are ballooning due to the prevalence of cost-plus contracts, a system under which the more the contractor spends, the more he makes. In cost-plus, every company in a chain of subcontractors simply adds its own percentage profit charge to whatever moneys have been spent—as high as 30 or 40 percent in some cases—so that a $150,000-per-year security guard may end up costing the government $600,000 or more. Henry Bunting, a former Halliburton purchasing officer, recently said that he often heard officials at Halliburton subsidiary KBR say, "Don't worry about price. It's cost-plus."

It's clear that there is a lot of money to be made in Iraq—soldiers who are miserable will come back for a few years to get themselves a house or a boat or two. A lot of the contractors seem to be guys like Bob and Ray—southern or western ex-cops or ex-military personnel (according to one report, 32 percent come from a few southern states) who come to the Middle East with halos over their heads "to help," and go home a few years later with that big score tucked away.

Americans are a missionary people; we cannot resist wanting to help other nations. Of course, the Iraqis know, instinctively, that nothing on earth is more dangerous than an American who visits your land and suddenly gets that goofy-ass Tim Allen *Home Improvement* fixer-upper look in his eyes. And it's comical to see how powerful that philanthropic urge becomes when it is attached to 4 million potential dollars. Pleading their case to Currier in the air-conditioned quiet of their trailer offices (plywood furniture, beat-up couch, bookshelf full of Christian hymnals and Michael Crichton novels), the pair began their pitch by comparing their plight to that of a similar training facility the army apparently had in Jordan, where some $12 million had apparently been spent just on a staff recreation center.

"I mean, if you're going to do that," said Bob, an older man with silver hair, "you might as well just take the money and go light a match to it."

"And here we ask for just four million dollars!" complained Ray, a younger type with a slight potbelly stretching from a striped artificial-fabric polo shirt. "And the money is just very hard to get our hands on."

Diplomatically, Currier said nothing, and the conversation shifted to a discussion of widespread problems with recruits across the province. Seeing Currier's despair at the long list of obstacles, Bob smelled an opening and pounced like an animal.

"I think the thing to do is invest another ten to fifteen million right here and do it right," he said bluntly.

A bold move but it fell flat. Nothing from the colonel. Bob and Ray were physically leaning forward in their chairs by this point.

Currier: "Do we have training for NCOs, commissars, et cetera?"

Bob: "It would be wonderful to run a class for these guys. We'd do some training for them, sure."

Bob smiled. It was the smile of a vacuum-cleaner salesman face-to-face with a housewife. Training? We can do training. Heck, this little baby cleans carpets of all types, from shag to Persian. . . . Let me show you what I mean, ma'am. . . .

Bob smiled again. It was time for him to bring out his ace in the hole, Major General Sabah Jalal Gharib, head of local law enforcement. I would see a number of these inspection-budgetary meetings, and the playbook was almost always the same. The local official, a toothy personage with a lit cigarette, a gray suit, and a mustache, was usually introduced by the American bureaucrat-privateer, propped up as the second coming of Fiorello La Guardia or Augusto Pinochet or both, and praised to the heavens for his hatred of Saddam and his devotion to the cause. He is invited to speak briefly. When he finishes he is applauded, called a "good guy," and then shuffled to the side. Finally, a request for funding is made. It's the same every time.

In this case Gharib asked Currier for money to build more police stations, at a cost of just half a million bucks or so per station. Then he sat smoking a cigarette, leaving the rest of the meeting to Bob and Ray.

"We only received a thousand rounds of ammo in the last shipment," said Bob. "You yourself know what a thousand rounds is good for."

"Every time we ask supply for new cars," said Ray. "And every time it's the same refusal. Look at us. We have old, beat-up cars!"

The memory of having just paid a monstrous tax bill burned in my skull as the sound of Ray complaining about having to drive an old car in Iraq bounced around in my ear. It dawned on me that this was how the appropriation process works in Iraq—your Bob and your Ray just have to ask for the money, and it arrives!

I would later be told that this particular training academy had been funded out of a nonmilitary appropriation called the International Narcotics League. More than a month after that, I would visit Congress and learn from several congressional aides that there was no way for even a U.S. congressman to find a budget where these programs exist—they're simply not in the public record. Unless you fall onto the info by parachute, there is no way to find out what is being built in Iraq, and for how much.

When the meeting ended, Gharib suddenly decided to take his important guest on a long, winding tour of the natural wonders of Sulimaniyah, which included a twisting skyline roadway that climbed beehive-style up a small mountain overlooking the city. The trip involved a large convoy of vehicles, and I was wedged into an SUV with an eclectic group that included Ray (who was driving) and a few other soldiers.

The talk in the car turned to the local population. The general theme of the conversation was that the Kurds were great folks, just like us, except when they weren't and were still a backward bunch of primitives.

"They're so advanced here," said Ray. "They're always looking to the future. All schooling here is free, even the university. They even pay the students, so that . . ."

"So that they can concentrate on their studies," said one passenger, Sergeant Arne Eastlund, approvingly. He laughed. "That's great. I wonder where they got that idea?"

"They dress more in the Western fashion here," noted Ray.

"That's good," said Eastlund.

Suddenly, a sergeant named Pistone chimed in. "You don't see many joggers or Rollerbladers here," Pistone said, looking out the window at the flow of Kurdish pedestrians trudging through their markets. "Or mountain bikers. Weird."

"Yeah, you're right," said Eastlund.

At the top of the hill, we drove through a recreation area full of picnickers. The Kurds sat on the hillside on carpets and sheets, drinking, smoking and eating homemade meals.

"You don't see many concession stands or salesmen here," said Pistone. "In America, in a place like this, there would be salesmen and concession stands everywhere." There was a tinge of empathetic regret in his voice.

"Hmm," said Eastlund.

Just then we drove past a young Kurd who, upon seeing the convoy of Americans, stood up from his picnic and very deliberately pulled out his middle finger to show to each and every one of us.

"Jesus Christ," said Pistone. "Did he just flip us off?"

"We should tell the Peshmerga," said Ray. "They'll take care of him. They'll send us his fingers in the mail."

"Yeah, we should," said Eastlund.

"Motherfucker," snarled Pistone.

We drove higher and came across a bunch of Kurdish children playing on a swing set that had been constructed high up on the mountainside.

"Oh, that's good," chuckled Pistone. "Just let your kids fall off the mountain. I mean, who's gonna herd the sheep tomorrow?"

"I wonder if they even have DUI laws in this country," mused Eastlund, watching the traffic come down the hill.

"Yeah, I doubt it," said Pistone. We drove further and he looked over at a bunch of teenagers dancing and snorted, "Yeah. Drinking and dancing on the side of a mountain—a real good idea." Near the top of the hill Pistone raised an eyebrow as he looked out the car window. "They got trash baskets up here. Surprising."

For those of us who still wonder why it is that we actually invaded this country in the first place—and this is a question that even the most creative conspiracy theorist will still have trouble answering convincingly—all it takes is a few scenes like this to understand that this isn't just about oil.

There is a certain psychologically inevitable quality to our blundering overseas, a kind of burning, insane desire to fuck with people we don't like or respect in the slightest, to cure the disease of their cultures, as it were, by drying them out in the sun of our creepy suburban enlightenment. What kind of madmen come to the ancient territory of mountainous Kurdistan and search expectantly for Rollerbladers out the window of an armored vehicle? This kind of weirdness comes far too naturally to us for this to be an accidental consequence of the invasion; it has to be part of the reason we're here, too.

It was a long twenty minutes down the hill and back into the city downtown, where we arrived just in time to see a small crowd of bubbly college-age girls walking home from one of the local institutes.

"Hey, how about that?" said Eastlund.

"Yup," said Ray cheerfully. "They dress almost like American girls here!"

III. LOST IN BAGHDAD

A Bet on the Wrong Horse

Back to Baghdad, which they say is one of the largest cities in the world. I wouldn't know. For most Americans in the capital, life in Baghdad just means a bigger FOB—one with walls twice as high, twice the number of guards, bigger cafeterias with twice as many varieties of pie. Beyond the barricades is a complex city of ten million, in whose streets a subterranean civil war is played out in daily assassinations between religious sects; one soldier, whose responsibilities included visiting a city morgue, told me that there were dozens of bodies to pick up every morning, many missing heads or kneecaps. But all of this is theoretical to most Americans, for whom the biggest difference life in the capital offers is the much higher number of nitpicking officers who never leave the FOB—called "fobbits" in army parlance. In the rougher regions, you will not find many officers who patrol the grounds looking for soldiers who forget to salute or commit the crime of bringing a book into the cafeterias (there might be an IED inside).

Upon returning to Baghdad from my trip north, I had a— vision. The vision coincided with my transfer out of the unit of charmed Okies in the vast Camp Liberty suburb and into a far more miserable and serious situation in a smaller FOB across town.

The whole vibe of my embed changed the moment that transfer went through. It was almost as if some spell had been cast around me. With the fun-loving Oklahoma crew, I never felt in danger for a second; even driving through some of the more notorious stretches of Iraqi highway, I felt as safe as a pixie in the Rose Bowl parade. But when my transfer came through, the skies darkened and I found myself standing in a carport in the marbled luxury of Camp Victory (with its absurd artificial lake and Saddam's ornate pink Alexandrian palaces, now commandeered by no-nonsense officers of the Middle American managerial type), and suddenly I could hear a tense and serious-sounding Bostonian lieutenant colonel named Alfred Bazzinotti yelling questions over the Humvee engines about my blood type, asking if I had signed the proper release forms indemnifying the army in case of whatever, and then finally telling me to get the hell in the truck because we were moving out.

Before long, though, our convoy got lost. In an attempt to stay one step ahead of the insurgents, soldiers took strange roads and byways, trying as often as possible to take advantage of the Humvee's off-road capabilities, and in this case the convoy tried to sneak across southern Baghdad at night by crossing what appeared to be an old dried-up lake bed, along a "road" that looked to me like the top edge of an ancient dam that rose steeply twenty feet off the ground on both sides. It was slow, dangerous going along this semi-cliff without streetlights, and it was no surprise to anyone when the "road" suddenly came to an end and the convoy was left looking at a precipice that stared back at us in the darkness like a bad joke. We doubled back and made it to the Baghdad city streets, where we moved through an abandoned marketplace full of cats and other feral animals that were feeding on garbage and whose eyes glowed yellow in the headlights as we drove past. Packs of wild dogs chased us, barking at every turn.

It was just then that I saw it, off in the distance, far in front of the trucks. It was a horse—a bright white horse, so horribly emaciated that you could see all of its ribs sticking out. It was wobbling, as though using every ounce of energy in its bones to stay standing. Sick as it looked, its white coat shone through the night, arrestingly pure, like the belly of a fish. It was also blocking the road, which pissed off the soldiers. American soldiers understandably do not like to stop their trucks for any reason, much less some raggedy-ass old horse. Our driver reached down and blasted the Humvee siren—*WOOO-EEEEEEEE!*—which startled the animal, causing it to lope off to the left shoulder of the road.

"Watch out for the . . . what the fuck is that?" shouted a sergeant named Vasquez.

"It's a horse," said the driver.

"Jesus. Somebody call the ASPCA," Vasquez said, looking at the miserable creature with pity.

"Or the glue factory," cracked the driver.

I looked out the Humvee window. For the first time I noticed that the horse's hind legs were blood-streaked. It appeared to be bleeding out of its ass. As we drove past it, it lumbered to the edge of the median strip, stopped, and fell over.

"Hey," I said. "That horse just fucking died."

Nobody up front in the truck heard me. We drove on.

IV. DON'T ASK WHY

The How Is Hard Enough

"Lower the big black dick?" asked Sergeant Cavanaugh.

"Yeah," said Sergeant Hennes. "Lower the Big Black Dick."

The Big Black Dick was a long black iron prod with a big square head at the end that the army had devised as a method of preventing vehicle-borne suicide bombers from ramming army convoys head-on. Technically it was called the RINO, but in this group of the 519th MP, a police transition squad on the eastern side of Baghdad, they called it the Big Black Dick.

Everyone hated the Big Black Dick. It turned urban driving into an unpleasantly approximate experience, like steering a yacht with a wedding cake balanced on the foredeck. Moreover, if something came up and you had to make a sudden turn down an alley, there was always the possibility that you'd have to stop the truck and send one or even two people out into the open air to put the thing back in the up position, which sort of defeated the purpose of traveling under armor in the first place.

Sergeant Jeremy Cavanaugh, a laconic young MP with a wry smile, jumped out of the Hummer, ran to the front of the truck, and lowered the unwieldy thing.

"Dick in place," he said sarcastically, returning to his seat.

"Must be uncomfortable, driving with that thing," I said.

"Sergeant Cavanaugh has it down to a science," noted Sergeant Jonathan Hennes.

"This dick is getting a lot of action," cracked Cavanaugh.

He hit the accelerator and we rolled out. This was early on the afternoon of Friday, May 5; the FOB we were leaving was called Rustimayah, a dank shithole that I'd been transferred to some two weeks into my embed. Not far from the vicious, chaotic ghetto known as Sadr City, Rustimayah is the smelliest, foulest, most vermin-infested base in the whole American military archipelago. A converted Republican Guard compound, the smallish FOB is sandwiched between a trash-burning facility and a sewage-treatment plant, and when you breathe the air here it feels like drinking a dog-shit milkshake.

Unlike the gleaming, futuristic prefab trailer camp at Liberty, which with its extensive creature comforts and vast white uniformity recalled a Holiday Inn version of Auschwitz, Rusti-mayah is just a jumble of old converted Iraqi buildings, filled to the cracks with crud and shit and larvae. An old bookshelf in one of the soldiers' dorms here discharged thousands of tiny fruit flies every time I tried to pull a book out; another time, I exited a latrine and stepped in what I thought was black topsoil, only to have the "soil" explode into a cloud of tiny tsetse flies. Even the half-assed attempts to make the place cheery—like the Internet café-store-hangout called Baghdaddy's! not far from the company headquarters—just made this stinky, edge-of-the-city outpost feel that much sadder.

Hennes, the squad's team leader, sighed as he glanced out the front passenger-side window of the truck. We were on our way to yet another police-station inspection and the road we were taking out of the FOB was not a particularly safe one— but then a lot of things about Rustimayah were not particularly safe. There were no gangs that never got hit in Rustimayah. Guys here got hit and they looked bummed out about it. Unlike the rah-rah atmosphere in sprawling Camp Liberty, there was an aura of depressed fatalism that stuck to everyone and everything on this base.

That was even true of Hennes, a smallish, sharp-witted, clean-cut young man from Florida. I liked him right away, mainly because he made no attempt to be my friend. When we first met and I gave him my usual goofy handshake and smile—Hey, guys, I'm just here to check out this war thing you've got going over here!—he'd recoiled slightly, his face crinkling as though a refrigerator full of rotted cheese had just been thrown open in front of him. At work Hennes had the mildly pissed-off, perpetually put-upon look of a man who has been asked to run a McDonald's in an insane asylum. "I don't do this for the glory," he cracked. "I do it to pay the bills."

He looked out the window now, saying nothing. The road we were on was a stretch with a bad recent record for small arms and IED incidents. There was all the usual potentially troublesome shit on both sides of the road, along with lots of Iraqi pedestrian traffic—young men in cheap slacks with mustaches and missing teeth, women in various states of religiously mandated cover, Pigpen-faced children running back and forth and belonging, hopefully, to someone.

We roared through it and I wondered what Hennes was thinking. Here he was, thousands of miles from home, riding in a truck with a preposterous fifteen-foot black phallus pointed provocatively straight out in a street full of unsmilingly dirty people who might or might not be trying to kill him at that very minute. And all of this in order to go . . .

To go where? Did that question cross his mind? Loosely speaking, the mandate of this and other police transition teams was construction and training, in other words seeing that police stations got built and teaching the Iraqi police whatever it is that we teach the Iraqi police. But I was beginning to wonder even about that. There is a thing that happens in bureaucracies—and the Iraq War is nothing if not a great and monstrous bureaucratic endeavor—in which things cease to happen for reasons and begin to happen just for the sake of happening. The nature of the colossal industrial apparatus that is the American military is that it fixes problems; upon encountering difficulties, it is not designed to give up, retreat, or rethink—it must conquer every obstacle in its path; it's a reflexive drive toward triumph hardwired in the very spine of the bureaucracy.

The primitive, single-plated Humvee that was first used for these patrols originally proved too vulnerable to IEDs and especially EFPs (explosively formed projectiles, copper-coated charges that are proficient at penetrating armor and were rumored to come from Chechnya). So the vehicle has been modified, and modified again, and then the modifications have been modified; it has been sent to the shop and affixed first with a Big Black Dick, then a Bigger Black Dick, and then extra armor and then extra armor on top of that. When the new triple-armored, Dick-bearing Humvee proved so heavy that the doors fell off their hinges, the army was forced back to the drawing board again, and doubtless a new kind of Humvee door will soon roll off the line.

Like the endless, inconclusive wars in Orwell's *1984*, this interminable technological back and forth assumes its own logic after a while, and it may be that, nine or ten versions of the Humvee down the road, no one will even remember anymore why we needed to go to the police stations in the first place. So now Hennes and his convoy are driving to the police stations with big iron dicks in their grilles, avoiding alleys and keeping their doors shut so that they don't fall off, while all the time trying not to get killed. That's a complicated and hazardous enough mission for a bunch of twenty-year-olds, and it is not surprising that most of them don't spend a whole lot of time thinking about the what or the why of the mission. When the how is as difficult and problematic as it is for most soldiers in Iraq, why becomes a luxury that almost no one, not even the people in charge, can afford.

We rolled through a section of eastern Baghdad that was a logistical nightmare—narrow, congested streets, high buildings lining both sides, debris and disabled vehicles everywhere—and finally reached the Bab-Al-Moudam police station and its garbage-strewn courtyard. Hennes excused himself and jumped out of the truck, indicating that I should wait.

"You should have been here last time we were here," said Cavanaugh, who as a Buffalo native appeared not to be shocked by Iraq.

"Oh, yeah?" I said.

"Yeah," he said. "Last time we were here, the IPs were shooting pigeons off the wall. This one guy shot a pigeon, it fell to the ground, and he went over and ripped its head off, squeezed its guts out, and fed it to a motherfucking cat."

"No shit," I said.

Hennes came back. "Let's go," he said.

We inspected the station and things seemed in order except for one thing—a gigantic pile of canned sodas tossed haphazardly in one corner of the weapons room, amid a row of neatly stacked automatic weapons. The police had probably, I thought, just been thirsty and confiscated someone's soda stash. Hennes sighed, like he'd seen this before, and asked the IP on duty what the deal was with the cans. Our translator, a masked Iraqi we called Johnny Bravo, who dreamed of being a Hollywood actor like Mel Gibson, explained.

"Expired merchandise," Johnny Bravo said. "You know, it's the poison, man."

"Poisoned," Hennes snorted. "Right. Whatever." He shook his head and we went back to the precinct offices to meet with the bigwigs.

Anyway, mask on—many of the translators do not trust

even Iraqi police to know their identity—Johnny Bravo and I followed Hennes upstairs, where he was to meet with a pair of local police chiefs named Colonel Adnan and Lieutenant Colonel Qazoen.

It was the by now familiar scene—a pair of mustachioed officials sitting with lit cigarettes and glasses of hot chai ready for their visitors, smiling and folding their hands. At first the meeting went well, as the two chiefs seemed to have the right answers for every question, punctuating their responses with occasional plaintive requests for equipment and money, but Hennes was noncommittal. Then he moved on to the subject of the "expired" cans in the pantry.

"Johnny," Hennes said, "ask him if he knows that there's a whole bunch of cans of soda in the armory."

Johnny translated and Qazoen frowned, thought for a moment, then answered, his eyes looking sad and earnest.

"He says yes, he knows," Johnny said. "The cans are expired. They're poisonous."

"Poison, right," Hennes said.

"He doesn't want the people poisoned by expired soda," Johnny said.

"Right," Hennes said.

Banal as this scene was, it got right to the heart of the peculiar dysfunctionality of the occupation. After observing many interactions like this, I had taken to asking both sides exactly what the Americans' authority was, legally, to tell the Iraqis to do anything. In this situation, for instance, could Sergeant Hennes order Colonel Adnan to throw out the soda? Or could he just suggest it? Given the fact that the whole ostensible thrust of our nation-building effort here is to impart historically despotic Iraq with a tradition of rule of law, this was a conundrum underlying our occupation that, to me anyway, seemed to threaten to reduce the entire exercise to an absurd paradox.

One of the first Americans I'd asked this question of was Colonel Currier, the mellow intellectual CO/roving inspector those Oklahoma boys had been driving around the country. Currier is a model commander, attentive to even the smallest concerns of the lowest-ranking soldiers in his unit; he habitually manipulated his schedule, for instance, to make sure the soldiers he traveled with never missed hot meals.

The colonel had worked out a coherent, logical case for every aspect of the mission. But even he was a little stumped by the legality question. Once, after he had given instructions and suggestions to some police officials in Tal Afar, I asked what his legal authority was to do so. "Well," he said, shrugging, "it's not an easy question to answer. I guess ultimately it's like Mao said: Power comes from the barrel of a gun. I mean, we're here, we've got the authority. It's implicit."

When I suggested that America seemingly had stepped into the exact role of the Ba'ath party, the colonel naturally did not like that comparison. "Let's just say it's kind of a gray area," he said finally.

For most of the officers and NCOs who deal with Iraqi officials on the micro level, that uncertainty is a daily reality. "Yeah, it's kind of a gray area," conceded Hennes, after the soda-can exchange with the two chiefs was over. "You ask what my authority is in these situations, and the answer is, technically not much," he said.

Almost everything about the Iraq War is a gray area, beginning with the question of whether the soldiers are at war or not in the first place. Can they shoot or can't they? When driving through the city, is the show of force intended to intimidate or reassure? Soldiers regaled me with stories of units that had been asked to remove their shoulder armor so as not to look "too scary" to the population. In other units, M-4 rifles were taken away from the Humvee gunners, to prevent an excess of warning shots—leaving soldiers with only the massive and lethal .50-caliber machine gun to defend themselves.

To the soldiers, all of these contradictory initiatives testified to a confusion on high about what the army is doing in Iraq. Is this mission political or military? "Either don't waste our time coming here or, if we are here, let us put the heat down," one soldier told me. "There's just too much gray area."

On a practical level, watching soldiers like Hennes and petty Iraqi officials like Colonel Adnan stumble over the political elephant in the room—the illusion of Iraqi sovereignty—is at times a painfully uncomfortable spectacle. Complicating matters is the strange disconnect between the two cultures. As ubiquitous as our presence in the country is, the actual commerce between Americans and Iraqis is far rarer than one might expect. Soldiers still characterize locations using the old slang terms "inside" or "outside the wire," but the ironic thing is that by "outside the wire" what everyone really means is "Iraq." "Inside the wire," of course, generally means "inside the FOB," and the FOB, with its high walls and stringent security, is a hermetically sealed universe that aims for the sanitary purity of one of those oxygenated, boy-in-a-bubble biospheres. Except in rare cases, Iraqis are not really welcome on the FOBs, and even in those instances—such as the case of the "host-country nationals" whom the army hires to clean up garbage inside the walls of Abu Ghraib—they're likely to be kept under constant surveillance by *Cool Hand Luke*–style walking bosses who can have them changed into yellow jumpsuits at the snap of a finger.

There are exceptions, obviously—the translators, the local politicos, the guests of the occupation—but for the most part the suburban American purity of the FOB, with its volleyball courts, cookouts, and Burger Kings, is kept closely guarded, meaning that Iraq is no longer a whole country but a pool of water marred by a rapidly expanding archipelago of oil slicks. According to the army, there are some eighty-two coalition FOBs spread across Iraq. As a result of all this, communication in those few instances where our culture meets theirs tends to be dysfunctional and sad—like a pair of Down syndrome kids rolling a ball back and forth across a shag rug.

"Okay," said Hennes. "Last time we were here, there were some IPs shooting BB guns. . . ."

He recounted the whole story of the pigeon massacre. Johnny Bravo translated. The Iraqi colonel listened, then frowned.

"He says," said Johnny Bravo, "that this was my hobby, but that if you don't want me to, I won't do it anymore."

"Well," said Hennes graciously, "I like to shoot BB guns, too, I just don't like to do it at work. Let's try to keep it professional."

Johnny Bravo translated. Upon hearing the admonition about professionalism, the colonel seemed to sour; his face changed and he began gesticulating forcefully as he answered.

"He says," said Johnny, "that his men work long hours, and you have to give them a chance to breathe."

Hennes sighed. "Well, of course . . ."

"He says," continued Johnny, "that nowadays they're always getting hit by IEDs, and it used to be rarely. So the men, they need to have a little fun and you don't want us to have any fun."

Hennes looked momentarily perplexed by this answer. "Well, I understand needing a release," he said. "But I just didn't think that was very professional."

The next day I was due to fly out of Rustimayah by helicopter, but something came up and so instead I spent the entire day at the helipad, waiting for a flight out. It was late in the long, hot afternoon when Hennes showed up, along with some of the other NCOs in the unit, including his friend Sergeant Brian Stake and another of the unit's translators, a slightly older man named Salim. Hennes was wide-eyed and in a state of highly agitated sarcasm; I could see right away that something had happened.

"Gee, too bad you missed us today," he said. "We got in a firefight."

We went to the cafeteria for dinner. Listening to the conversation between Stake and Hennes, fresh from an afternoon of combat, made me powerfully aware of the gulf that separates soldiers and civilians. Whatever our reasons for doing so— whether it's academics anxious to test beloved theories, or politicians making gambits out of self-interest, or even patriotic civilians voting for sacrifices that others have to make— whenever society makes life-or-death decisions, the burden always ends up with these guys, right here.

"Why did they attack us?" Hennes asked sarcastically. "They attacked us because they didn't get their morning paper."

"Yeah," said Stake. "They didn't find out who won the Sabres-Flyers game."

I bit my lip, the thought involuntarily popping into my head: Who did win that game?

"Wait, I don't understand," said Salim. "They attack because of a paper?"

Hennes shook his head, resisting the urge to laugh. "No," he said. "It's just . . ."

"Actually," deadpanned Sergeant Stake, "when it was over, we just ordered some chai and talked things over."

"Yeah," said Hennes. "Let's be peaceful."

Salim looked up helplessly. Were they being serious? No one bothered to straighten him out.

As often as the soldiers get attacked, there is surprisingly little discussion among the troops about who is actually doing the shooting. Is it Al Qaeda? The Mahdi army? Foreign Shia fighters from Iran? Sunni extremists? There are literally hundreds of possibilities; one intelligence operative told me that each and every day, fighters came in claiming to belong to groups with new names. "You might get five young guys in a town, just playing at being bad guys," he said. "They'll call themselves the Grandmother's Brigade or something. But they're basically just gangbangers." The distinctions interest the intelligence guys, but to most soldiers it doesn't really matter who's doing the shooting. They all go by one name—Hajii, a name we use the same way we used Charlie a few decades ago.

I left Rustimayah that night, but I was back a week later. For a memorial service. Two soldiers from that same battalion had been killed when a bomb hit them en route to a police station. I was told that it was an EFP that tore straight through the Humvee armor and that there was nothing left of the men but ash.

V. YOU CAN STEAL WI-FI ANYWHERE

Three Days in Abu Ghraib

Early one Sunday morning I met up with a man I'll call the Commando. He had his own Humvee, but he was driving in a military convoy. As far as I knew, no Westerner drives in Iraq without the military anymore—not even an intrepid ex-military international black-operations expert who claims to be a close personal friend of Alice Cooper's, like the Commando. The convoy rolled out of a Baghdad FOB and moved slowly into the city, taking a serpentine route around an IED location reported just an hour earlier.

In the car, the Commando explained something to me. "There is no offensive operation in the regular army here," he said. "The intelligence guys, the special ops, they are the force here. It's all on us."

The Commando is the kind of guy who would stand out in a crowd of civilians, like a lion tamer wandering the aisles of a Circle K. Tall, deeply tanned, with a silver Fu Manchu mustache and the build of a heavyweight karate champion (which he probably was, for all I know), he has a booming voice and a garrulous character, unnervingly intense and almost too quick to make intimate friendships; he'd found me in a military cafeteria, where I guess I'd looked scruffy and pathetic amid all the armed soldiers, and had decided to adopt me. "You should disembed, come with me," he said, patting my back violently. "I'll take you somewhere that'll blow your fucking mind."

Now that I'd actually come to meet him I was regretting it. The Commando looked like he just might be crazy. He was moving his lips as he whispered some song to himself. His huge sunglasses betrayed nothing in his eyes, which I suspected were darting back and forth. The convoy moved out of the city limits; I sank in the Humvee seat.

"Hey, Commando," I said finally. "They're going to hang me by my balls for this."

He leaned over and smiled. "You're going to be looking bad guys right in the eye," he said. "Trust me."

After about a half hour drive, we came to a large walled facility, marked on each corner with lookout towers. FOB Abu Ghraib. My asshole puckered violently. "I could spend the next year standing on a box with a hood over my head and wires coming out of my ass," I thought. But my entrance into the facility was smooth and uneventful. Abu Ghraib's closing had been announced long ago. When I arrived it was about a month away from what personnel there expected would be its last days as a functioning military prison.

The place looked like a ghost town—like one of those abandoned factory sites in Rust Belt cities, where giant industrial structures once teeming with people now sit mute on the lakeshores. It was home, seemingly, to more birds than people; the old prison blocks were now populated every ten feet or so with buzzing nests of beautiful barn swallows, lending the facility, with its portraits of a bereted Saddam crumbling away piece by piece from the concrete walls, a strangely peaceful and beneficent air.

The FOB itself is a large, squarish, walled camp with an odd layout. On the right side as you enter is another walled-off section within the prison grounds that used to contain political cells in Saddam's time. The main "hard site" where terror suspects were still being held was in a complex of buildings that included a rec center, a chapel, a restaurant (the Mortar Cafe), a first-class field hospital, even a Green Bean, which is sort of like an army version of Starbucks. (Before I left I would indulge in the perverse thrill of ordering a double cappuccino with a vanilla shot at Abu Ghraib.) Years of American occupation have left this place in a relatively clean state, although remnants of the horrific squalor still exist, most notably in the form of sweeping piles of trash and junk along the walls of the facility.

There is not much I can tell about my Abu Ghraib experience, except to say that I was there for three of the very weirdest days of my entire life. The Commando dumped me in an abandoned cell block and shut the door behind me almost immediately upon arrival. Three times a day he would bring me food—ribs and chicken and other delights from the typically well-stocked FOB cafeteria—and then leave me alone for fifteen hours or more to devour the piles of trashy books he left for me as entertainment (how the Erica Jong novel *Sappho's Leap* made it to Abu Ghraib I'll never figure out). I was to avoid all people, keep quiet, and when he took me out of my cell for tours of the FOB—once a day or so—I was to watch my mouth and look like some mysteriously high-ranking spook. Who would know in a place like this?

"You go where I go," he said on the first day. "And don't ask any fucking questions. In the meantime, stay here and don't move."

He shut the cell door. I stood for a moment in the middle of my cell, staring at the white concrete walls; it took exactly ten seconds for me to burst out laughing. The next hours were taken up with a variety of absurd activities: push-ups, line drawings of dogs, experimentation with a mime routine. Late in the evening I turned on my laptop and discovered, to my absolute amazement, that there was a functioning wireless hub in the building. I got online and promptly spent most of that night filling out sunny customer-survey responses for various state-side corporations.

Dear Krispy Kreme Corporation . . . Thank you for being YOU.

Outside my room, behind the boarded-up barred window, I could hear residents of the village just beyond the prison walls chanting their evening prayers. Later at night I would hear something else entirely—the sounds of mortar shells crashing close by, two biggish blasts shaking the room.

Abu Ghraib is the symbol of American mistakes in Iraq, the place where the weird criminal perversions of bored, porn-surfing American teenagers clashed spectacularly with fastidious, sexually inviolate Islamic culture. It was also a most powerful symbol of our misguided perception of ourselves and our place in the world.

We came into this war expecting to be treated like the GIs who went into France a half century ago—worshipped, instantly excused for the occasional excess or foible, and handed the keys to both the castle wine cellar and the nurses' dormitory. Instead we were treated like unclean monsters by the people we liberated, and around the world our every move was viciously scrutinized not only by those same Europeans we rescued ages ago but by our own press.

The failure of Abu Ghraib was the failure to accept the role we had created for ourselves as new masters of subject peoples. We wanted to rule absolutely and also to be liked, which was why our first reaction after the scandal broke was to issue profuse apologies, call for a self-flagellating round of investigations, and demand the prison's closure. A hegemonic power more comfortable with ruling would have just shot the reporter who broke the story and moved on.

But America has never been able to stomach that kind of thing, which is why, incidentally, this occupation of Iraq is probably not going to work. We are too civilized to make ourselves truly feared in public, but not civilized enough to properly restrain our power in private.

On my second day in the facility, the Commando roused me out of my bunk and dragged me out for a tour. Beyond one wall of the facility there stood a clearly visible row of residential apartments, a neighborhood called Khandari, which the Commando explained was a hotbed of activity. "Hajiis looking right over the wall," he said. "They have gunfire there two or three times a week."

We drove around. The Commando pointed out a small hole through which a group of prisoners had made a daring escape some months back. "Now, no American male could ever have made it through that hole," he said. "But three of those stinky little bastards slid through here." He laughed as he recounted the story. One of the escapees, he said, made it over the wall. The other two, however, stayed behind and tried to blend in by putting on some civilian clothes. When a squad of soldiers confronted them, they tried to talk their way out of trouble by claiming to be employees of KBR. "They were like, 'KBR! KBR!'" he laughed. "They still had on their jumpsuits under their civilian clothes. Yeah, right, KBR."

We made our way around. A helicopter was landing in the middle of the compound and a small group of American soldiers led out a group of six dark-skinned men in FlexiCuffs. A female soldier arranged them in lock step, then marched them off toward the hard site. We followed them and along one wall were boxes of prefab halal food. At least proper care was taken to meet the prisoners' dietary restrictions.

"They'll be given a number, then interviewed," the Commando said. "As for these influxes . . . on a good day, we'll have that helicopter full of guys land ten to twelve times."

He threw me back in my cell. This time I read *The Corrections* by Jonathan Franzen. If there is a worse way to spend a day than being locked in Abu Ghraib prison reading Jonathan Franzen I'm not aware of it. In the early evening the Commando came back. "Sandstorm," he said. "Come on out."

I climbed up a flight of stairs to the rooftop. I looked around in all directions. The place looked like Mars—a sea of red sand, impenetrable beyond fifty yards or so. "Wow," I said.

"It gets much redder than this," he said admiringly. "It gets fucking beet red. I got pictures."

He took me back to my cell. The next day it was more of the same. The Commando spoke much and often about the bravery of the men who were out risking their lives to bring terror suspects to this facility. He explained to me that many men like him were moved to pitch in after 9/11. They live outside the public view, their accomplishments never noted by anyone, much of what they do for a living a secret even from their own families. I never did find out exactly what he did at the facility, although I had a few ideas. But I was struck suddenly that what I was looking at here wasn't a portrait of American iniquity in Iraq but the offensive side of our war. What is public about Iraq is the pounding our soldiers take, the day-in, day-out IED attacks against teenagers in Humvees. Most of the men our reporters know in embeds are on the defensive from sunup to sundown.

There is an impression that we are not fighting back, but we are. Here in Abu Ghraib and places like it, away from public view, we swoop down in the night and snatch people out of their homes by the half dozen. I would imagine that rules are bent. But what rules can there be in a place like this? (The Commando's take on the Geneva Convention: "While you're beating his ass, don't take his picture.") I asked the Commando at one point what the goal was: "Is the idea that we'll keep capturing these guys, until there won't be any more of them?"

"Who knows?" he said. "I guess."

One last long night in the hooch. I read a military-equipment magazine with an article about the psychological importance of leaving a big hole in the enemy when you shoot him. "A big hole is more devastating than a little pucker," it noted. I wrote that down, for future reference. In the morning the Commando dragged me out for the last time and tossed me in the Hummer. We picked up coffee from the Green Bean and settled into the convoy line. On the way back the Commando regaled me with stories of his personal exploits. He hinted at access to the kind of information that would keep all of America awake if it knew, even blurting out one threat he'd heard about that made me very uncomfortable being a New Yorker. Americans are a sheltered people, but our secret warriors are not— even if it's only as an adversary, they've at least looked the world in the eye. But they never get to share their experience. In Iraq, half of our fight is always going to be in the shadows.

The convoy rolled on until we reached another FOB, where we stopped for one last lunch. He told me stories of comrades he'd lost in Afghanistan, and the lengths he'd gone to for one man's family. I was not sure I agreed with the Commando's take on the Iraq War or what the possibilities were for its success; I got the feeling, in fact, that he was only dimly interested in who the other side or sides even were—the most important thing being who was giving the orders to fight. But his devotion to his friends and allies was powerful and unmistakable. "It's like a little community," he said, "where people do things for each other."

"Good luck," I said, shaking his hand.

"You too."

He left the cafeteria and I never saw him again. I left Iraq a week and a half later. Just in time. It took exactly four weeks to get tired of the sounds of IED blasts outside the wall. Against that backdrop, the appeal of getting in a truck every morning is extremely limited. I felt for the guys who have to stick it out a year or more.

VI. DOWN THE RABBIT HOLE

No Way Out as a Way of Life

The Iraq War, the central political event of this generation, this crazy flash point that will find a way to touch the lives of almost everyone in the world before it's over, is here to stay. We must come to grips with the reality of this monstrous, rapidly expanding thing that is fast taking on far greater dimensions and meaning than a mere foreign-policy blunder.

This is the place where two existential dead ends have come around in a circle to meet in an irreconcilable explosion of violence—the bureaucratic ennui and intellectual confusion of modern civilized man versus the recalcitrant, prehistoric fanaticism of Al Qaeda's literally cave-dwelling despotic mob. Human history has traveled in two exactly opposite directions for the past thousand years, and the supreme irony is that both paths led straight here, to this insane stalemate in the Mesopotamian desert.

Beyond the walls of the FOB the chaos of Iraq is just a fresh take on the same old totalitarian doublethink from the last century that sent Nazis and Communists on crazed quests for paradise by sanctioning the violence buried in their dumb hearts. All bloody revolutions rely for their success on ideologies that dehumanize the nonbeliever, and these Islamic fanatics roaming the streets of Baghdad, piously chanting "*Allahu Akbar!*" as they watch the bodies of ice salesmen or infidel teenagers cook, are no different. On top of everything else, they're not even original.

Nothing like that abject savagery is evident on the American side. But there is something very unsettling in the way that the war effort has re-created the cozy isolationism of the American suburbs in its giant military outposts. It's a concentrated dose of our culture, where Mom, her tennis lesson awaiting, sends the kids off to school and Dad, the sweetest guy you'll ever meet, brings home a paycheck earned on the backs of industrial slaves from China.

Walking the peaceful streets of Anytown, you'd never guess this—although at night the family purges unconscious guilt by watching morality plays like *The O.C.* and *Desperate Housewives,* in which Middle America ritualistically confesses to a sizzling sex life it's never come close to having. Our defining characteristic is that despite a creeping fear, we know ourselves very poorly and have willfully turned a blind eye to the world outside our easy, cocoonlike consumer lives.

In the same way, our soldiers on the FOB may be forgiven for not understanding the discontent over the wall, because the "Iraq" of their experience is not much different from the cable-ready communities, with the Burger King just down the street, that many of them came from in the first place.

Life is good and happy down the rabbit hole, but outside it something is going terribly wrong. What's horrifying about Iraq is that none of our people, not even the ones running things, seem to understand why that might be. It's a terrible thing to be blind. Terrible—and frightening.

Not long after I got home, I got an e-mail from Wilkerson in the 158th, the good-luck Oklahoma boys: *hey man, how ya doin? we are doin good. we got hit the other day and it wasnt good at all. i cant give you details or anything but just know all our boys are good . . . but im gonna go get for now, so you be good and drink a beer for me. Hahaha later steve-o*

The gang that never gets hit had been on its way home to Baghdad from Baqubah on the evening of June 5 when the third truck in the convoy was rocked by an explosion. Spicer and Wilkerson, in the second truck, accelerated through the cloud and made it to safety. But Specialist Issac Lawson, a Californian I hadn't met in my time with the squad, was hit badly. He died on arrival after an airlift to a nearby field hospital.

In war good luck always runs out. The only thing no one runs out of is more people. And when one of the sides is America, not even the money is exhaustible. The thing just keeps spinning, spitting out more bodies, and you find yourself ashamed of being glad it isn't someone you know.

Bush's Favorite Democrat

In Connecticut's Democratic primary, Joe Lieberman
claims he's facing a leftist "jihad," but there are two
words the senator can't duck: "Iraq" and "war"

August 10, 2006

Early Sunday afternoon, Beulah Heights First Pentecostal
Church, New Haven, Connecticut. A hot summer day with an
all-black congregation, a big hall in a tough neighborhood packed
full to the last pew, with the faithful cooling themselves with
old-fashioned handheld fans. Senator Joe Lieberman, a pale animal with a balloon head, stands at the podium and smiles, his
gnomish Wallace Shawn mini-fingers piously clasped before him.

As an orator, Lieberman is a pro's pro. No matter what the
crowd, his rap always has the feel of a barroom Casanova's
metronome come-on. He talks and talks, and five minutes later
you can't figure out how his hand got that far up your skirt.
He is especially brilliant in this particular environment, an
absolute master of the "my heart is as black as yours" honkie-
in-church act. He swoops in, tells a story about meeting Dr.
King back in the day, shakes his head solemnly at the scourge
of racism, and then coasts to a Scripture-packed dismount.
Clear throat; assume sonorous, preacherly intone; dream aloud
of a better day ahead, a day when . . .

"When the mountains will be made low, when the valleys
will be raised up, when the rough road will be made smooth
and the crooked path will be made straight," he says. "Because
on that day, with God's help, the earth truly will be full of the
knowledge of the Lord."

Jesus, I think. This guy's good. He pauses, smiling, for applause. Then: "Thank you! Enjoy lunch!"

And he's outta there. The whole thing takes about eight minutes. You can keep your political speeches pretty short in the year 2006 if you don't once mention the words "war" or "Iraq." Next stop: firemen in Fairfield. I'm still gathering my shit in the church foyer when I see his caravan zooming past the entrance, back toward the highway.

The scene says everything you need to know about the modern Democratic Party. It spends its weekdays sucking off the Pentagon and Wall Street and the pharmaceutical industry, and on the weekends it comes out and spends five minutes getting teary-eyed for the "I have a dream" speech and thinks you owe it your vote because of it. Some party members agree, but quite a few don't, which is why Joe Lieberman— the hawkish onetime vice presidential candidate who has made himself the most visible symbol of the "new" Democrats—is facing a surprising primary challenge on August 8. Like Lieberman himself, the "I was there in the sixties" act is finally getting old.

"I hate the sixties, and I'm tired of hearing about it—what have you done for me lately?" says Regina Meade, one of the churchgoers. She shakes her head. "I lost a cousin in the war. Twenty-nine years old. What about that? What about that?"

Billed as a preview to the midterm elections later this fall, with implications for the '08 presidential race, the Democratic primary for the Senate in Connecticut is a hot little turd attracting, for the first time since November '04, the exiled flies of national campaign journalism. They are here in Connecticut now, searching angrily for good coffee and road maps in precious little towns like Wallingford, Fairfield, and Danbury, where Lieberman is currently even in the polls with an antiwar challenger in the person of a wide-eyed political rookie named Ned Lamont.

If you believe the propaganda emanating from Lieberman and his coterie of whore-cronies in the Democratic Leadership Council, Lamont is a dangerous, pillar-crushing revolutionary, a preppy, tanned mixture of Lenin and the Ayatollah. The Democrat insiders' strategy vis-à-vis Lamont is very similar to the one used to dispose of Howard Dean a few years back, only it's even more savage this time around. They have chosen to go after Lamont's supporters in the blogosphere, deriding the likes of "Daily Kos" founder Markos Moulitsas Zuniga and the wackos at MoveOn.org as "liberal fundamentalists" bent on liquidating poor Lieberman for the sake of radical leftist orthodoxy. The DLC started the smear campaign in June with an editorial called "The Return of Liberal Fundamentalism" that used the word "purge" no fewer than eight times, in case you missed the KGB motif the first seven times.

Since then, a spate of similar editorials has appeared in the national media, with anyone and everyone jumping on the theme of blood-hungry blogger leftists scheming to take over the world via the Lamont campaign—from *New York Times* elitist fuckhead David Brooks ("The Liberal Inquisition") to Jonathan Chait at the *Los Angeles Times* ("Purely Foolish Democrats") to those always-predictable bards of conventional wisdom at *Newsweek* ("The War's Left Front"). The whole campaign was a classic bit of bait and switch. Rather than face up to its own record on the war, the party tried to defend its own by making the race into a referendum on "leftist" Internet pests, some with suspiciously foreign-sounding names.

And just like three summers ago, when the media cheerfully regurgitated party-concocted code words like "angry," "shrill," "testy," and "strident" when discussing the doomed Howard

Dean, reporters this time around made sure to repeat the same terrorist/communist–themed code words in their campaign coverage, with nearly every major media outlet including some combination of the words "purge" or "fundamentalist" in their Lamont stories. *New York* magazine went so far as to call Lamont's Net-roots supporters the "Blogitburo," and Lieberman himself, in an interview, derided his opponents' supporters as being on a "jihad."

This witch-hunting horseshit was preposterous enough, when the DLC and its ilk somehow succeeded in painting a tepid, pro-business centrist from the Hamptons like Dean as the second coming of Karl Marx. But that was nothing compared to the stretch they're making in playing the red-baiting game with Lamont, a Richie Rich Harvard capitalist from the socioeconomic Olympus of Greenwich whose expensively wavy haircut and crisp, supernaturally clean chinos would bring a tear to the eye of the mannequin in the Pebble Beach Pro Shop.

The only thing radical about Lamont is his opposition to the Iraq War policies of George Bush and Lieberman, and in this vague "radicalism" he is joined by upwards of 91 percent of all Democrats, according to recent polls; otherwise, he is as vanilla and unthreatening as a politician could possibly be, the human incarnation of the white line in the middle of the road. Lamont's non-Iraq politics are not much more than a cautious presentation of already-tried mainstream party ideas, like permitting the uninsured to buy into the congressional health plan, and his stump humor is the gentlest kind of aw-shucks Americana— when he gets applause or cheers from the back of the room, he calls out, "Thanks, Mom!"

When I sat down and talked with Lamont on a park bench after an appearance in Wallingford, he was plainly horrified when I compared the attacks against him to the campaign against Dean. "I hadn't thought about that," he said, adding quickly, "What you have to remember is that I'm a business guy from central Connecticut."

He talked about the assault from the party regulars: "Well, I've got grassroots support that is perceived as a threat to the established order," he said. Then he scratched his head. "But it's weird. It's like there's a signal sent down from somewhere. The other day I was with this reporter from the *New York Observer*, and he was reading down a list of talking points: Why is it that bipartisanship can't exist in the party? Are you a pacifist? And so on. And I was like, 'Man, where is this coming from?'"

Of course it's fairly obvious where it's coming from. Even the most casual Democratic voters understand by now that there is a schism within the party, one that pits "party insiders" steeped in the inside-baseball muck of Washington money culture against . . . well, against us, the actual voters.

The insiders have for many years running now succeeded in convincing their voters that their actual beliefs are hopeless losers in the general electoral arena, and that certain compromises must be made if the party is ever to regain power.

This defeatist nonsense is sold to the public in the form of beady-eyed party hacks talking to one another in the opinion pages of national media conglomerates, where, after much verbose and solemn discussion, the earnest and idealistic candidate the public actually likes is dismissed on the grounds that "he can't win." In his place is trotted out the guy the party honchos insist to us is the real "winner"—some balding, bent little bureaucrat who has grown prematurely elderly before our very eyes over the course of ten or twenty years of sad, compromise-filled service in the House or the Senate.

This "winner" is then given a lavish parade and sent out there on the trail, and we hold our noses as he campaigns in our name on a platform of Jesus, the B-2 bomber, and the death penalty for eleven-year-olds, consoling ourselves that he at least isn't in favor of repealing the Voting Rights Act. (Or is he? We have to check.) Then he loses to the Republicans anyway and we start all over again—beginning with the next primary election, when we are again told that the antiwar candidate "can't win" and that the smart bet is the corporate hunchback still wearing two black eyes from the last race.

No one has played the role of that "winner" more enthusiastically, or more often, than Joe Lieberman. He is everything a Washington insider loves in a politician. He is pompous, pious, and available. Routinely one of the very top recipients of campaign donations from the insurance, pharmaceutical, and finance sectors, and a man whose wife, Hadassah, is a pharmaceutical-industry lobbyist for Hill and Knowlton, Lieberman has quietly become one of the greatest allies corporate America has in Washington.

For example, Lieberman, who as chairman of the DLC in the mid- to late nineties presided over an organization heavily subsidized by companies such as AIG and Aetna (the latter of which also contributes lavishly to his campaigns), sponsored a bill that limited auto insurance suits by permitting the offering of lower rates to consumers who forfeited their right to sue. He has fought for similar antilawsuit laws for tobacco, for HMOs, for pharmaceutical companies. Victor Schwartz, general counsel for the American Tort Reform Association, once bragged that "if it were not for Lieberman, there would never have been a Biomaterials Access Act"—a 1998 law that protected companies like Dow Chemical and DuPont (also big

DLC contributors) from lawsuits filed for the production of defective medical implants. Yes, that's right: Joe Lieberman fought for the principle of manufacturing faulty fake tits with impunity.

In a move that was perfectly characteristic of everything he stands for, Lieberman in 2001 offered a piece of legislation, S. 1764, that purported to provide incentives to companies that develop medicines to treat the victims of bioterror attacks but, more important, extended the patent life of a wide range of drugs for several years, delaying the introduction of more cost-friendly generic drugs. Shilling for the socialist subsidy of drug companies while masquerading as a Churchillian, tough-on-security Democrat in the war on terror age: that's Joe Lieberman, and the modern Democratic Party, in a nutshell.

In the midst of all this whoring for business interests, Lieberman has preposterously marketed himself to the public as a stern guardian of "morality" and "traditional values," along the way taking some admirably mean-spirited positions. He once supported a bill denying funding to public schools that counseled suicidal teens that it is okay to be gay, a remarkable position for a man whose response to the Enron scandal was to say that "government will never be able to legislate or regulate morals."

Lieberman also signed the American Council of Trustees and Alumni, the notorious organization founded by Lynne Cheney that published a baldly McCarthyite list of "anti-American academics." In 1997, Lieberman pushed for warning labels on CDs, getting the Senate to take up the issue under the title "Music Violence: How Does It Affect Our Youth?" in the hopes of snagging the votes of a few grandmas by wagging a finger at Marilyn Manson—yes, Lieberman was one of those asshole politicians who tried to pin Columbine on rock music. And rather than denounce Ken Starr for the most egregious misuse of prosecutorial authority since the House Un-American Activities Committee, Lieberman's response to the Lewinsky scandal was to attack Bill Clinton in one of the lamest "O the children!" acts of all time, saying, "It is hard to ignore the impact of the misconduct the president has admitted to on our children, our culture, and our national character."

A few years later, faced with a similar political choice, he chose to stand fast by Bush on the issue of Iraq, saying, "We undermine the president's credibility at our nation's peril." Apparently the president deserves absolute loyalty only when his mistakes result in teenagers getting their heads shot off.

It was this last position of Lieberman's that forced the candidacy of Lamont into being. "We're trying to determine what the right boundary is on a Democrat," says Lamont spokesman Robert Johnson. "We know what the left boundary is. But what is it on the right? At some point, when a Democrat is sucking up to a president like George Bush, you have to put your foot down. Lieberman does not stop at a 'center.' The further right they go, he just follows."

But, of course, Lieberman's crowning insult—and perhaps his last fatal mistake as an (ostensible) member of the Democratic Party—was his recent decision to register and run as an independent in case he loses the primary to Lamont. Finally taking his mask off and revealing himself as a baldly self-interested political creature, this final-act version of Lieberman plans on dying hard, forcing liberal voters to kill him twice in the same movie, like Jason in *Friday the 13th*.

With his hideous fake folksiness, much-celebrated "great sense of humor," and relentless Beltway hype as just the nicest guy you'd ever want to meet (David Brooks calls him "transparently the most kindhearted and well-intentioned of men"),

217

Joe Lieberman is easy to hate—which makes him easy to hate for the wrong reasons. Sure, he's an arrogant, condescending prude; sure, he's a willing, energetic censor who outrageously poses as an aggrieved champion of "decent people everywhere"; and sure, he reminds you very much of the lecturing, overbearing high school vice principal you once had who ended up getting busted on a kiddie-porn rap ten years after you graduated.

Yet all of that means nothing. What is important to remember about Joe Lieberman is that his individual personality is incidental. Lieberman is just another "winner" to be rolled off the line and served up to Democratic voters by the behind-the-scenes corporate masters bent on controlling both sides of Washington politics, using whatever scare tactics necessary to ensure success. He's a pawn and a stooge whom they've gotten good mileage out of so far because he happens to have a special talent for being just the kind of officious, self-righteous prick you have to be to sell their muddled policies in public—but his time is up now, and not because of him but because of them. People are tired of being told who can and cannot win. As it turns out, they get to decide that for themselves.

The Worst Congress Ever

How our national legislature has become a stable of thieves and perverts—in five easy steps

November 2, 2006

There is very little that sums up the record of the U.S. Congress in the Bush years better than a half-mad boy-addict put in charge of a federal commission on child exploitation. After all, if a hairy-necked, raincoat-clad freak like Representative Mark Foley can get himself named cochairman of the House Caucus on Missing and Exploited Children, one can only wonder: What the hell else is going on in the corridors of Capitol Hill these days?

These past six years were more than just the most shameful, corrupt, and incompetent period in the history of the American legislative branch. These were the years when the U.S. parliament became a historical punch line, a political obscenity on par with the court of Nero or Caligula—a stable of thieves and perverts who committed crimes rolling out of bed in the morning and did their very best to turn the mighty American empire into a debt-laden, despotic backwater, a Burkina Faso with cable.

To be sure, Congress has always been a kind of muddy ideological cemetery, a place where good ideas go to die in a maelstrom of bureaucratic hedging and rank favor trading. Its whole history is one long love letter to sleaze, idiocy, and pigheaded, glacial conservatism. That Congress exists mainly to misspend our money and snore its way through even the direst political crises is something we Americans understand instinctively.

219

"There is no native criminal class except Congress," Mark Twain said—a joke that still provokes a laugh of recognition a hundred years later.

But the 109th Congress is no mild departure from the norm, no slight deviation in an already underwhelming history. No, this is nothing less than a historic shift in how our democracy is run. The Republicans who control this Congress are revolutionaries, and they have brought their revolutionary vision for the House and Senate quite unpleasantly to fruition. In the past six years they have castrated the political minority, abdicated their oversight responsibilities mandated by the Constitution, enacted a conscious policy of massive borrowing and unrestrained spending, and installed a host of semipermanent mechanisms for transferring legislative power to commercial interests. They aimed far lower than any other Congress has ever aimed and they nailed their target.

"The 109th Congress is so bad that it makes you wonder if democracy is a failed experiment," says Jonathan Turley, a noted constitutional scholar and the Shapiro Professor of Public Interest Law at George Washington Law School. "I think that if the framers went to Capitol Hill today, it would shake their confidence in the system they created. Congress has become an exercise of raw power with no principles, and in that environment corruption has flourished. The Republicans in Congress decided from the outset that their future would be inextricably tied to George Bush and his policies. It has become this sad session of members sitting down and drinking Kool-Aid delivered by Karl Rove. Congress became a mere extension of the White House."

The end result is a Congress that has hijacked the national treasury, frantically ceded power to the executive, and sold off the federal government in a private auction. It all happened before our very eyes. In case you missed it, here's how they did it—in five easy steps.

STEP ONE

RULE BY CABAL

If you want to get a sense of how Congress has changed under GOP control, just cruise the basement hallways of storied congressional office buildings like Rayburn, Longworth, and Cannon. Here, in the minority offices for the various congressional committees, you will inevitably find exactly the same character—a Democratic staffer in rumpled khakis staring blankly off into space, nothing but a single lonely "Landscapes of Monticello" calendar on his wall, his eyes wide and full of astonished, impotent rage, like a rape victim. His skin is as white as the belly of a fish; he hasn't seen the sun in seven years.

It is no big scoop that the majority party in Congress has always found ways of giving the shaft to the minority. But there is a marked difference in the size and the length of the shaft the Republicans have given the Democrats in the past six years. There has been a systematic effort not only to deny the Democrats any kind of power-sharing role in creating or refining legislation but to humiliate them publicly, show them up, pee in their faces. Washington was once a chummy fraternity in which members of both parties golfed together, played in the same pickup basketball games, probably even shared the same mistresses. Now it is a one-party town—and congressional business is conducted accordingly, as though the half of the country that the Democrats represent simply does not exist.

American government was not designed for one-party rule but for rule by consensus—so this current batch of Republicans has found a way to work around that product design. They have scuttled both the spirit and the letter of congressional procedure, turning the lawmaking process into a backroom deal, with power concentrated in the hands of a few chiefs behind the scenes. This reduces the legislature to a Belarus-style rubber stamp, where the opposition is just there for show, human pieces of stagecraft—a fact the Republicans don't even bother to conceal.

"I remember one incident very clearly—I think it was 2001," says Winslow Wheeler, who served for twenty-two years as a Republican staffer in the Senate. "I was working for [New Mexico Republican] Pete Domenici at the time. We were in a Budget Committee hearing and the Democrats were debating what the final result would be. And my boss gets up and he says, 'Why are you saying this? You're not even going to be in the room when the decisions are made.' Just said it right out in the open."

Wheeler's very career is a symbol of a bipartisan age long passed into the history books; he is the last staffer to have served in the offices of a Republican and a Democrat at the same time, having once worked for both Kansas Republican Nancy Kassebaum and Arkansas Democrat David Pryor simultaneously. Today, those Democratic staffers trapped in the basement laugh at the idea that such a thing could ever happen again. These days, they consider themselves lucky if they manage to hold a single hearing on a bill before Rove's well-oiled legislative machine delivers it up for Bush's signature.

The GOP's "take that, bitch" approach to governing has been taken to the greatest heights by the House Judiciary Committee. The committee is chaired by the legendary Republican monster James Sensenbrenner Jr., an ever-sweating, fat-fingered beast who wields his gavel in a way that makes you think he might have used one before in some other arena, perhaps to beat prostitutes to death. Last year, Sensenbrenner became apoplectic when Democrats who wanted to hold a hearing on the Patriot Act invoked a little-known rule that required him to let them have one.

"Naturally, he scheduled it for something like nine a.m. on a Friday when Congress wasn't in session, hoping that no one would show," recalls a Democratic staffer who attended the hearing. "But we got a pretty good turnout anyway."

Sensenbrenner kept trying to gavel the hearing to a close, but Democrats again pointed to the rules, which said they had a certain amount of time to examine their witnesses. When they refused to stop the proceedings, the chairman did something unprecedented: he simply picked up his gavel and walked out.

"He was like a kid at the playground," the staffer says. And just in case anyone missed the point, Sensenbrenner shut off the lights and cut the microphones on his way out of the room.

For similarly petulant moves by a committee chair, one need look no further than the Ways and Means Committee, where Representative Bill Thomas—a pugnacious Californian with an enviable ego who was caught having an affair with a pharmaceutical lobbyist—enjoys a reputation rivaling that of the rotund Sensenbrenner. The lowlight of his reign took place just before midnight on July 17, 2003, when Thomas dumped a "substitute" pension bill on Democrats—one that they had never read—and informed them they would be voting on it the next morning. Infuriated, Democrats stalled by demanding that the bill be read out line by line while they recessed to a side room to confer. But Thomas wanted to move forward—so he called the Capitol police to evict the Democrats.

Thomas is also notorious for excluding Democrats from the conference hearings needed to iron out the differences between House and Senate versions of a bill. According to the rules, conferences have to include at least one public, open meeting. But in the Bush years, Republicans have managed the conference issue with some of the most mind-blowingly juvenile behavior seen in any parliament west of the Russian Duma after happy hour. GOP chairmen routinely call a meeting, bring the press in for a photo op, and then promptly shut the proceedings down. "Take a picture, wait five minutes, gavel it out—all for show" is how one Democratic staffer described the process. Then, amazingly, the Republicans sneak off to hold the real conference, forcing the Democrats to turn amateur detective and go searching the Capitol grounds for the meeting. "More often than not, we're trying to figure out where the conference is," says one House aide.

In one legendary incident, Representative Charles Rangel went searching for a secret conference being held by Thomas. When he found the room where Republicans closeted themselves, he knocked and knocked on the door but no one answered. A House aide compares the scene to the famous "Land Shark" skit from *Saturday Night Live,* with everyone hiding behind the door afraid to make a sound. "Rangel was the land shark, I guess," the aide jokes. But the real punch line came when Thomas finally opened the door. "This meeting," he informed Rangel, "is only open to the coalition of the willing."

Republican rudeness and bluster make for funny stories, but the phenomenon has serious consequences. The collegial atmosphere that once prevailed helped Congress form a sense of collective identity that it needed to fulfill its constitutional role as a check on the power of the other two branches of government. It also enabled Congress to pass legislation with a wide mandate, legislation that had been negotiated between the leaders of both parties. For this reason Republican and Democratic leaders traditionally maintained cordial relationships with each other—the model being the collegiality between House Speaker Nicholas Longworth and Minority Leader John Nance Garner in the 1920s. The two used to hold daily meetings over drinks and even rode to work together.

Although cooperation between the two parties has ebbed and flowed over the years, historians note that Congress has taken strong bipartisan action in virtually every administration. It was Senator Harry Truman who instigated investigations of war-time profiteering under FDR, and Republicans Howard Baker and Lowell Weicker Jr. played pivotal roles on the Senate Watergate Committee that nearly led to Nixon's impeachment.

But those days are gone. "We haven't seen any congressional investigations like this during the last six years," says David Mayhew, a professor of political science at Yale who has studied Congress for four decades. "These days, Congress doesn't seem to be capable of doing this sort of thing. Too much nasty partisanship."

One of the most depressing examples of one-party rule is the Patriot Act. The measure was originally crafted in classic bipartisan fashion in the Judiciary Committee, where it passed by a vote of thirty-six to zero, with famed liberals such as Barney Frank and Jerrold Nadler saying aye. But when the bill was sent to the Rules Committee, the Republicans simply chucked the approved bill and replaced it with a new, far more repressive version, apparently written at the direction of then attorney general John Ashcroft.

"They just rewrote the whole bill," says Representative James McGovern, a minority member of the Rules Committee. "All that committee work was just for show."

To ensure that Democrats can't alter any of the last-minute changes, Republicans have overseen a monstrous increase in the number of "closed" rules—bills that go to the floor for a

vote without any possibility of amendment. This tactic under-
cuts the very essence of democracy. In a bicameral system, allowing bills to be debated openly is the only way that the
minority can have a real impact, by offering amendments to
legislation drafted by the majority.

In 1977, when Democrats held a majority in the House, 85
percent of all bills were open to amendment. But by 1994, the
last year Democrats ran the House, that number had dropped
to 30 percent—and Republicans were seriously pissed. "You
know what the closed rule means," Representative Lincoln
Diaz-Balart of Florida thundered on the House floor. "It means
no discussion, no amendments. That is profoundly undemo-
cratic." When Republicans took control of the House, they
vowed to throw off the gag rules imposed by Democrats. On
opening day of the 104th Congress, then Rules Committee
chairman Gerald Solomon announced his intention to institute
free debate on the floor. "Instead of having seventy percent
closed rules," he declared, "we are going to have seventy percent open and unrestricted rules."

How has Solomon fared? Of the 111 rules introduced in the
first session of this Congress, only twelve were open. Of those,
eleven were appropriations bills, which are traditionally open.
That left just one open vote—H. Res. 255, the Federal Deposit
Insurance Reform Act of 2005.

In the second session of this Congress? Not a single open
rule, outside of appropriations votes. Under the Republicans,
amendable bills have been a genuine Washington rarity, the
upside-down eight-leafed clover of legislative politics.

When bills do make it to the floor for a vote, the debate generally resembles what one House aide calls "preordained Kabuki."
Republican leaders in the Bush era have mastered a new congressional innovation: the one-vote victory. Rather than seek-

ing broad consensus, the leadership cooks up some hideously expensive, favor-laden boondoggle and then scales it back bit by bit. Once they're in striking range, they send the fucker to the floor and beat in the brains of the fence sitters with threats and favors until enough members cave in and pass the damn thing. It is, in essence, a legislative microcosm of the electoral strategy that Karl Rove has employed to such devastating effect.

A classic example was the vote for the Central American Free Trade Agreement, the union-smashing, free-trade monstrosity passed in 2005. As has often been the case in the past six years, the vote was held late at night, away from the prying eyes of the public, who might be horrified by what they see. Thanks to such tactics, the 109th is known as the "Dracula" Congress: twenty bills have been brought to a vote between midnight and 7 a.m.

CAFTA actually went to vote early—at 11:02 p.m. When the usual fifteen-minute voting period expired, the nays were up, 180 to 175. Republicans then held the vote open for another forty-seven minutes while GOP leaders cruised the aisles like the family elders from *The Texas Chainsaw Massacre,* frantically chopping at the legs and arms of Republicans who opposed the measure. They even roused the president out of bed to help kick ass for the vote, passing a cell phone with Bush on the line around the House cloakroom like a bong. Representative Robin Hayes of North Carolina was approached by House Speaker Dennis Hastert, who told him, "Negotiations are open. Put on the table the things that your district and people need and we'll get them." After receiving assurances that the administration would help textile manufacturers in his home state by restricting the flow of cheap Chinese imports, Hayes switched his vote to yea. CAFTA ultimately passed by two votes at 12:03 a.m.

Closed rules, shipwrecked bills, secret negotiations, one-vote victories. The result of all this is a Congress where there is little or no open debate and virtually no votes are left to chance; all the important decisions are made in backroom deals, and what you see on C-Span is just empty theater, the world's most expensive trained-dolphin act. The constant here is a political strategy of conducting congressional business with as little outside input as possible, rejecting the essentially conservative tradition of rule-by-consensus in favor of a more revolutionary strategy of rule by cabal.

"This Congress has thrown caution to the wind," says Turley, the constitutional scholar. "They have developed rules that are an abuse of majority power. Keeping votes open by freezing the clock, barring minority senators from negotiations on important conference issues—it is a record that the Republicans should now dread. One of the concerns that Republicans have about losing Congress is that they will have to live under the practices and rules they have created. The abuses that served them in the majority could come back to haunt them in the minority."

STEP TWO

WORK AS LITTLE AS POSSIBLE—AND
SCREW UP WHAT LITTLE YOU DO

It's Thursday evening, September 28, and the Senate is putting the finishing touches on the Military Commissions Act of 2006, colloquially known as the "torture bill." It's a law even Stalin would admire, one that throws habeas corpus in the trash, legalizes a vast array of savage interrogation techniques, and generally turns the president of the United States into a kind of turbocharged Yoruba witch doctor, with nearly unlimited snatching powers. The bill is a fall-from-Eden moment in American history, a potentially disastrous step toward authoritarianism— but what is most disturbing about it, beyond the fact that it's happening, is that the senators are hurrying to get it done.

In addition to ending generations of bipartisanship and in- stituting one-party rule, our national legislators in the Bush years are guilty of something even more fundamental: they suck at their jobs.

They don't work many days, don't pass many laws, and the few laws they're forced to pass they pass late. In fact, in every year that Bush has been president, Congress has failed to pass more than three of the eleven annual appropriations bills on time.

That figures into tonight's problems. At this very moment, as the torture bill goes to a vote, there are only a few days left until the beginning of the fiscal year—and not one appropria- tions bill has been passed so far. That's why these assholes are hurrying to bag this torture bill. They want to finish in time to squeeze in a measly two hours of debate tonight on the half- trillion-dollar defense-appropriations bill they've blown off until now. The plan is to then wrap things up tomorrow before split- ting Washington for a month of real work, i.e., campaigning.

Senator Pat Leahy of Vermont comments on this rush to tor- ture during the final, frenzied debate. "Over two hundred years of jurisprudence in this country," Leahy pleads, "and follow- ing an hour of debate, we get rid of it?"

Yawns, chatter, a few sets of rolling eyes—yeah, whatever, Pat. An hour later the torture bill is law. Two hours after that, the diminutive chair of the Defense Appropriations subcom- mittee, Senator Ted Stevens, reads off the summary of the military-spending bill to a mostly empty hall; since the mem- bers all need their sleep and most have left early, the "debate" on the biggest spending bill of the year is conducted before a largely phantom audience.

"Mr. President," Stevens begins, eyeing the few members present. "There are only four days left in the fiscal year. The 2007 defense appropriations conference report must be signed into law by the president before Saturday at midnight. . . ."

Watching Ted Stevens spend half a trillion dollars is like watching a junkie pull a belt around his biceps with his teeth. You get the sense he could do it just as fast in the dark. When he finishes his summary—$436 billion in defense spending, including $70 billion for the Iraq "emergency"—he fucks off and leaves the hall. A few minutes later, Senator Tom Coburn of Oklahoma—one of the so-called honest Republicans who has clashed with his own party's leadership on spending issues—appears in the hall and whines to the empty room about all the lavish pork projects and sheer unadulterated waste jammed into the bill. But aside from a bored-looking John Cornyn of Texas, who is acting as president pro tempore, and a couple of giggling, suit-clad pages, there is no one in the hall to listen to him.

In the sixties and seventies, congress met an average of 162 days a year. In the eighties and nineties, the average went down to 139 days. This year, the second session of the 109th Congress will set the all-time record for fewest days worked by a U.S. Congress: 93. That means that House members will collect their $165,000 paychecks for only three months of actual work.

The current Congress will not only beat but shatter the record for laziness set by the notorious "Do-Nothing" Congress of 1948, which met for a combined 252 days between the House and the Senate. This Congress—the Do-Even-Less Congress—met for 218 days, just over half a year, between the House and the Senate combined.

And even these numbers don't come close to telling the full story. Those who actually work on the Hill will tell you that a great many of those "workdays" were shameless mail-ins, half days at best. Congress has arranged things now so that the typical workweek on the Hill begins late on Tuesday and ends just after noon on Thursday, to give members time to go home for the four-day weekend. This is borne out in the numbers. On nine of its workdays this year, the House held not a single vote—meeting for less than eleven minutes. The Senate managed to top the House's feat, pulling off three workdays this year that lasted less than one minute. All told, a full 15 percent of the Senate's workdays lasted under four hours. Figuring for half days, in fact, the 109th Congress probably worked almost two months less than that "Do-Nothing" Congress.

Congressional laziness comes at a high price. By leaving so many appropriations bills unpassed by the beginning of the new fiscal year, Congress forces big chunks of the government to rely on "continuing resolutions" for their funding. Why is this a problem? Because under congressional rules, CRs are funded at the lowest of three levels: the level approved by the House, the level approved by the Senate, or the level approved from the previous year. Thanks to wide discrepancies between House and Senate appropriations for social programming, CRs effectively operate as a backdoor way to slash social programs. It's also a nice way for congressmen to get around having to pay for expensive-ass programs they voted for, such as No Child Left Behind and some of the other terminally underfunded boondoggles of the Bush years.

"The whole point of passing appropriations bills is that Congress is supposed to make small increases in programs to account for things like the increase in population," says Adam Hughes, director of federal fiscal policy for OMB Watch, a

231

nonpartisan watchdog group. "It's their main job." Instead, he says, the reliance on CRs "leaves programs underfunded."

Instead of dealing with its chief constitutional duty—approving all government spending—Congress devotes its time to dumb bullshit. "This Congress spent a week and a half debating Terri Schiavo—it never made appropriations a priority," says Hughes. In fact, Congress leaves itself so little time to pass the real appropriations bills that it winds up rolling them all into one giant monstrosity known as an Omnibus bill and passing it with little or no debate. Rolling eight-elevenths of all federal spending into a single bill that hits the floor a day or two before the fiscal year ends does not leave much room to check the fine print. "It allows a lot more leeway for fiscal irresponsibility," says Hughes.

A few years ago, when Democratic staffers in the Senate were frantically poring over a massive Omnibus bill they had been handed the night before the scheduled vote, they discovered a tiny provision that had not been in any of the previous versions. The item would have given senators on the Appropriations Committee access to the private records of any taxpayer—essentially endowing a few selected hacks in the Senate with the license to snoop into the private financial information of all Americans.

"We were like, 'What the hell is this?'" says one Democratic aide familiar with the incident. "It was the most egregious thing imaginable. It was just lucky we caught them."

STEP THREE

LET THE PRESIDENT DO WHATEVER HE WANTS

The Constitution is very clear on the responsibility of Congress to serve as a check on the excesses of the executive branch. The House and Senate, after all, are supposed to pass all laws—the president is simply supposed to execute them. Over the years, despite some ups and downs, Congress has been fairly consistent in upholding this fundamental responsibility, regardless of which party controlled the legislative branch. Elected representatives saw themselves as beholden not to their own party or the president but to the institution of Congress itself. The model of congressional independence was Senator William Fulbright, who took on McCarthy, Kennedy, Johnson, and Nixon with equal vigor during the course of his long career.

"Fulbright behaved the same way with Nixon as he did with Johnson," says Wheeler, the former Senate aide who worked on both sides of the aisle. "You wouldn't see that today."

In fact, the Republican-controlled Congress has created a new standard for the use of oversight powers. That standard seems to be that when a Democratic president is in power, there are no matters too stupid or meaningless to be investigated fully—but when George Bush is president, no evidence of corruption or incompetence is shocking enough to warrant congressional attention. One gets the sense that Bush would have to drink the blood of Christian babies to inspire hearings in Congress—and only then if he did it during a nationally televised State of the Union address and the babies were from Pennsylvania, where Senate Judiciary chairman Arlen Specter was running ten points behind in an election year.

The numbers bear this out. From the McCarthy era in the 1950s through the Republican takeover of Congress in 1995, no Democratic committee chairman issued a subpoena without either minority consent or a committee vote. In the Clinton years, Republicans chucked that long-standing arrangement and issued more than one thousand subpoenas to investigate alleged administration and Democratic misconduct, reviewing more than two million pages of government documents.

Guess how many subpoenas have been issued to the White House since George Bush took office? Zero—that's right, zero, the same as the number of open rules debated this year; two fewer than the number of appropriations bills passed on time.

And the cost? Republicans in the Clinton years spent more than $35 million investigating the administration. The total amount of taxpayer funds spent, when independent counsels are taken into account, was more than $150 million. Included in that number was $2.2 million to investigate former HUD secretary Henry Cisneros for lying about improper payments he made to a mistress. In contrast, today's Congress spent barely half a million dollars investigating the outright fraud and government bungling that followed Hurricane Katrina, the largest natural disaster in American history.

"Oversight is one of the most important functions of Congress—perhaps more important than legislating," says Representative Henry Waxman. "And the Republicans have completely failed at it. I think they decided that they were going to be good Republicans first and good legislators second."

As the ranking minority member of the Government Reform Committee, Waxman has earned a reputation as the chief Democratic muckraker, obsessively cranking out reports on official misconduct and incompetence. Among them is a lengthy document detailing all of the wrongdoing by the Bush administration that should have been investigated—and would have been, in any other era. The litany of fishy behavior left uninvestigated in the Bush years includes the manipulation of intelligence on Saddam Hussein's weapons of mass destruction, the mistreatment of Iraqi detainees, the leak of Valerie Plame's CIA status, the award of Halliburton contracts, the White

House response to Katrina, secret NSA wiretaps, Dick Cheney's energy task force, the withholding of Medicare cost estimates, the administration's politicization of science, contract abuses at Homeland Security, and lobbyist influence at the EPA.

Waxman notes that the failure to investigate these issues has actually hurt the president, leaving potentially fatal flaws in his policies unexamined even by those in his own party. Without proper congressional oversight, small disasters like the misuse of Iraq intelligence have turned into huge, festering, unsolvable fiascoes like the Iraq occupation. Republicans in Congress who stonewalled investigations of the administration "thought they were doing Bush a favor," says Waxman. "But they did him the biggest disservice of all."

Congress has repeatedly refused to look at any aspect of the war. In 2003, Republicans refused to allow a vote on a bill introduced by Waxman that would have established an independent commission to review the false claims Bush made in asking Congress to declare war on Iraq. That same year, the chair of the House Intelligence Committee, Porter Goss, refused to hold hearings on whether the administration had forged evidence of the nuclear threat allegedly posed by Iraq. A year later the chair of the Government Reform Committee, Tom Davis, refused to hold hearings on new evidence casting doubt on the "nuclear tubes" cited by the Bush administration before the war. Senator Pat Roberts, who pledged to issue a Senate Intelligence Committee report after the 2004 election on whether the Bush administration had misled the public before the invasion, changed his mind after the president won reelection. "I think it would be a monumental waste of time to replow this ground any further," Roberts said.

Sensenbrenner has done his bit to squelch any debate over Iraq. He refused a request by John Conyers and more than fifty other Democrats for hearings on the famed "Downing Street Memo," the internal British document that stated that Bush had "fixed" the intelligence about the war, and he was one of three committee chairs who rejected requests for hearings on the abuse of Iraqi detainees. Despite an international uproar over Abu Ghraib, Congress spent only twelve hours on hearings on the issue. During the Clinton administration, by contrast, the Republican Congress spent 140 hours investigating the president's alleged misuse of his Christmas-card greeting list.

"You talk to many Republicans in Congress privately, and they will tell you how appalled they are by the administration's diminishment of civil liberties and the constant effort to keep fear alive," says Turley, who testified as a constitutional scholar in favor of the Clinton impeachment. "Yet those same members slavishly vote with the White House. What's most alarming about the 109th has been the massive erosion of authority in Congress. There has always been partisanship, but this is different. Members have become robotic in the way they vote."

Perhaps the most classic example of failed oversight in the Bush era came in a little-publicized hearing of the Senate Armed Services Committee held on February 13, 2003—just weeks before the invasion of Iraq. The hearing offered senators a rare opportunity to grill Secretary of Defense Donald Rumsfeld and top Pentagon officials on a wide variety of matters, including the fairly important question of whether they even had a fucking plan for the open-ended occupation of a gigantic hostile foreign population halfway around the planet. This was the biggest bite that Congress would have at the Iraq apple before the war, and given the gravity of the issue it should have been a beast of a hearing. But it wasn't to be.

In a meeting that lasted two hours and fifty-three minutes, only one question was asked about the military's readiness on the eve of the invasion. Senator John Warner, the committee's venerable and powerful chairman, asked General Richard Myers if the United States was ready to fight simultaneously in both Iraq and North Korea, if necessary.

Myers answered, "Absolutely."

And that was it. The entire exchange lasted fifteen seconds. The rest of the session followed a pattern familiar to anyone who has watched a hearing on C-Span. The members, when they weren't reading or chatting with one another, used their time with witnesses almost exclusively to address parochial concerns revolving around pork projects in their own districts. Warner set the tone in his opening remarks; after announcing that U.S. troops preparing to invade Iraq could count on his committee's "strongest support," the senator from Virginia quickly turned to the question of how the war would affect the budget for navy shipbuilding, which, he said, was not increasing "as much as we wish." Not that there's a huge navy shipyard in Newport News, Virginia, or anything.

Other senators followed suit. Daniel Akaka was relatively uninterested in Iraq but asked about reports that Korea might have a missile that could reach his home state of Hawaii. David Pryor of Arkansas used his time to tout the wonders of military bases in Little Rock and Pine Bluff. When the senators weren't eating up their allotted time in this fashion, they were usually currying favor with the generals. Warner himself nicely encapsulated the obsequious tone of the session when he complimented Rumsfeld for having his shit so together on the war.

"I think your response reflects that we have given a good deal of consideration," Warner said. "That we have clear plans in place and are ready to proceed." We all know how that turned out.

STEP FOUR

SPEND, SPEND, SPEND

There is a simple reason that members of Congress don't waste their time providing any oversight of the executive branch: there's nothing in it for them. "What they've all figured out is that there's no political payoff in oversight," says Wheeler, the former congressional staffer. "But there's a big payoff in pork."

When one considers that Congress has forsaken hearings and debate, conspired to work only three months a year, completely ditched its constitutional mandate to provide oversight, and passed very little in the way of meaningful legislation, the question arises: What do they do?

The answer is easy: they spend. When Bill Clinton left office, the nation had a budget surplus of $236 billion. Today, thanks to Congress, the budget is $296 billion in the hole. This year, more than 65 percent of all the money borrowed in the entire world will be borrowed by America, a statistic fueled by the speed-junkie spending habits of our supposedly "fiscally conservative" Congress. It took forty-two presidents before George W. Bush to borrow $1 trillion; under Bush, Congress has more than doubled that number in six years. And more often than not, we are borrowing from countries the sane among us would prefer not to be indebted to. The United States shells out $77 billion a year in interest to foreign creditors, including payment on the $300 billion we currently owe China.

What do they spend that money on? In the age of Jack Abramoff, that is an ugly question even to contemplate. But let's take just one bill, the so-called energy bill, a big, hairy, favor-laden bitch of a law that started out as the wet dream of Dick Cheney's energy task force and spent four long years leaving grease tracks on every set of palms in the Capitol before finally becoming law in 2005.

Like a lot of laws in the Bush era, it was crafted with virtually no input from the Democrats, who were excluded from the conference process. And during the course of the bill's gestation period we were made aware that many of its provisions were more or less openly for sale, as in the case of a small electric utility from Kansas called Westar Energy.

Westar wanted a provision favorable to its business inserted in the bill—and in an internal company memo it acknowledged that members of Congress had requested Westar donate money to their campaigns in exchange for the provision. The members included former Louisiana congressman Billy Tauzin and current Energy and Commerce chairman Joe Barton of Texas. "They have made this request in lieu of contributions made to their own campaigns," the memo noted. The total amount of Westar's contributions was $58,200.

Keep in mind, that number—fifty-eight grand—was for a single favor. The energy bill was loaded with them. Between 2001 and the passage of the bill, energy companies donated $115 million to federal politicians, with 75 percent of the money going to Republicans. When the bill finally passed, it contained $6 billion in subsidies for the oil industry, much of which was funneled through a company with ties to Majority Leader Tom DeLay. It included an exemption from the Safe Drinking Water Act for companies that use a methane-drilling technique called "hydraulic fracturing," one of the widest practitioners of which is Halliburton. It included billions in subsidies for the construction of new coal plants and billions more in loan guarantees to enable the coal and nuclear industries to borrow money at bargain-basement interest rates.

Favors for campaign contributors, exemptions for polluters, shifting the costs of private projects on to the public—these are the specialties of this Congress. Its members seldom miss an opportunity to impoverish the states we live in and up the bottom line of their campaign contributors. All this time—while Congress did nothing about Iraq, Katrina, wiretapping, Mark Foley's boy-madness, or anything else of import—it has been all about pork, all about political favors, all about budget "earmarks" set aside for expensive and often useless projects in their own districts. In 2000, Congress passed 6,073 earmarks; by 2005 that number had risen to 15,877. They got better at it every year. It's the one thing they're good at.

Even worse, this may well be the first Congress ever to lose control of the government's finances. For the past six years it has essentially been writing checks without keeping an eye on its balance. When you do that, unpleasant notices eventually start appearing in the mail. In 2003, the inspector general of the Defense Department reported to Congress that the military's financial-management systems did not comply with "generally accepted accounting principles" and that the department "cannot currently provide adequate evidence supporting various material amounts on the financial statements."

Translation: the Defense Department can no longer account for its money. "It essentially can't be audited," says Wheeler, the former congressional staffer. "And nobody did anything about it. That's the job of Congress, but they don't care anymore."

So not only does Congress not care what intelligence was used to get into the war, what the plan was supposed to be once we got there, what goes on in military prisons in Iraq and elsewhere, how military contracts are being given away and to whom—it doesn't even give a shit what happens to the half trillion bucks it throws at the military every year.

Not to say, of course, that this Congress hasn't made an effort to reform itself. In the wake of the Jack Abramoff scandal, and following a public uproar over the widespread abuse of earmarks, both the House and the Senate passed their own versions of an earmark reform bill this year. But when the two chambers couldn't agree on a final version, the House was left to pass its own watered-down measure in the waning days of the most recent session. This pathetically, almost historically half-assed attempt at reforming corruption should tell you all you need to know about the current Congress.

The House rule will force legislators to attach their names to all earmarks. Well, not all earmarks. Actually, the new rule applies only to nonfederal funding—money for local governments, nonprofits, and universities. And the rule will remain in effect only for the remainder of this congressional year—in other words, for the few remaining days of business after lawmakers return to Washington following the election season. After that, it's back to business as usual next year.

That is what passes for "corruption reform" in this Congress—forcing lawmakers to put their names on a tiny fraction of all earmarks. For a couple of days.

STEP FIVE

LINE YOUR OWN POCKETS

Anyone who wants to get a feel for the kinds of beasts that have been roaming the grounds of the congressional zoo in the past six years need only look at the deranged, handwritten letter that convicted bribe taker and GOP ex-congressman Randy "Duke"

Cunningham recently sent from prison to Marcus Stern, the reporter who helped bust him. In it, Cunningham—who was convicted last year of taking $2.4 million in cash, rugs, furniture, and jewelry from a defense contractor called MZM— bitches out Stern in the broken, half-literate penmanship of a six-year-old put in time-out.

"Each time you print it hurts my family And now I have lost them Along with Everything I have worked for during my 64 years of life," Cunningham wrote. "I am human not an Animal to keep whiping [sic]. I made some decissions [sic] Ill be sorry for the rest of my life."

The amazing thing about Cunningham's letter is not his utter lack of remorse, or his insistence on blaming defense contractor Mitchell Wade for ratting him out ("90% of what has happed [sic] is Wade," he writes), but his frantic, almost epic battle with the English language. It is clear that the same Congress that put a drooling child chaser like Mark Foley in charge of a House caucus on child exploitation also named Cunningham, a man who can barely write his own name in the ground with a stick, to a similarly appropriate position. Ladies and gentlemen, we give you the former chairman of the House Subcommittee on Human Intelligence Analysis and Counterintelligence:

"As truth will come out and you will find out how liablest you have & will be. Not once did you list the positives. Education Man of the Year . . . hospital funding, jobs, Hiway funding, border security, Megans law my bill, Tuna Dolfin my bill . . . and every time you wanted an expert on the wars who did you call. No Marcus you write About how I died."

How liablest you have & will be? What the fuck does that even mean? This guy sat on the Appropriations Committee for years—no wonder Congress couldn't pass any spending bills!

This is Congress in the Bush years, in a nutshell—a guy who takes $2 million in bribes from a contractor, whooping it up in turtlenecks and pajama bottoms with young women on a contractor-provided yacht named after himself (the *Duke-Stir*), and not only is he shocked when he's caught, he's too dumb even to understand that he's been guilty of anything.

This kind of appalling moral blindness, a sort of high-functioning, sociopathic stupidity, has been a consistent characteristic of the numerous Republicans indicted during the Bush era. Like all revolutionaries, they seem to feel entitled to break rules in the name of whatever the hell it is they think they're doing. And when caught breaking said rules with wads of cash spilling out of their pockets, they appear genuinely indignant at accusations of wrongdoing. Former House majority leader and brazen fuckhead Tom DeLay, after finally being indicted for money laundering, seemed amazed that anyone would bring him into court.

"I have done nothing wrong," he declared. "I have violated no law, no regulation, no rule of the House." Unless, of course, you count the charges against him for conspiring to inject illegal contributions into state elections in Texas "with the intent that a felony be committed."

It was the same when Ohio's officious jackass of a (soon to be ex-) congressman Bob Ney finally went down for accepting $170,000 in trips from Abramoff in exchange for various favors. Even as the evidence piled high, Ney denied any wrongdoing. When he finally did plead guilty, he blamed the sauce. "A dependence on alcohol has been a problem for me," he said.

Abramoff, incidentally, was another Republican with a curious inability to admit wrongdoing even after conviction; even now he confesses only to trying too hard to "save the world."

But everything we know about Abramoff suggests that Congress has embarked on a never-ending party, a wild daisy chain of golf junkets, skybox tickets, and casino trips. Money is everywhere and guys like Abramoff found ways to get it to guys like Ney, who made the important discovery that even a small entry in the Congressional Record can get you a tee time at St. Andrews.

Although Ney is so far the only congressman to win an all-expenses trip to prison as a result of his relationship with Abramoff, nearly a dozen other House Republicans are known to have done favors for him. Representative Jim McCrery of Louisiana, who accepted some $36,000 from Abramoff-connected donors, helped prevent the Jena band of Choctaw Indians from opening a casino that would have competed with Abramoff's clients. Representative Deborah Pryce, who sent a letter to Interior Secretary Gale Norton opposing the Jena casino, received $8,000 from the Abramoff money machine. Representative John Doolittle, whose wife was hired to work for Abramoff's sham charity, also intervened on behalf of the lobbyist's clients.

Then there was DeLay and his fellow Texan Representative Pete Sessions, who did Abramoff's bidding after accepting gifts and junkets. So much energy devoted to smarmy little casino disputes at a time when the country was careening toward disaster in Iraq: no time for oversight but plenty of time for golf.

For those who didn't want to go the black-bag route, there was always the legal jackpot. Billy Tauzin scarcely waited a week after leaving office to start a $2-million-a-year job running PhRMA, the group that helped him push through a bill prohibiting the government from negotiating lower prices for prescription drugs. Tauzin also became the all-time poster boy for pork absurdity when a "greenbonds initiative" crafted in his Energy and Commerce Committee turned out to be a sub-sidy to build a Hooters in his home state of Louisiana.

The greed and laziness of the 109th Congress has reached such epic proportions that it has finally started to piss off the public. In an April poll by CBS News, fully two-thirds of those surveyed said that Congress has achieved "less than it usually does during a typical two-year period." A recent Pew poll found that the chief concerns that occupy Congress—gay marriage and the inheritance tax—are near the bottom of the public's list of worries. Those at the top—education, health care, Iraq, and Social Security—were mostly blown off by Congress. Even a Fox News poll found that 53 percent of voters say Congress isn't "working on issues important to most Americans."

One could go on and on about the scandals and failures of the past six years; to document them all would take . . . well, it would take more than ninety-three fucking days, that's for sure. But you can boil the whole sordid mess down to a few basic concepts. Sloth. Greed. Abuse of power. Hatred of democracy. Government as a cheap backroom deal, finished in time for thirty-six holes of the world's best golf. And brains too stupid to be ashamed of any of it. If we have learned nothing else in the Bush years, it's that this Congress cannot be reformed. The only way to change it is to get rid of it.

Fortunately, we still get that chance once in a while.

Acknowledgments

Obviously first and foremost I want to thank all of my editors and coworkers at *Rolling Stone* for helping put together the stories in this book, with particular thanks to Jann Wenner, Eric Bates, Sean Woods, Coco McPherson, Peter Kenis, Eric Magnuson, Phoebe St. John, Amanda Trimble, and most of all to Will Dana, who gave me my start at the magazine at a time when I was really a mess personally. I am very grateful to everyone at the *Stone* for their patience and professionalism through what is often a very frantic and frustrating production process. Some of those people ought to have shot me a long time ago.

I traveled a great deal during the course of the time period covered in this book, and in that time there was only one person with whom I talked every day. P' Nira, thank you for always picking up the phone. *Kid Tung.*